Fantastical CAKES

INCREDIBLE CREATIONS for THE BAKER IN ANYONE

GESINE BULLOCK-PRADO

PHOTOS BY JULIA A. REED and RAYMOND PRADO

RUNNING PRESS
PHILADELPHIA

Running Press
Hachette Book Group
1290 Avenue of the Americas, New York, NY 10104
www.runningpress.com
@Running_Press

Printed in China

First Edition: November 2018

Published by Running Press, an imprint of Perseus Books, LLC,
a subsidiary of Hachette Book Group, Inc. The Running Press name
and logo is a trademark of the Hachette Book Group.

The Hachette Speakers Bureau provides a wide range of
authors for speaking events. To find out more, go to
www.hachettespeakersbureau.com or call (866) 376-6591.

The publisher is not responsible for websites (or their content)
that are not owned by the publisher.

Photographs by Julia A. Reed: cover, back cover
(except for bottom left corner), and pages 43, 53, 54, 82, 95, 96, 99, 113, 151,
153, 187, 196, 205, 209, 211, 213, 216, 220, 222, 226, 230-1, 237, 239, 240, 245,
249, 250, 254, 257, 274, 276, 278, 281, 284, 291, 292-3, 296, 300, 303.
All other photographs by Raymond Prado.
Print book cover and interior design by Amanda Richmond.

Library of Congress Control Number: 2018944246

ISBNs: 978-0-7624-6343-5 (hardcover), 978-0-7624-6342-8 (ebook),

RRD-S

10 9 8 7 6 5 4 3 2 1

To Louis & Laila:

you make life so much sweeter

Contents

PART TWO:

FILLING...118

PART THREE:

THE CAKES...210

Introduction

When I was a kid visiting my aunt's house in Maryland in the '80s, I battled with my big sister over possession of the single greatest tome ever written in all of these great United States: *Cake Decorating!* If I could get my grubby little hands on it first, I spent every minute engrossed in that puny book, a pamphlet, really, dedicated to piping spastic ruffles and neon flowers on lumpy box cakes. *Cake Decorating!* promised that with only a few specialty tips and a relatively steady hand, you, too, could make delightfully decorated treats. It was exactly the kind of book that my own baking snob mother would never allow in her kitchen, a book that celebrated wicked things like excessive sugar!

Preservative-packed boxed cake mixes! Artificial dyes! Cakes in the shape of stuffed toys!

Looking at it again, so many years later (I found myself a well-loved copy on eBay), I'm astounded not only by how damn ghastly the cakes inside looked (it was pre-Instagram, after all), but that it never occurred to me how odd it was that the book didn't contain a single real *recipe*. Instead, listed in the tools section, the author(s) recommended which flavor of box mix and canned frosting worked best with each style of cake. From scraggly, demon-possessed-looking teddy bears whose eyes have been applied in a haphazard manner, to square blocks of cake piped with jittery numbers to approximations of recalled children's toys, to cakes with waxy white icing tinted in an array of colors never to be found in nature, I did not see a single decorating idea or finished cake in the book that didn't look to be a permanent resident of the Island of the Misfit Cakes. Although not a single confection in that book is remotely appetizing, the magic, the *promise* of learning to make a cake truly spectacular still beckons to me from within those pages.

Since I grew up to become the pastry chef and baking instructor that I was clearly genetically engineered to be (what ten-year-old spends five hours meticulously reading over a twenty-page book dedicated to piping squiggly lines and lopsided flowers?), I've been looking for the modern version of that little book, one that combined some of the whimsy and clever ideas (make grass *and* animal fur with the same piping tip!) of *Cake Decorating!* with the added culinary backbone, skills, and elegant recipes you might find in a Julia Child tome or a professional pastry text. I always came up empty-handed.

I wrote the book I was yearning for with my students in mind every step of the way. In my little baking school, Sugar Glider Kitchen, I bring together all kinds of bakers, from rank beginners who can't tell a yolk from a white to experienced chefs who need a refresher on croissant. No matter the skill level, every baker that walks through my door wants to walk out with something beautiful in his or her hands because baking is as much a visual experience as it is a treat for the taste buds. Cake carries this burden to the extreme. It's gotta be gorgeous, otherwise you can't Instagram it. And if you don't Instagram it, it doesn't really exist. But joking aside, we eat with our eyes first and a beautiful cake relays important informa-

tion: (1) that the baker gives a damn; (2) the baker knows what he or she is doing; and (3) if it's half as tasty as it is pretty, it's going to be the best cake ever.

So, when a student asked in a class whether I was writing another book and I answered, "Yup. It's going to focus on creating and decorating beautiful cakes," all the members of the class looked up in unison, their butter and flour-encrusted hands motionless, hovering over their unfinished quick puff.

"Did you say cakes? And decorating? A whole book?" someone asked from the back of the classroom.

"Well, that's the plan," I said. There was a silence and then an explosion of glee.

"Yes! Yes yes yes!" I'm not exaggerating. That was the response. Along with a few "Thank God"s.

Turns out that while I've been teaching my students insanely complicated pastry techniques that I insist they need in their repertoire, I've also been listening to them and what they really want to get out of their baking life. Sometimes they do want a big challenge, a multistep extravaganza. Most of the time, however, they want to keep their baking projects simple and manageable. Here's the rub, though. They also want their baked goods to be super scrumptious and to look gorgeous. In chatting with my students, they've expressed time and again that they want fewer and less complicated steps, but they still want the "wow" factor. And if there are a few steps involved, they want them simple and fail-safe—they want to know what they can make ahead, what can be kept frozen, and when they can skip a step without ruining everything. These are my *Cake Decorating!* soul brothers and sisters. It's for them, for you, for all of us, that I've written this book.

Getting Started

Meet the B.A.D.A.S.S. Method

What I'm best known for, what my students travel across the country to learn, are the baking techniques and decorating tips and tricks that straddle the worlds of fine pastry art and down-home baking. Specifically, I'm asked to teach bakers the skills to make cakes look professional and elegant, that taste amazing, but that don't require days on end to finish. Here's the thing, I developed these fast and efficient approaches for *me*. It's actually a selfish motivation because I've made and I make a *lot* of cakes and I want every single one of them to look gorgeous and tasty. . . but I want gorgeous without too much fuss.

I've also created a method to get great results every time. Some steps might seem like overkill at first, but once you get into the routine of it and see the results, the steps will move quickly, and you'll come to realize that things like prepping pans and getting ingredients to room temperature are as important to the recipe as measuring out the flour correctly. So, I'd like to introduce you to the B.A.D.A.S.S. method of making cakes: Bake Ahead, Dam and Assemble, Smooth Coat, and Spruce Up. This is information you can take into your general cake life, and I know you live a very full cake-filled existence, so these techniques you can use on every cake, not just the cakes in this book. Each step ensures success:

First, bake delicious, even layers that you can make ahead and freeze. If you opened my freezer right now, you'd spy eight 6-inch rounds of chocolate cake, four 8-inch rounds of confetti cake, and two 10-inch squares of WASC (White Almond Sour Cream Cake) waiting for me in the freezer. Some are there because I'm getting ahead of a big baking project. Some I ended up not needing and forgot were there and I get really excited when I stumble upon them. But most of the layers are there because I wanted to get my bake on and I know that if I feed that urge by baking some perfect layers, they'll never be wasted. A moment always arrives when there's urgent need for a confetti cake and fast. I have never felt more like Wonder Woman than when a cake emergency arises and I turn to my freezer in triumph to reveal perfect layers, ready and waiting for my finishing touches.

Second, take the precaution of damming the filling with a ring of sturdy (and delicious) frosting so that every type of filling stays put, from liquidy curds that haven't yet set, to whole pieces of fruit to delicate mousse.

Taking the time to create that dam with each succeeding layer is essential to the perfectly finished layer cake and when you're assembling a cake from baked ahead layers, straight from the freezer, everything sets faster, from the frosting dam to the liquidy filling. Remember, the outside of your cake will not look great if your filling is busting out the sides. Piping a sturdy ring to keep all that deliciousness inside, where it belongs, is your insurance policy to a gorgeous finished cake.

Third, you must apply a smooth crumb coat to lock in any crumbs and to guarantee that the tops and sides of the cake are level.

All of this leads to my favorite part, the final smoothing of the cake. Sometimes you want to stop at the damming step and present a truly "naked" cake. Sometimes you want a crumb coat that gives your guests just a peek of the deliciousness that's hidden inside. But my favorite cake takes one giant step up from the crumb with an additional smooth coat: another layer of frosting to encase your cake in impeccable frosting perfection. I start by piping an even layer of buttercream to the top of the cake, using the same pastry bag and tip I used to dam the cake. It's an insurance policy for a level top. Then I take a hot (and dry) offset spatula and smooth the top.

I then pipe stripes around the sides of the cake.

They don't have to be perfect. It's more fun when they aren't because the reveal when you smooth the sides is that much more dramatic. Using the smoothing technique with a dry and hot icing scraper, you get a flawlessly finished cake.

Other times you want the works, the full spruce: a cake with a perfect coat of icing, an impeccable layer of ganache or marzipan, and a spray of realistic sugar flowers.

Fantastical Cakes is divided into three sections (cake layers, fillings and frostings, and assembly) that will get you exactly where you want to be in your cake life from naked to fantastical. Feel free to mix and match!

A List of Tools and Ingredients

The right tools and ingredients will get the job done. That's the maxim in carpentry, the tool part at least, and it holds true for baking as well. Some of those tools even cross the two spectrums. Home Depot *faux bois* (wood grain) tools, finishing trowels, and high butane torches bring me such glee when I consider the prospect of playing with them in the bakery. But you already have tools in your kitchen that will help you get started without having to run out and plop down a ton of cash. Tools you trust that you already use every day, and you probably can't live without.

TOOLS
Oven and
Oven Thermometer

I'm sorry to be the one to tell you this, but the most necessary implement in your baking (and cooking) arsenal is probably not being truthful. I'll just say it. Your oven is lying to you. Okay, fine. There are some ovens that are true, that hold temperature properly, but that's a rare oven indeed. Some ovens are off by only a few degrees, barely enough to make much of a difference in a finished product. However, others can vary by 20°, even 50°. Some more. Now that's a big problem.

If you have spent any time reading the comments section of major food magazines' recipe sites (and who hasn't?), you'll find a single complaint that reappears over and over again: the timing on the recipe was wrong and therefore, the recipe was wrong. Hate to tell you this, but as the kids say, "The call is coming from inside your house." Inside your oven, more specifically. It wasn't the recipe that was at fault. It was the oven being used to make the recipe. Like I said, ovens are big fat liars. If your cakes crater, you've probably got an oven problem. If your custard pies take days to set, it's an oven problem. If your croissants leak, there's a darn good chance that it's an oven problem. The big solution is to get a new oven. That's pretty extreme. The easy solution is to get an oven thermometer. They cost a few bucks and they work. I had a student who designed a brand-new kitchen, fitting her dream workspace with the best appliances. She'd heard me harp about lying ovens for years now and despite the fact that the manufacturer of this otherwise very lovely oven said, in no uncertain terms, that its ovens were expertly calibrated and were true to temperature, my student chose to heed my repeated warnings. She put an oven thermometer inside. The knob read

350°F/180°C). The oven thermometer read 320°F/160°C. Knowledge is power, friends. You can make adjustments when you know what the problem is.

So, if your cake craters—rising properly, or so it seems, and then collapsing in the middle—you've got an oven that runs too hot. The cake batter sides get an extra-hot blast of heat, and rise and set too quickly, while the middle of the cake is still rising and has nothing to hold on to because the sides have already taken a vacation way down south. So, the middle goes *boom*. The solution is to get an oven thermometer, find out exactly how off your temperature is, and make the adjustment. It also helps to wrap your cake pans in my DIY cake strips to prevent collapse and create an even rise without a giant dome (see "Pan Prep," page 30).

Scale

Yes, a decent kitchen scale comes before an electric mixer. Ideally, you'd have both. I think they're equally important, but to stress how important I think scales are, I've put them higher on the chain of baking command. Scales give you accuracy and they make the process easier. Yes, easier. For instance, with a paste method cake where the dry ingredients are combined all at once, there's nothing easier than just sticking your mixing bowl on a scale and weighing the ingredients straight into the bowl, one on top of the other. No extra dirty dishes. No question about accuracy.

To use most food scales, find the "Unit" button, which will help you toggle between ounces and grams. Make sure you're on the unit you're meant to be using. Next,

look for the "Tare" or "Zero out" button. This allows you to start at zero and clear between additions. I choose a scale based on the range of weight it can measure as well. I look for accuracy at lower units, and whether it can read up to a few pounds. It's no fun getting to the very last few critical ounces of an ingredient and having your scale yell, "*Error!*" I also look for scales that can be plugged in *and* can be used off battery power. Preferably, the battery called for will be a standard AA or AAA rather than the flat, round variety that's a pain to find and costs a ton.

Stand Mixer/Hand Mixer

Creaming and foaming mixing methods are virtually impossible to achieve well, or at all, without an electric mixer. Hand mixers can get the job done. They take a while longer to mix properly, but they'll get you there. A good stand mixer, however, is best. It is an investment. A good one is never cheap, but if you are a baker of any regularity, a mixer is essential.

Cake Pans

This is pretty obvious, isn't it? I like my cake pans made of lighter metals, not dark nonstick materials. The lighter the pan, the lighter the crust on your cake. Nine-inch/23 cm pans seem to be the most common size available and used, but if you only buy one set of cake pans, get two 8-inch/20.5 cm round pans. That one inch/2.5 cm is the difference between a shorter, squatter cake or a taller, more lithe cake.

Cake Turntable

Even *think* of covering a cake with a smooth coat of frosting and you'll need a turntable to make it come out as it does in your daydream. You don't need bells and whistles. Don't splash out on motorized and tilting turntables; they are a waste of cash. Instead, look for a sturdy, well-balanced turntable that turns smoothly. Plastic turntables are nice and cheap, but tend to fall apart easily. Stay away from turntables whose base is far too small compared to the diameter of the top. This means it will be top-heavy with a cake on it and is a guaranteed tipping hazard. There's nothing sadder than achieving a perfectly smooth finished coat, gently shifting the cake off the turntable so you can transfer it to the fridge, only for the whole thing to tip over, and your cake goes *splat!* Instead, look for cake turntables that have nice and wide stands that are larger than half the diameter of the top.

Offset Spatulas

I have a baking school, so I'm up to my eyeballs in spatulas, but I recommend you have at least three small offset spatulas and one large offset spatula on hand.

Icing Scraper

The most common icing scraper is also known as a bench scraper. They work in a pinch for shorter cakes. However, if you like to build 'em high as I do, get yourself a larger icing scraper. You can buy taller icing scrapers (up to 12 inches/30.5 cm high) at any cake decorating store and many craft stores. The most common type has a flat metal "blade" and others are made from acrylic. In a pinch, you can use a finishing trowel from the hardware store, but use a new one, not one that's been used for tiling, and wash it with soapy water before its first use. Food safety first. Always. For best results, use a scraper with a clean 90° angle so you can rest the shorter end on the cake stand and provide a level guide as you smooth the sides of the cake with the longer end.

Knives and Sharp Things

A small paring knife for running along the edge of a pan and cake is so handy in releasing cakes and a very thin and long serrated knife is perfect for "torting" layers (cutting them in half on the horizontal). I also keep an X-ACTO blade for cutting fondant, gum paste, and trimming paper templates.

Large Spatulas

There are times when you need to lift tender and fragile cakes, and a large offset spatula just won't cut it. A large cake lifter is the only thing that can really save you and keep your layers intact.

Sheet Pans

Half sheet pans are crucial in baking. Many manufacturers make off-size and flimsy versions that don't conform to most baking standards. The correct size of a half sheet pan is 18 x 13 inches/45.5 x 33 cm and will have a lip around the entire pan, which will fit in almost any oven.

Liquid Measure Cup

The most common liquid measure cup is the Pyrex glass measure. If you've got one, you're golden. Be aware, however, that these cups are meant for liquid measures only. My favorite liquid measure cup is the plastic Perfect Beaker. It's the perfect shape for reading the volume properly.

Dry Measure Cups

Any standard measuring cup will do in a pinch, but make sure that the handle of the cup does not impede you from knocking off the flour with a straight edge.

Candy Thermometer

Thermometers, like ovens, can be liars. I've found the thermometer that makes it all better: the ThermoWorks flip thermometer. It's guaranteed calibrated and accurate to a wonderfully small degree. But it's damn expensive (if it helps with the pricing issue, it's also a fabulous meat thermometer). Otherwise, cheaper clip-on thermometers work in a pinch, even if they are wildly inaccurate. Thankfully, you can put one in a pot of boiling water and check for accuracy. At sea level, boiling water is 212°F/100°C. If the thermometer reads 220°F/104.5°C at boiling, you need to subtract 8°F/4.5°C from the reading to get to the right temperature. Sometimes doing math can take too long and by the time you've subtracted, you've already overshot your desired number. If you're mathematically zippy, you'll be fine. Otherwise, it's worth investing in a thermometer that actually works every time. You'll end up saving money because you won't be wasting ingredients.

Small Wares

There are a host of tools that make baking life easier.

- Parchment paper and silicone mats to keep things from sticking
- Rubber spatulas for gently mixing ingredients
- Bowl scrapers to get every last drop of batter from the bowl
- Whisks to distribute ingredients
- Sieves to ensure your finest custards and curds are smooth as can be
- Large metal bowls for setting atop simmering water to gently melt chocolate or whisk together a delicate curd
- Scissors to snip off the tip of a disposable piping bag or trim a round of parchment for the bottom of a cake pan
- Tweezers to pluck out errant eyebrow hairs that jump from your head into the batter
- Piping bags for adding a band of icing to the perimeter of your cake layer to keep the filling inside and for piping lifelike flowers
- Piping tips for making sure those flower petals are just right
- Fondant smoothers for doing the obvious
- Cardboard rounds to make a sturdy base for the bottom of your assembled cake
- Flower nails to make piping those beautiful flowers simpler

If you make cake regularly, you tend to collect these bits and bobs over time.

INGREDIENTS
Flour

Flour is the foundation of almost all baked goods. It forms the basis of "baker's math." I won't bore you with the particulars, but it's truly interesting stuff! The reason it's considered the foundational element of baking is that flour is most often the largest measure of all the ingredients, with sugar coming in as the second-largest measure, and because it contains gluten, proteins that when combined with moisture form strong bonds that provide structure in baked goods. This is why it's darn hard to find a decent gluten-free bread.

In the United States, we grade flour differently than in other countries where there are often just a few wheat flour options: plain flour and self-rising flours, for example. We get a whole host of options, which is fabulous but can also be very confusing. The first thing to keep in mind is that, in the United States, if a recipe doesn't specify the *type* of flour you can usually assume that all-purpose is being called for. If "cake" flour is called for, assume it's bleached cake flour.

Different types of flour have higher or lower percentages of gluten proteins. For example, King Arthur Flour brand bread flour clocks in at 12.7 percent protein content, its all-purpose contains 11.7 percent protein, and its unbleached cake flour contains 10 percent gluten protein.

(The average bleached cake flour contains 8 to 9 percent gluten protein.)

When you add water to flour and agitate, you "activate" the gluten and the more you agitate the mixture, the more gluten is produced. So, when you read in a recipe not to "overmix" or "overwork" a batter or dough, you're really being told not to produce too much gluten.

In some cases, when a mixing method calls for you to mix the flour, other dry ingredients, and fats together (also called the paste method) before adding moisture, you coat some of the gluten proteins with fat and essentially deactivate them. When you use a very low-protein flour, such as cake flour, in that scenario, you'll often have to mix the batter for a few minutes after adding moisture (e.g., water, milk, or buttermilk) to produce enough gluten strength to give the batter structure when it bakes.

Be aware, however, that flours aren't interchangeable and there will be a demonstrable change to the outcome of the cake. If a recipe calls for all-purpose flour and you only have bleached cake flour, the lower-protein-quotient cake flour will result in a cake that has an iffy structure and will likely fall apart very easily, and that will be gummy from all that gelatinized starch.

Another thing with flours is that they all aren't created equally. I stick with King Arthur Flour because they are, for my money and experience, the most consistent flours on the market. King Arthur guarantees the gluten protein levels of each of its flours. Frequently, large manufacturers will not calibrate the protein percentages when they change from winter wheat to summer wheat, so the same bag of flour can have vastly different levels of protein in it, leading to wonky outcomes in your finished product. Often, if a student comes to me with a baking problem where the lead-up is, "I did it exactly the same way as I always do with exactly the same brand of ingredients and it didn't turn out right," I always ask what flour was used. Check the packaging of your flour to see if it offers the gluten percentages on the bag or box itself, or on the company's website.

The second general flour rule is to measure it properly if you choose not to weigh the flour. (Weighing is always the best and most accurate measure.) If you are measuring by the cup, there is a very good chance that you've been doing it all wrong. The first step to a proper measure is to fluff the flour with a large spoon. Take a scoop of that fluffed flour and gently sprinkle the flour into your dry measure cup—making sure never to shake, shimmy, or stomp down the flour during the process. That also means that you should not knock the cup against the counter to pack in the flour or wiggle the cup to get that mound to straighten out. Simply sprinkle the flour into the cup, let it naturally mound, and then scrape off the excess with a straight edge—such as the back of a dinner knife. Tamping or wiggling will pack down the flour and give you a larger measure of flour than the recipe calls for.

In this book, I've included recipes that call for either unbleached or bleached cake flours, and for all-purpose flour. At first glance, it would seem that cake flour is cake flour and that swapping one out for the other isn't a big deal. However, there is a textural difference between the two. Bleached cake flour goes through a bleaching process and during this process the gluten is denatured, making much of it unavailable to provide its traditional structural bonds. However, the starches in the flour are magnified.

1st column: all-purpose flour, bleached cake flour, fine sea salt
2nd column: granulated sugar, brown sugar, confectioners' sugar, and maple sugar
3rd column: egg, European (high fat content) and American butter, bittersweet chocolate morsels, Dutched cocoa powder
4th column: baking powder, gel dye (Americolor and Wilton), Gum-Tex Tylose Powder
5th column: dry milk powder, buttermilk powder, almond flour

Sugar

When sugar is called for in a recipe, use traditional granulated sugar. Different brands may use different varieties of base sugar from either sugar cane or sugar beets, and both are processed differently based on their various plant origins. The resulting two granulated sugars are pretty much interchangeable in most recipes without a perceived difference. Some people swear to the superiority of cane sugar, saying that it caramelizes better. The test most often used to compare the two types is the burning during crème brûlée. Cane sugar is said to have a superior caramelization for the purpose of the wonderfully crackly surface on the custard. However, if you are a strict vegan or baking for a strict vegan, the traditional processing of cane sugar uses char from animal bones to break down and bleach the granules, which makes the sugar "unvegan."

For the purposes of this book, white granulated sugar is interchangeable with cane or beet.

Confectioners', or 10X, sugar is a finely milled sugar with added cornstarch. Several brands use tapioca flour/starch instead of cornstarch; they will work just as well.

When brown sugar is called for, use light brown sugar. Brown sugar, both light and dark, are processed white sugars that have had the molasses extracted and replaced to varying degrees, depending on whether the sugar is labeled as light or dark.

And then there's maple sugar, which is simply maple sap evaporated into a dry powder. It's magical. Here in Vermont and in New England, it's pretty easy to find the stuff in grocery stores, but in the rest of the world, the Internet is the place to go for all your maple sugar needs.

Eggs

When eggs are called for in a recipe, unless it says otherwise, use large eggs at room temperature. If the eggs are to be separated, it's best to separate them cold, which helps keep the yolk from breaking, and then allow the separated portions to come to room temperature before using. Cover the yolks with a piece of plastic wrap so that the wrap touches the surface of the yolks, to keep the yolk from forming a skin. Much of mixing in the baking process is about balance and keeping things

emulsified. Having the ingredients at the same temperatures is key to keeping the balance. If a right-from-the-refrigerator egg is added to other room-temperature ingredients, such as creamed butter and sugar, it can lead to the butter's seizing up and getting chunky. I often keep eggs out overnight if I'm going to be baking first thing in the morning. Otherwise, you can place them in a bowl of warm water to speed along the process.

In our organic, farm-to-table, backyard chicken world it's easy to assume that a free-range, farm-fresh egg is best. Often it is. The albumen in the white is nice and perky, giving you all its most potent protein powers. The yolk is often larger than the standard grocery store egg and is a deep orange and creamy. This all sounds great, right? But there are a few things that can go wrong with those eggs in baking. First, I know from my own hens, that these eggs often vary in size from medium to extra-extra-large. You can guesstimate how much to use but, obviously, it's not very exact. That gorgeous yolk can also be a pain if you're making things with delicate color balances. The patterned Swiss Roll cake (page 298) is the perfect example of this. That bright orange in the yolk can really throw off the final color, changing pink to peach and blue to green.

Butter

When butter is called for in a recipe, assume it's for standard American butter with a butterfat content which comes in at 81 to 82 percent. European butters, or high-fat butters, come in at more like 83 to 84 percent. Those few percentage points can make a difference.

While European butters make for gorgeous pastries and cakes, they are not a requirement for a great product. If you like to use European butter, feel free to use your favorite brand in a one-to-one swap with the American butter in the cake recipes. However, do not add European butter in recipes for buttercream or ganache, where that extra fat can upset the emulsification: the delicate balance of proteins, fats, and liquids.

And yes, use unsalted butter and not salted butter. A recipe will have a precise measure of salt specified. Salted butter has an *unspecified* amount of salt included as a preservative. Baking is precise and guesstimating how much more or less salt you should add to balance the salt in the butter is the height of unbakerly conduct and can lead to an anemic-tasting pastry in the event you add too little to compensate, or just downright salty, if you add too much.

Chocolate

Most modern recipes will specify the percentage of chocolate that best suits the recipe. The percentage identifies the amount of cacao liquor (which is the terminology used in the chocolate industry for the ground cacao bean) present in the bar, chips, or callets of chocolate. The higher the number, the more cacao liquor. The lower the number, the higher the percentage of sugar and lower amount of cacao liquor. The percentage doesn't signify whether the chocolate will be good, though. Different beans produce different taste qualities. I recommend taste testing to see what you like best. Best. Test. EVER!

Cocoa

All the recipes in this book specify whether natural or Dutched cocoa powder is called for. Natural cocoa is an unprocessed cocoa that's a rust color. It's high in acid and brings with it an almost harsh, citrusy flavor. Dutched cocoa neutralizes the alkalinity present in natural cocoa, making it beautifully dark, very rich in flavor, and mellow. Natural cocoas have the available acidity to work with baking soda, creating carbon dioxide and that *lift*! Recipes with Dutched cocoa most often use baking powder or a combination of baking powder and soda. So, if you used a Dutched cocoa instead of natural cocoa in a recipe that used baking soda for leavening, the outcome would fall flat, quite literally.

Like chocolate, different cocoas have different flavors. I have distinct favorites after years of testing, but you may find that your taste varies towards a fruitier-flavored cocoa versus the dark, mellow sort that I prefer. So, bake up a few chocolate cakes using different cocoas.

Gelatin

In the United States, powdered gelatin is the norm but in other parts of the world and in pastry, leaf gelatin is the more common form used to set everything from *cremeux* to curd. Leaf gelatin can be intimidating to the uninitiated because it's so darn different from the powdered stuff, but once you get to using it, you'll fall in love. Leaf gelatin comes in a variety of setting strengths ranging from bronze, silver, gold, and platinum. They are rated by their "bloom" or setting strength. Silver-grade leaf gelatin is the closest to using powdered gelatin and it's also the easiest to find in cake shops and on the Internet.

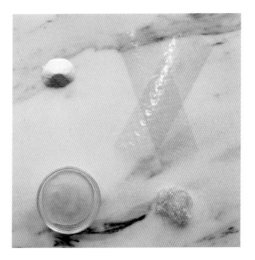

The conversion is simple: one 7-gram packet of gelatin equals 1 tablespoon of powdered gelatin, which then equals three leaves of silver leaf gelatin. Before you use the leaf gelatin, you are going to bloom it, which means to soften it in water or another liquid, much in the same way as you would powdered gelatin. Then, instead of incorporating the leaf gelatin along with its softening water as you would with powdered gelatin, you take the leaf gelatin from the water and squeeze out the excess moisture. I find that leaf gelatin is simply easier to use, incorporates into things more easily without any lumpiness, and sets beautifully.

Artificial Leavening

Baking powder and baking soda are both artificial leaveners, unlike yeast, which is a natural leavener. Both baking powder and baking soda use similar methodologies to create lift in cakes, cookies, and other yummies. However, just because they are both categorized as artificial doesn't mean that they are the same. You can't swap out one for the other. Baking soda is straight-up sodium bicarbonate. If you mix baking soda, which is basic, with an acid, then *kaploowee!*—you have liftoff. So, when a recipe calls for baking soda, it will also contain an acid. For example, in your favorite Toll House chocolate chip cookies, the acid comes from the molasses present in the brown sugar. Baking soda is about three to four times stronger than baking powder and the standard ratio for using baking soda is ¼ teaspoon baking soda per cup/120 grams of flour. Too much of it and the finished product tastes metallic. So, if you'd ever done a one-to-one swap, adding the same amount of baking soda as the amount of baking powder called for in a recipe because you were strapped, you've added *way* too much leavening and you would have also needed to include an acid in the recipe.

Baking powder is a combination of sodium bicarbonate (baking soda), cornstarch, and an acid (most often cream of tartar). The general ratio for using baking powder is 1 teaspoon per cup/120 grams of flour. Both soda and powder can lose their efficacy over time. To test baking soda, do my favorite science trick: Combine a little baking soda and cider vinegar. If it fizzles like crazy, you're good. For baking powder, add ½ teaspoon to ¼ cup/56 ml of water. The reaction won't be half as dramatic as baking soda and acid, but you should get some fizzling action. If nothing happens, you'll need a new can.

Food Coloring

The most common options are liquid, gel, and powdered. You might also find candy gel colors, but those are used for airbrushing colors onto cakes and pastries, and there are also natural dyes. It gets confusing when you find yourself in a cake decorating emporium and you don't know what's what. Personally, I stick with the gel colors. The two brands I use most often are Americolor and Wilton. Both are heat-safe, which means that when you add them to a steaming hot mixture, they won't burn. Both also have very saturated colors and the gel is thick, which means that you'll get a lot of color bang for your buck. The food coloring that you typically find in the grocery store is liquid color. The best example to show how the two differ is to look at the Royal Purple Velvet Mirror Glaze Cake (page 306). You only need a few hearty drops of gel to get decent purple, but you'll need the whole darn bottle if you use the liquid.

The next thing you need to know about all of the colors in the "artificial" spectrum is that the darker the hue—think: Royal Blue and Forest Green—the more bitter the flavor. If you plan on using a dark-colored fondant, for instance, I recommend that you buy a brand that's already tinted in a shade close to what you're going for, so you only have to use a smidge of artificial coloring to get to the right shade.

Gums and Glycerin

I'm not going to lie; both are weird ingredients. Tylose Gum powder is used in making gum paste. It hardens the sugar mixture so you can make realistic flowers that hold their shape for months if well stored. It is a common mistake to think that all gums are similar but, much as with flour, you cannot substitute one thickening/hardening gel for another because they are used for very different things. For instance, guar gum and xanthan gums are used in gluten-free baking as a thickening agent but they won't perform the same function as the Tylose, which hardens the finished product. While it is edible, if you've ever eaten anything made from gum paste, you're probably well aware that the stuff isn't exactly delicious.

Glycerin is used in soaps and in candies to add extensibility, or stretchiness. Glycerin is often added to fondant recipes to keep it from tearing. It is food safe and edible. Don't worry.

Dry Milk Powder

I use dry milk powders in my "Better than Box Cake" recipes. You can find both whole milk powder and buttermilk powder in most grocery stores. I use Carnation brand milk powder, which comes in an envelope, and the Saco Pantry brand buttermilk powder that comes in a sweet little box or in a round carton. Avoid milk powders that look like large granules (that kind usually comes in a box the size of a cereal box). The brands I use are powdery soft and very fine, so they combine with the other ingredients smoothly.

Nut Flours

I use almond, pistachio, and hazelnut flours in the nut meringue layers of a desert called *dacquoise*. They are naturally gluten-free but it's a misnomer to call them "flour" because they aren't. Many people feel that it's okay to swap in nut flours when wheat flours are called for—it's not. Although the nuts do contain protein (and loads of oil), they don't contain the gluten proteins necessary for baking and they won't have the requisite structural capacity and fine siltiness of flour that lends traditional baked goods refinement and structure. But don't worry; we will use nut flours to build some beautiful gluten-free cakes.

Part One

LAYERS *of* LOVE

Pan Prep

I have a system of prepping pans from which I do not stray. I regret it when I do. At first, this might seem over the top or too much work. But I'll show you how I do it and I'll tell you why, and once you get the hang of it, it will be like second nature to you.

The first thing I do, before dealing with the pans, is preheat the oven per the recipe instructions. Then, I take out my pans. Usually two 8-inch/20.5 cm pans. I take a little knob of unsalted butter and smear it in a light coat along the bottom of the pan. This method might appeal to you if you aren't all too confident about being able to contain nonstick spray to just the bottom of the pan. It's pretty easy to accidently get the nonstick stuff along the sides. The reason I avoid greasing the sides of the pan is that I want to keep the cake from shrinking too much from its intended size. An 8-inch/20.5 cm cake can become a 7½-inch/19 cm cake when the sides are too liberally sprayed, as the batter never adheres to the confines of the pan and

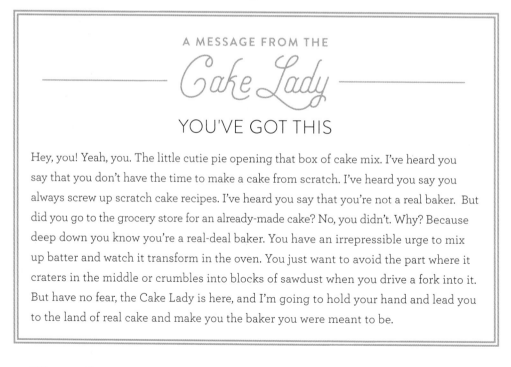

A MESSAGE FROM THE

Cake Lady

YOU'VE GOT THIS

Hey, you! Yeah, you. The little cutie pie opening that box of cake mix. I've heard you say that you don't have the time to make a cake from scratch. I've heard you say you always screw up scratch cake recipes. I've heard you say that you're not a real baker. But did you go to the grocery store for an already-made cake? No, you didn't. Why? Because deep down you know you're a real-deal baker. You have an irrepressible urge to mix up batter and watch it transform in the oven. You just want to avoid the part where it craters in the middle or crumbles into blocks of sawdust when you drive a fork into it. But have no fear, the Cake Lady is here, and I'm going to hold your hand and lead you to the land of real cake and make you the baker you were meant to be.

just shrinks as it grows up. This is also the reason I choose "stick" pans and not non-stick pans. I can always run a paring knife or small offset spatula along the sides of the pan to release it, but I can't make the cake magically grow once it's out of the oven.

I then cut a piece of parchment to fit the bottom of the pan and gently brush the top of the parchment with more butter. You can also spray the bottom, and only the bottom, of the pan. Not the sides, just the bottom. But we know why that's tricky.

But I don't stop at just prepping the inside of the pan. I prep the outside of the pan.

You might have noticed in baking supply shops that things called "cake strips" are being hawked as the fix to cake doming (doming is when the cake rises higher in the middle than on the sides). They do actually work, by creating something of a steam environment that regulates the temperature of the cake batter—keeping the sides from setting too quickly, and then having the batter settle all in the middle dome. Unfortunately, I find the commercial strips tend to work too well and can steam some cakes to the point where they have a gummy texture. But there's a happy medium and that's making homemade cake strips with things you likely already have at home.

I cut a few lengths of an old, but clean, terry cloth towel. I make the strips about 2½ inches/6.5 cm tall and I make sure the length is at least as long as the circumference of my biggest baking pan. I usually need two strips for this and it's okay if they overlap a bit when wrapped around the pan. I wet the pieces and then, using safety pins, I secure the strips snugly around the outer sides of my cake pan. To create an insulated environment, I wrap aluminum foil around the pan to cover the strips, keeping them from drying out too quickly.

Another tool I use is waterproofing repair tape that has a reflective, metal outer surface and a very sticky contact surface, just like a regular piece of tape. I use a small piece to keep aluminum strips together. It's heat-safe because the outside is faced in metal, but make sure to only use just enough tape to secure the aluminum, as the sticky side can melt a bit onto the pan or the oven rack. It's easy enough to scrape off once cooled. Using cake strips not only stops doming, which gives you an even layer of cake that is easily torted, but also keeps the edges of the cake from overbrowning.

Cake Pan Size and Batter Amounts

Most of the cake recipes here are developed for two 8- or 9-inch/20.5 or 23 cm layers, either round or square, unless otherwise stated. However, there will be a time when you want to make a 6-inch/15 cm cake or a 10- or 12-inch/25.5 or 30.5 cm cake. Traditionally, for an 8-inch cake, the standard amount of batter for two pans is 6 cups/1.4 L (3 cups/710 ml of batter in each pan). That's give or take ½ to 1 cup/120 to 235 ml. For a 10-inch cake, 12 cups/2.8 L are standard (6 cups/1.4 L per pan), and then for a 12-inch, 14 to 15 cups/3.3 to 3.5 L (7 to 7 ½ cups/1.65–1.75 L per pan). And then, of course, there's the 6-inch/15 cm cake, which requires 4 cups/950 ml (2 cups/475 ml per pan). When it comes to 6-inch cakes, I usually have three pans available or I bake off all the cake batter in a half sheet pan and use a cake ring to stamp out 6-inch rounds.

Cake Lady

POKE IT. DON'T STAB IT.

Many a cake recipe will recommend that to check for a cake's "doneness" you should stab the poor thing with a toothpick. In the event it comes away with wet batter on it, it's not done. If it appears from within the depths of cake either clean or subtly speckled with moist crumbs, it's done. The thing is, it might not be done. There's a slight chance that the cake hasn't completely set and taking it out of the oven will cause the middle to fall a bit. That's not fair to either you or the cake.

That's why I recommend gently poking the cake to see whether it springs back. If it does spring back, it's done. If the cake feels set, not at all goopy, but while poking you leave a small indentation that doesn't leave, the cake's not yet ready and needs about five more minutes. Another indication of doneness, if you prepare the pan as I recommend with fat spread on the bottom of the pan and not on the sides of the pan, is you'll often see the sides of the cake just starting to pull away from the pan. With cakes made from the foam method, sponge cakes, the cake will often "tell" you when you poke it that it's not ready. You'll hear a crackling noise, a message from the sweet beyond that the cake needs a few more minutes to set before it leaves the warmth of the oven. If you are especially persnickety, you can also use an instant-read thermometer, which means you *have to* stab your cake. When the temperature reads between 200° and 210°F/90° and 100°C, the cake is baked through. All this said, if I had to make a choice, I'd rather my cake be slightly underdone than overdone. I'll take an ultra-moist cake over a dry cake any day.

You will have to make more than one batch of batter if you wish to make a larger cake than 8 to 9 inches/20.5 to 23 cm, and then the timing changes, doesn't it? In general, for every 2 inches/5 cm larger the cake gets I add fifteen to twenty minutes more to the baking time, but please start checking after ten minutes past the original baking time for an 8-inch cake. A 6-inch/15 cm cake will be about ten minutes less than the 8-inch batter equivalent. But here's the thing, and you are likely going to hate this: baking times are *never* exact. Every oven is different and most are liars. You have to start checking for visual cues in all your baking, even if you're using exactly the pan that's called for. I give the oven a little hip check, a very slight one, just enough to see whether the cake is jiggly through the oven door. If you knock the oven too hard, you could make the cake fall. If the cake has set, you can open the door and give the cake a poke. If it springs back when gently prodded, it's done. If it feels set but there's a slight indentation left behind, give it five more minutes. If you notice that the cake is pulling away from the sides of the pan, that's a sure indicator it's done.

Serving Amounts per Cake

Serving sizes are standard in just about every publication and I think they are stingy as all get out. Keep in mind that the standard serving suggestion is for a two-layer cake as well, which I find just unfair as a cake glutton. I stick to the standards as far as the cake diameter goes, but as a rule (that I sometimes break) I make my cakes four layers, not two. I think that makes up for the miserly approach of the number of slices per cake. So, I'm giving you the normal servings but feel free to halve them, based on how cake crazy your guests are.

6-inch/15 cm round/square cake = 12 servings

8-inch/20.5 cm round/square cake = 24 servings

10-inch/25.5 cm round/square cake = 38 servings

12-inch/30.5 cm round/square cake = 56 servings

Different Cake Types and When to Use Them

A friend of mine, fellow baker, and former specialty cake maker, Michele, lamented at the fact that all the tear sheets her former clients would bring in were pictures of Australian cakes, but the layers and fillings they wanted inside were 100 percent American. You may wonder what this means but I understood immediately and it explained quite a bit about why she quit the cake-for-hire business. Some of the most amazing new cake designs come from Down Under and with Instagram and social media allowing pictures of the newest and yummiest to be transmitted across the globe in record time, brides-to-be in other parts of the world see the beauty and want some of it for their own. However, to "build" some of these compli-cated cakes, you often need a very sturdy interior. That means using a very dense cake, almost like a pound cake, that's sturdy enough to handle being stacked and presented in the heat of an Australian summer. You'll also need a sturdy filling, no whipped cream or curd. Ganache or buttercream, even a smear of jam, works best. Not knowing the mechanics of these cakes, most American brides ask that their cakes be built with the most tender and moist of cakes with soft and luscious fillings that could collapse under the weight of so many tiers or feel the strain of heavy décor and then teeter or tear.

If you've got a cake in mind and aren't sure what type of layer to use, have no fear. You'll find it in here.

The
MIX REMIX

Years ago, when I was of a mind to open another pastry shop (this time in Texas instead of Vermont), I took a tour of an existing bake shop that had secretly gone on the market. The establishment was well known for its custom cakes. The front of the house was lined with pictures of multitier, fondant-heavy creations next to local notables, such as the governor. This was the go-to bakery to hire if you needed to order a special event cake for a fancy Austinite. I anticipated finding some top-notch equipment in the back, considering the kind of work it was putting out.

Great mixers, the best in refrigeration, top-tier flour and sugar bins, perhaps a list of contacts with the finest local purveyors of high-fat butters and cream. Instead, I found row after row, shelf after shelf, of box mix cakes. I did a double take to make sure I hadn't taken a wrong turn and wandered into the baking aisle of the local Piggly Wiggly. I looked down to find giant pails of premixed "buttercream." I felt as if my breath had been knocked out of me. Call me naive, but I'd never seen the evidence of such a crime with my own eyes and on such a large scale. The place had "bakery" written out front. How could it get away with not really baking?

I had heard that such things went on with small "cottage industry" cake decorators who were juggling families, full-time jobs, and taking cake orders on the side. These busy entrepreneurs use box mixes for consistency and economy so they can get to the business of decorating. Those tear sheets from bridal magazines customers come in with of bedazzled and beruffled cake perfection take work. Hours of decorating work. The whole "baking a decent cake" part really puts a damper on all that painstaking decoration if you're taking cake orders as a side business. I'll also tell you a secret about those glossy, out-of-this-world gorgeous, cakes in the magazine: they are most likely Styrofoam inside, or "cake dummies" as we call them in the profession. When looks are everything and you'll never see the inside of the thing, why bother with cake? Just decorate on a dummy. Especially if you'll only see a picture of a slice out on a plate on the following page, no need to make the real, multitier deal. Any busy home baker can be forgiven for using a box mix from the grocery store. Cake decorators, baking from home, taking orders as a side gig, can be forgiven for taking one variable off their busy plate and using box cake mix. But I can't lend this kind of forgiveness to a "bakery" charging the big bucks and selling itself as a preeminent custom cake maker. It has no business not baking from scratch. But I've got another secret for you aspiring home bakers—making a better cake from scratch is just as easy and fast as using a box mix.

WHITE CAKE HOMEMADE BOX MIX

White cake is the standard in pretty layers. It's genuinely white because it uses primarily egg whites for protein structure (I add one whole egg to my mix for tenderness.) You won't miss the extra yolks in this beautifully moist (and pretty) cake.

DRY MIX

2½ cups plus 1 tablespoon/300 g bleached cake flour

1½ cups/300 g granulated sugar

⅓ cup plus 2 teaspoons/40 g whole milk powder

2 teaspoons/8 g baking powder

1 teaspoon/7 g salt

½ teaspoon/2 g cream of tartar

Sift all the dry ingredients into a large mixing bowl and whisk to combine or place them in a blender or food processor and pulse until very fine and combined. Store in a large jar in a cool, dark place until you're ready to bake.

Note: You can double, triple, or quadruple this recipe as long as you have a very large storage bin in which to keep it. Simply measure 23¼ ounces/660 g of the dry mix (the weight of the above ingredients) for two 8- or 9-inch/20.5 or 23 cm or three 6-inch/15 cm layers.

COCONUT CAKE HOMEMADE BOX MIX

Add coconut milk and a hint of coconut extract to a batter in lieu of regular old milk and vanilla and you've got yourself a cracking good coconut cake. It's really that easy (and delicious). Make sure you shake-shake-shake that can of coconut milk before you add it, though. The milk separates into a thick layer of cream on top and a watery soup on the bottom in the can and you want both to make this cake tender *and* coconutty. It's so coco-nutty that I use it in my Coconut Snowball Cake (page 241).

DRY MIX

- 2½ cups plus 1 tablespoon/300 g bleached cake flour
- 1½ cups/300 g granulated sugar
- 2 teaspoons/8 g baking powder
- 1 teaspoon/7 g fine sea salt
- ½ teaspoon/2 g cream of tartar

Sift all the dry ingredients into a large mixing bowl and whisk to combine or place in a blender or food processor and pulse until very fine and combined. Store in a large jar in a cool and dark place until you're ready to bake.

Note: You can double, triple, or quadruple this recipe as long as you have a very large storage bin in which to keep it. Simply measure out 23¼ ounces/660 g of the dry mix (the weight of the above ingredients) for two 8- or 9-inch/20.5 or 23 cm layers or two 8-inch/20.5 cm half spheres.

TO BAKE

Unsalted butter or baker's nonstick
  spray for pans

1 recipe (23¼ ounces/660 g) dry mix

4 large egg whites, at room temperature
  (totaling 160 g)

1 large egg, at room temperature

⅔ cup/150 ml canned coconut milk

¾ cup/1½ sticks/170 g unsalted butter,
  much softer than room temperature,
  yet not melted

1 tablespoon unrefined coconut oil

1 teaspoon coconut extract

1 teaspoon pure vanilla extract

Preheat the oven to 350°F/180°C for conventional, 325°F/170°C convection. Butter or spray two 8- or 9-inch/20.5 or 23 cm uncoated cake pans on the bottom of the pan only. Dab any areas of pooling with a paper towel. Line the bottom of each pan with a round of parchment. Attach soaked DIY cake strips to the outer sides of the pans (see page 31) and set aside.

Place the dry mix in the bowl of a stand mixer fitted with the paddle attachment. In a separate bowl or glass measuring cup, combine the egg whites, whole egg, coconut milk, butter, coconut oil, coconut extract, and vanilla. Whisk well. With the mixer on low speed, slowly add the wet ingredients to the dry. This should take about 30 seconds. Once added, turn the mixer speed to medium or medium-high speed (medium speed for a professional 6-quart/5.7 L mixer and medium-high for a standard 4-quart/3.8 L mixer). Mix for 1 minute total. This may seem excessive. But this mixing time is crucial (see my notes on bleached cake flour, page 20).

Divide the batter evenly between the prepared pans. Drop each round pan from a 12-inch/30.5 cm height onto the counter, twice, to release any large bubbles. For half spheres, gently tap on the countertop to release large bubbles. Bake in the middle rack of the oven, slightly separated, for 30 to 35 minutes, or until the cake springs back when gently poked.

YELLOW CAKE HOMEMADE BOX MIX

Golly, this is such a lovely cake. It's one of those gems that is so yummy, I eat it without any frosting at all. But when I do pair it with something, I'll combine it with an equally delightful filling and frosting. Don't be fooled by the simplicity of a yellow cake, it can be as sophisticated as you want.

DRY MIX

3⅓ cups/400 g unbleached cake flour
2 cups/400 g granulated sugar
1 tablespoon/14 g baking powder
1 teaspoon/7 g fine sea salt
½ teaspoon/2 g cream of tartar
⅓ cup plus 2 teaspoons/40 g cultured buttermilk powder

Sift all the dry ingredients into a large mixing bowl and whisk to combine or place in a blender or food processor and pulse until very fine and combined. Store in a large jar in a cool and dark place until you're ready to bake.

Note: You can double, triple, or quadruple this recipe as long as you have a very large storage bin in which to keep it. Simply measure out 30½ ounces/863 g of the dry mix (the weight of the above ingredients) for two 8- or 9-inch/20.5 or 23 cm layers.

TO BAKE

Unsalted butter or baker's nonstick spray for pans

1 recipe (30½ ounces/863 g) dry mix

1 cup/2 sticks/226 g unsalted butter, much softer than room temperature, yet not melted

4 large eggs, at room temperature

2 teaspoons pure vanilla extract

¾ cup/175 ml water

Preheat the oven to 350°F/180°C for conventional, 325°F/170°C convection. Butter or spray two 8- or 9-inch/20.5 or 23 cm uncoated cake pans on the bottom of the pan only. Dab any areas of pooling with a paper towel. Line the bottom of the pans with a round of parchment. Attach soaked DIY cake strips to the outer sides of the pans (see page 31) and set aside.

Place the dry mix in the bowl of a stand mixer fitted with the paddle attachment. Add the soft butter and mix on low speed until the mixture resembles wet sand.

In a separate bowl or glass measuring cup, combine the eggs, vanilla, and water. Whisk to combine. With the mixer on low speed, slowly add the wet ingredients to the dry. This should take about 30 seconds. Once added, turn the mixer speed to medium or medium-high (medium speed for a professional 6-quart/5.7 L mixer and medium-high for a standard 4-quart/3.8 L mixer). Mix for 1 minute total.

Divide the batter evenly between the prepared pans. Drop each pan from a 12-inch/30.5 cm height onto the counter, twice, to release any large bubbles. Bake in the middle rack of the oven, slightly separated, for 35 to 40 minutes, or until the cake springs back when gently poked.

Allow to cool 10 minutes in the pans, then run a small offset spatula or paring knife along the edge of each pan and the cake to release the sides.

CHOCOLATE CAKE HOMEMADE BOX MIX

You want a rich, dark chocolate cake without any fuss? This is your cake. And while the whole "box mix" thing might lead you to think that this cake would pale in comparison to a more convoluted chocolate cake recipe, don't believe it. It's all in the ingredients. If you choose a high-quality cocoa that's deep in color and flavor, you'll be gifted with a chocolate gem that's as good as any chocolate cake out there.

DRY MIX

2½ cups plus 1 tablespoon/300 g
  unbleached cake flour

2 cups/400 g granulated sugar

1 cup/85 g Dutched cocoa powder

3 tablespoons/19.5 g buttermilk powder

1½ teaspoons/8 g baking powder

½ teaspoon/3 g baking soda

Place all the dry ingredients in a blender or food processor and pulse until very fine and combined. Store in a large jar in a cool and dark place until you're ready to bake.

Note: You can double, triple, or quadruple this recipe as long as you have a very large storage bin in which to keep it. Simply measure out 28¾ ounces/815.5 g of the dry mixture (the weight of the above ingredients) for two 8- or 9-inch/20.5 or 23 cm or three 6-inch/15 cm layers.

TO BAKE

Unsalted butter or baker's nonstick
  spray for pans
1 recipe (28¾ ounces/815.5 g) dry mix
½ cup/1 stick/115 g unsalted butter,
  much softer than room temperature,
  yet not melted
⅓ cup/75 g neutral oil, such as canola
4 large eggs, at room temperature
1 cup/223 ml brewed coffee
1 teaspoon pure vanilla extract

Preheat the oven to 350°F/180°C for conventional, 325°F/170°C convection. Butter
or spray two 8- or 9-inch/20.5 or 23 cm or
three 6-inch/15 cm uncoated cake pans on
the bottom of the pan only. Dab any areas of
pooling with a paper towel. Line the bottom
of each pan with a round of parchment.
Attach soaked DIY cake strips to the outer
sides of the pans (see page 31) and
set aside.

Place the dry mix in the bowl of a stand
mixer fitted with the paddle attachment. Add
the soft butter and oil and mix on low speed
until the mixture resembles wet sand.

In a large liquid measure cup, combine the
eggs, coffee, and vanilla. Whisk to combine.
With the mixer on low speed, slowly add the
wet ingredients to the dry. This should take
about 30 seconds. Once added, turn the
mixer speed to medium or medium-high
speed (medium speed for a professional
6-quart/5.7 L mixer and medium-high for
a standard 4-quart/3.8 L mixer). Mix for 1
minute total.

Divide the batter evenly between the
prepared pans. Drop each pan from a
12-inch/30.5 cm height onto the counter,
twice, to release any large bubbles. Bake
in the middle rack of the oven, slightly
separated, for 35 to 40 minutes for 8- or
9-inch/20.5 or 23 cm pans, or 30 to 35
minutes for 6-inch/15 cm pans, until the cake
springs back when gently poked.

Allow to cool 10 minutes in the pans, then
run a small offset spatula or paring knife
along the edge of each pan and the cake to
release the sides.

The
NEXT STEP IN LAYERS
The Paste Method

One of the simplest mixing methods is the paste method, also known as reverse creaming. Does this sound intimidating? Well, I fooled you. You've already done it if you've ever made a box mix cake. And that's what my Homemade Box Mix cake method is based on. Paste method is exactly what it sounds like: you make a paste with the dry ingredients and the fats. Most often, when the first measure of fat in the form of butter, shortening or oil is added, the mixture will look a lot like wet sand.

What's so lovely about it is that, aside from its being dead simple, you also get an incredibly tender cake out of the bargain. There's another name for this kind of cake. It's called a high-ratio cake, which means that there's a higher ratio of sugar to flour. If you look at dry measure recipes exclusively, you might not have realized

that you've been making high-ratio cakes because a cup of flour measures out to 4¼ ounces/120 g, whereas a cup of sugar checks in at 7 ounces/198 g. So, while it might look as if the flour outweighs the sugar in a recipe using dry cup measure, by weight it could be the other way around. That higher dose of sugar does more than make a cake sweet, it makes it super-duper tender. Combine that with a low-protein flour and you get a delicate, sweet, and supple beauty of a cake layer.

Using the paste method, you want to pay attention to the timing of the mixing. When you combine the dry ingredients with the fats first, you're coating the flour with that fat. Not all of it, but a lot of it. When you coat flour in fat, you make it unavailable to produce gluten. In general, if a recipe says to do something (use room-temperature butter, divide the ingredients, sift the flour), it's for a darn good reason. In paste method recipes, that's doubly true. If the recipe says to mix for one minute after adding the wet ingredients, mix for one whole minute. Otherwise, you won't have the structure you need for the cake to rise and keep its shape. It's tough when you've spent a lifetime being told, "Don't overmix!" That still holds true, but in this case, you've got to agitate the batter enough to break loose some of the gluten to create structure. When you've mixed correctly, you'll get a tender, tightly crumbed cake. It's also delicate, which means it's great in a layer cake but it doesn't hold up well to being tiered as it's not quite sturdy enough. At least, not for a bottom tier.

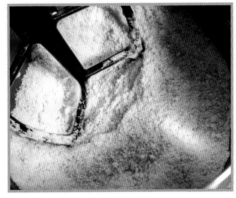

WHITE PARTY CAKE

When I think of the perfect slice of cake, inevitably it's a snowy white cake that comes to mind. It has a tight and tender crumb structure that pairs perfectly with everything from citrus to berry to chocolate. And since the cake is so pearly, almost all your filling options will create a lovely visual contrast; each slice will look like a work of art. To kick up the fun meter a notch, I add rainbow jimmies to the batter to make the party official.

Unsalted butter or baker's nonstick
  spray for pans
2¾ cups/326 g unbleached cake flour
1⅔ cups/333 g granulated sugar
1 tablespoon baking powder
1 teaspoon salt
¾ cup/1½ sticks/170 g unsalted butter,
  very soft
4 large egg whites, at room temperature
1 large egg, at room temperature
1 cup/227 ml whole milk
1 teaspoon pure vanilla extract
¼ cup/40 g rainbow jimmies (optional)

Preheat the oven to 350°F/180°C. Butter or spray the bottom of two 8-inch/20.5 cm uncoated round cake pans and line with parchment or 1 half sheet pan *or* line a half sheet pan with parchment and spray the paper (half sheet cake is for the "Birthday Suit" cake, page 212). Set aside.

Whisk the cake flour, sugar, baking powder, and salt together in the bowl of a stand mixer fitted with the paddle attachment. Add the butter in pieces and mix on low speed until the mixture resembles damp sand.

Add the egg whites, one at a time, then the whole egg, scraping down the sides and bottom of the bowl and beating for 30 seconds between each addition.

Add the milk and vanilla in 3 additions, mixing for 1 minute after each addition, until fluffy. Fold in the jimmies. Divide the batter evenly between the two prepared 8-inch/20.5 cm pans or spread the batter onto the prepared half sheet pan. Bake 20 to 25 minutes, or until the cake just springs back.

Option : My all-time favorite naked cake is made with confetti layers, where you can see that the fun is baked right in the batter from the outside. (See page 212.)

YELLOW CAKE

This yellow cake is the quintessential layer cake. You know the one. The kind that Mrs. Cleaver would slather in chocolate icing and serve to the Beaver in huge slabs when he came home from school. It's tender, moist, and just slightly dense, in the best way. In fact, my favorite way to make this moist and dense beauty is to fill and finish it with my Fudgy Chocolate Frosting (page 186). Together, the cake becomes simple perfection.

Unsalted butter or baker's nonstick
  spray for pans
2 cups/397 g granulated sugar
3 cups/360 g all-purpose flour
1 tablespoon baking powder
1 teaspoon salt
1 cup/2 sticks/226 g unsalted butter,
  very soft
4 large eggs, at room temperature
1 tablespoon vanilla bean paste
1¼ cups/284 ml whole-fat buttermilk,
at room temperature

Preheat the oven to 350°F/180°C for conventional or 325°F/170°C convection. Butter or spray the bottom of two 8-inch/20.5 cm round cake pans and line with parchment. Set aside.

Whisk the sugar, flour, baking powder, and salt in the bowl of a stand mixer fitted with the paddle attachment. Whisk for 30 seconds to combine. Add the butter and mix on low speed until the mixture resembles wet sand.

Add the eggs, one at a time, mixing for 30 seconds between each addition. Scrape down the bottom and sides of the bowl.

Add the vanilla bean paste and mix just to combine. Add the buttermilk with the mixer on low speed. Once it's incorporated, scrape down the bottom and sides of the bowl and increase the speed to medium-high and beat for 30 seconds more.

Divide the batter evenly between the prepared pans and bake on the middle rack for 35 to 40 minutes, or until the cake just springs back when gently poked. Allow to cool for 10 minutes in the pans and then, using a paring knife or a small offset spatula, run the knife around the edge of the pans to release the cakes. Turn over onto parchment and allow to cool.

MAPLE CAKE

In early spring in Vermont, we're all but fed up with snow. Come late February, we've been shoveling our walkways and driveways at least once a week and there's always a very good chance that the biggest storm hasn't even dumped on us yet. But there's one thing that sustains us through those last months of cold up in the Green Mountains: sap. The second the sun shines on our maples and the mercury inches just past freezing, we drill a tap hole past the bark and into the meat of the tree and the celebration begins when a clear stream of sap starts pouring out. Ray and I hammer the metal taps in as fast we can and hang our buckets underneath them to collect the abundance. It takes 40 gallons/151 L of sap to make 1 gallon/3.8 L of maple syrup. Every drop is precious. When we finally boil down the good stuff to the point that it's amber and thick, I take the sweet party up a notch and make a cake to celebrate the bounty of our maples and the coming of spring. I pair this maple-sweet and slightly nutty-tasting gem of a cake with Maple Espresso Cream Cheese Frosting (page 190).

Unsalted butter or baker's nonstick spray

1 cup/213 g light brown sugar

1 cup/156 g maple sugar or 1 cup/235 ml maple syrup

3 cups/360 g all-purpose flour

1 tablespoon baking powder

1 teaspoon salt

1 cup/2 sticks/226 g unsalted butter, very soft

4 large eggs, at room temperature

1 teaspoon maple extract

1 teaspoon vanilla bean paste

1¼ cups/284 ml whole milk, at room temperature

Preheat the oven to 350°F/180°C for conventional or 325°F/170°C convection. Butter or spray the bottom of two 8-inch/20.5 cm or three 6-inch/15 cm round cake pans and line with parchment. Set aside.

Place the brown sugar, maple sugar, flour, baking powder, and salt in the bowl of a stand mixer fitted with the paddle attachment. If you're using maple syrup instead of maple sugar, hold it back until you've added the butter. Whisk the dry ingredients for 30 seconds to combine. Add the butter and mix on low speed until the mixture resembles wet sand.

Add the eggs, one at a time, mixing for 30 seconds between each addition. Scrape down the bottom and sides of the bowl. Add the maple syrup (if using), maple extract, and vanilla bean paste and mix just to combine. Add the milk with the mixer on low speed. Once it's incorporated, scrape down the bottom and sides of the bowl and increase the speed to medium-high and beat for 30 seconds more.

Divide the batter evenly between the prepared pans and bake on the middle rack for 35 to 40 minutes for 8-inch/20.5 cm layers or 30 to 35 minutes for 6-inch/15 cm layers, or until the cake just springs back when gently poked. Allow to cool for 10 minutes in the pans and then, using a paring knife or a small offset spatula, run the knife around the edge of the pans to release the cakes. Turn over onto parchment and allow to cool.

I LOVE THIS CHOCOLATE FUDGE CAKE

MAKES TWO 8-INCH/20.5 CM OR THREE 6-INCH/15 CM ROUND LAYERS

When I perfected this cake, having gone through version after version, the page upon which I'd been noodling around with the recipe in my special "Layers" notebook was splattered with alternating blotches of chocolate and coffee. I'd used all types of writing implements during the journey from black, blue, and red inks to pencil. But I saved my lucky green pen for when I'd landed on exactly the right ratio of ingredients and I wrote, next to a green jaunty star, "LOVE this cake." I underlined the sentiment just to make sure I'd remember just how much I loved this cake. Did I mention that I love this cake? I really do.

Unsalted butter or baker's nonstick
  spray for pans
2 cups/240 g all-purpose flour
2 cups/396 g granulated sugar
¾ cup/78 g Dutched cocoa powder
2 teaspoons baking powder
1 teaspoon baking soda
1 teaspoon salt
¼ cup/ ⅓ stick/57 g unsalted
  butter, very soft
⅓ cup/60 ml neutral oil, such as canola
2 large eggs, at room temperature
1 cup/240 ml buttermilk
1 cup/236 ml freshly brewed coffee,
  slightly cooled
1 teaspoon pure vanilla extract

Preheat the oven to 350°F/180°C for conventional or 325°F/170°C convection. Butter or spray the bottom of two 8-inch/20.5 cm or three 6-inch/15 cm round cake pans and line with parchment. Attach soaked DIY cake strips to the outer sides of the pans (see page 31). Set aside.

Place the flour, sugar, cocoa powder, baking powder, baking soda, and salt in the bowl of a stand mixer fitted with the paddle attachment. Whisk for 30 seconds to combine. Add the butter and oil and mix until the mixture resembles wet sand.

Add the eggs, one at a time, scraping down the bottom and sides of the bowl between each addition.

Combine the buttermilk, coffee, and vanilla in a small bowl. Add the buttermilk mixture in three additions, mixing for 30 seconds and scraping down the bottom and sides of the bowl between each addition.

Divide the batter evenly between the prepared pans. Bake for 30 to 35 minutes for 8-inch/20.5 cm layers or 25 to 30 minutes for 6-inch/15 cm layers, or until the cake just springs back when gently poked.

HUMMINGBIRD CAKE

The recipe for Hummingbird Cake made its first public appearance in *Southern Living* magazine in 1978. It was submitted by Mrs. L. H. Wiggins without any mention as to why exactly it was called Hummingbird Cake, but a reasonable guess is that its lovely sweetness would be the perfect nectar for those flying cuties. The original recipe called for 1½ cups/355 ml of oil, but I find that starting with a larger portion of butter and then adding a dose of moistening oil makes for a perfect, sweet layer cake. To finish, I pair this lovely confection with a cream cheese icing to keep the hummingbirds happy (page 190).

Unsalted butter or baker's nonstick spray for pans

3 cups/360 g unbleached cake flour

2 cups/396 g granulated sugar

1 teaspoon baking soda

½ teaspoon baking powder

1 teaspoon ground cinnamon

1 teaspoon salt

¼ teaspoon freshly grated nutmeg

1 cup/2 sticks/226 g unsalted butter, very soft

¼ cup/59 ml neutral oil, such as canola oil

1 teaspoon pure vanilla extract

4 large eggs, at room temperature

½ cup/125 g whole-fat Greek yogurt

1 cup/200 g mashed banana (from about 3 large bananas)

1 (8-ounce/26 g) can crushed pineapple, drained

½ cup/59 g chopped pecans, lightly toasted and cooled

Preheat the oven to 350°F/180°C for conventional or 325°F/170°C convection. Butter or spray the bottom of two 8-inch/20.5 cm round cake pans and line with parchment. Attach soaked DIY cake strips to the outer sides of the pans (see page 31). Set aside.

Place the flour, sugar, baking soda, baking powder, cinnamon, salt, and nutmeg in the bowl of a stand mixer fitted with the paddle attachment. Whisk for 30 seconds to combine. Add the butter and mix on low speed until the mixture resembles wet sand. Add the oil and vanilla and continue to mix until combined.

Add the eggs, one at a time, mixing thoroughly between each addition. Scrape down the bottom and sides of the bowl and add the yogurt. Mix on medium-high speed for 1 minute.

Take the bowl from the stand and scrape down the bottom and sides of the bowl with a large rubber spatula. Fold in the mashed banana, crushed pineapple, and pecans. Divide the batter evenly between the prepared pans and bake for 25 to 30 minutes, or until the cake springs back when gently poked.

ALMOND CAKE

I can't get enough of this cake. I'm a huge fan of almond and marzipan and this cake pretty much is the best of everything almondy and marzipany. It's a supermoist cake. I'm so sorry I keep using that word. I know it offends but it best describes the best kind of cake. And this is the best kind of cake. I layer it with Honey-Pear-Lavender Cremeux (page 141) and finish with honey buttercream (page 178) for a sophisticated finished confection, such as my Beehive Cake (page 236).

Unsalted butter or baker's nonstick
   spray for pan
1 cup/120 g all-purpose flour
½ teaspoon baking powder
½ teaspoon salt
10 ounces/283 g almond paste
1 cup/2 sticks/226 g unsalted butter,
   very soft
1 cup/198 g granulated sugar
¼ cup/57 g honey
6 large eggs, at room temperature
1 teaspoon almond extract

Preheat the oven to 325°F/170°C conventional or 300°F/150°C convection. Butter or spray a half sheet pan and line with parchment. Attach soaked DIY cake strips to the outer sides of the pan (see page 31). Set aside.

In a small bowl, combine the flour, baking powder, and salt.

Using the large holes of a box grater, finely grate the almond paste. Place the grated almond paste in the bowl of a stand mixer fitted with the paddle attachment. Mix on low speed until smooth. Add butter and mix until combined and smooth. Add the sugar and honey and continue to mix on low speed until the mixture resembles wet sand.

Scrape the bottom and sides of the bowl and add the eggs, one at a time, scraping down the bowl every now and again and then add the almond extract. Add the flour mixture slowly, on low speed, and mix until just combined.

Spread the batter evenly in the prepared pan and bake for 20 to 25 minutes, or until the cake is set and springs back when gently poked.

Note: Make sure that the almond paste you use is very soft. If the paste has dried on the grocer's shelf, put it in a plastic bag with a slice of apple and leave sealed together overnight.

FRENCH STRAWBERRY-LEMON YOGURT CAKE

MAKES TWO 8-INCH/20.5 CM ROUND LAYERS

When you think of fine pastry, you think of France. You just do. So, it may come as a surprise to you that home baking isn't a huge thing in France. There are so many fabulous bakeries and pastry shops that it's just easier to pop around the corner and pick up a lovely galette from the corner patisserie. But the one cake everyone does seems to bake at home is the simple yogurt cake. It's moist and bright. Most often it's baked in a loaf or a simple pan and served without much fanfare. Personally, I like to add fresh strawberries and a bit of lemon to bump up the sunny flavors. When I do layer this cake, I keep the filling light and bright.

Unsalted butter or baker's nonstick
  spray for pans
½ cup/125 g plain whole-fat Greek yogurt
¼ cup/59 ml whole-fat buttermilk
Grated zest of 1 lemon
1 teaspoon lemon extract
1½ cups/180 g all-purpose flour
2¼ teaspoons baking powder
½ teaspoon salt
1 cup/198 g granulated sugar
½ cup/1 stick/113 g unsalted butter,
  very soft
¼ cup/59 ml neutral oil, such as canola
2 tablespoons honey
2 large eggs, at room temperature
½ cup/85 hulled and finely
  chopped strawberries

Preheat the oven to 350°F/180°C for conventional or 325°F/170°C convection. Butter or spray the bottom of two 8-inch/20.5 cm round cake pans and line with parchment. Attach soaked DIY cake strips to the outer sides of the pans (see page 31). Set aside.

In a large liquid measure cup, combine the yogurt, buttermilk, lemon zest, and lemon extract and stir well. Set aside.

Place the flour, baking powder, salt, and sugar in the bowl of a stand mixer fitted with the paddle attachment. Whisk to combine. Add the butter, oil, and honey and mix on low speed until the mixture resembles wet sand.

Add the eggs, one at a time, mixing between each addition. Add the yogurt mixture in two additions, mixing on medium-high speed between each addition.

Take the mixing bowl from the stand mixer and, using a large rubber spatula, fold in the strawberry pieces.

Divide the batter evenly between the two prepared pans. Bake in the middle of the oven for 35 to 40 minutes, or until the cake springs back when gently poked. Allow to cool 10 minutes in the pan and then, using a paring knife or small offset spatula, run the knife between the pans and the cake to release the sides. Turn over the cake onto a piece of parchment and allow to cool completely.

The Creaming Method

I've been creaming together butter and sugar since I was old enough to scamper onto the kitchen countertop and reach into the highest cupboard where my mother hid her stash of illicit sugar that was meant for holiday baking only. Now, most recipes that call for creaming butter and sugar together just start with that procedure and then move on to include eggs and dry ingredients, and most often require the use of a stand mixer or a hand mixer. When I was a kid, I started and stopped with the sugar and butter and I did it by hand. And then I ate it with a spoon, really fast, because if my mother came home and caught me, there'd be hell to pay. But for a child born with a deep kinship with sugar and butter, growing up in a vegan, no-sugar household required such hijinks for said child to survive.

Because I was combining the sugar and butter together for the express purpose of inhaling the mixture, shall we say, "à la carte," I wasn't worried about suspending the two in a beautiful, creamy state of being that was optimal for creating beautiful cakes. I was just going for a decent mash-up. As I got older and discovered ways of accessing other ingredients and an oven (don't ask), I was able to produce slightly more palatable treats to feed my sweet soul. I started with cookies, in which case mixing together the butter and sugar isn't much more of an ordeal than what I'd already been accustomed to doing. Cookies don't require anything lofty from sugar and butter, since most cookies don't aspire to great heights. They are meant to be round (usually) and flat (almost exclusively).

A few years older still and I was on to cakes. I learned quickly that giving butter and sugar a cursory spin wasn't going to cut it. The cakes weren't as springy as I'd hoped. They were too dense and they were often riddled with molten pockets of crystallized sugar goo. It was then that I surmised that what "light and fluffy" meant was to get the mixture from what looked to be a very sad pile of damp sand into a state wholly different, as if I'd walked into the hair salon with my unruly mass of frizzy brown hair and exited in full Farrah Fawcett glory. Those kinds of transformations take a while. And so it is with creaming butter and sugar when you're mixing them for a cake.

When you're making a cookie or a traditional muffin recipe, dense is okay. You want something with a tight crumb structure and little lift. When you're creaming the butter and sugar for those kinds of treats, you need just a little agitation so that the air pockets you're creating during mixing are small and the leavening you've added to the recipe won't expand the batter too much beyond that little pocket. That wet, grainy look works for cookies.

When you're creaming butter and sugar for a cake, however, you want those pockets *big* so that the leavening can really do its job and expand those air pockets with all that lovely carbon dioxide. For that expansion to happen, you need your ingredients to be willing and able to perform. Sugar can just show up. Regular old granulated sugar is just fine. The butter, however, has to do some prep work. It must be at room temperature. This can take anywhere from thirty minutes to two hours, depending on how cool or warm your room is. You want to be able to easily make a dent in the butter with your finger. However, you don't want it melted. The sugar's job is to essentially punch holes in the butter as it's mixing. If the butter's too cold, the sugar can't make much of a dent.

The mixture will stay in that sad, damp sand state. If it's melted, there's nothing really there for the sugar to punch. It's like getting into a fistfight with pudding. On the other hand, a room-temperature butter will give the sugar something to work with, punching holes and dancing around the bowl, creating big bubbles and really expanding into a light and fluffy mess.

I find that if my butter's right on the money, temperature-wise, it takes three to four minutes to get to optimal light and fluffy. If my room temperature is just a little chilly, such as in the dead of winter, it can take quite a bit longer. Sometimes five minutes longer. But that extra time is crucial and definitely worth it if you want that perfectly moist and bouncy cake that's also perfect for stacking *high*. This is the cake that's born to be in a wedding cake. Creamed cakes are usually structurally sound enough to act as the foundational base in the tallest celebratory tiered wonder.

THE DEEP FREEZE

The whole point of "Baking Ahead" is that you can get your cake layers baked early and know that when you're ready to finish everything up, a day, a week, or a month later, your layers are waiting in tip-top condition for the party to commence. To do this properly, you'll need to allow your cake to cool completely. My method is to leave the cake to cool in the pan for ten minutes and then I use a paring knife or small offset spatula to release the cake from the sides of the pan and turn over the layer onto a piece of parchment. If you release a very tender cake too early, it can fall apart. Those ten minutes in the pan help keep things together when you eventually turn out the cake. When you do turn it out, the cake pan will still be very warm, so use oven mitts or kitchen towels to turn the cake pan over.

While the cake is still warm, remove the parchment from the bottom of the cake. Often, any browning will cling to the parchment, if it doesn't, take a small serrated knife (a steak knife is perfect for this) and gently scrape any browning from the bottom and sides of the cake layer.

Once the layer has completely cooled, gently flip the layer over. Often the browned portion on the top of the cake will have steamed off and will stick to the parchment. Whatever's left, scrape off with the steak knife.

I like to torte my cakes before wrapping and freezing them. Slip a cake board under the layers and place in the freezer for 30 to 45 minutes, just long enough for the cake layer to chill all the way through but not so much that it's frozen solid. This tightens the crumb structure of the cake and makes torting—cutting the layer in half horizontally—much easier and keeps the cake from shedding chunks as you cut it in half. (See more about torting on page 117.) Wrap each layer of cake individually in a double coating of plastic wrap and then wrap in foil. Freeze the cakes in a single layer; don't stack them. You can assemble the layers, filling and coating them, straight from the freezer. Cakes well wrapped and stored in a stable freezer (one that doesn't rise and drop in temperature constantly) can be left frozen for months.

GESINE'S TRIED-AND-TRUE YELLOW CAKE

This is the cake that became the foundation of my pastry shop, Gesine Confectionary. There's nothing this little cake couldn't do. It starred as the layers in most of the specialty cakes that left the shop and it was the base of my world-famous (or, at least, Vermont famous) Golden Eggs. This cake is moist and delicious and complements just about any filling and frosting you can throw at it. Ask anyone in Vermont. They'll agree.

Unsalted butter or baker's nonstick
  spray for pans
3 cups/360 g all-purpose flour
1 tablespoon baking powder
1 teaspoon salt
1 cup/2 sticks/226 g unsalted butter,
  at room temperature
2 cups/396 g granulated sugar
5 large eggs, at room temperature
1 tablespoon vanilla bean paste
1¼ cups/295 ml whole-fat buttermilk

Preheat the oven to 350°F/180°C for conventional or 325°F/170°C convection. Butter or spray the bottom of two 8-inch/20.5 cm round cake pans and line with parchment. Attach soaked DIY cake strips to the outer sides of the pans (see page 31). Set aside. In a small bowl, whisk together the flour, baking powder, and salt for 30 seconds. Set aside.

Place the butter and sugar in the bowl of a stand mixer fitted with the paddle attachment. Mix on high speed until light and fluffy, 3 to 4 minutes. Scrape down the bottom and sides of the bowl and make sure to scrape

down the paddle as well. Mix again for about 30 seconds.

Add the eggs, one at a time, mixing well between each addition and scraping down the bottom and sides of the bowl every few eggs. Add the vanilla bean paste and mix just to combine.

With the mixer running on low speed, add a third of the flour, then half of the buttermilk, then a third of the flour and the remaining buttermilk, finishing with the remaining flour. Mix until just combined. Don't overmix. Take the bowl from the mixing stand and, using a large rubber spatula, scrape the bottom and sides of the bowl and fold the batter a few times to ensure everything is well incorporated.

Divide the batter evenly between the prepared pans. Bake for 35 to 40 minutes, or until the cake just springs back when gently poked.

Variation: For a Butterscotch Cake, replace 1 cup/198 g of the granulated sugar with 1 cup/213 g of dark brown sugar.

Maple Sticky Bun Cake and Caramel Cake

MAPLE STICKY BUN CAKE

MAKES TWO 8-INCH/20.5 CM ROUND LAYERS

Who doesn't love a maple-infused sticky bun? I know I do. But sometimes it's fun to indulge in a little mash-up, inviting the breakfast treat to the cake party. This sweet and rich cake is delicious on its own. You can bake it in a large baking pan and top with crumble and you've got a brilliant coffee cake for breakfast. Or you can layer it with maple butter pecan frosting (page 190) and top it with an ooey-gooey caramel topping studded with roasted pecans and you've got a celebration (or breakfast...I totally wouldn't hold it against you for eating it for breakfast).

Unsalted butter or baker's nonstick spray for pans

CINNAMON-SUGAR RIBBON

¼ cup/53 g light brown sugar
¼ cup/30 g pecans, lightly toasted
½ teaspoon ground cinnamon

CAKE

3 cups/360 g all-purpose flour
1 tablespoon baking powder
1 teaspoon ground cinnamon
1 teaspoon salt
1 cup/2 sticks/226 g unsalted butter, at room temperature
1 cup/198 g granulated sugar
½ cup/106 g light brown sugar
½ cup/78 g maple sugar
1 tablespoon vanilla bean paste
5 large eggs, at room temperature
1¼ cups/295 ml buttermilk

Preheat the oven to 350°F/180°C for conventional or 325°F/170°C convection. Butter or spray the bottom of two 8-inch/20.5 cm round cake pans and line with parchment. Attach soaked DIY cake strips to the outer sides of the pans (see page 31). Set aside.

Prepare the cinnamon-sugar ribbon: Place the brown sugar, pecans, and cinnamon in a food processor and pulse until combined and very fine. Set aside.

Prepare the cake: In a small bowl, combine the flour, baking powder, cinnamon, and salt. Whisk for 30 seconds. Set aside.

Place the butter, granulated sugar, light brown sugar, and maple sugar in the bowl of a stand mixer. Mix on high speed until light and fluffy, 3 to 4 minutes. Scrape down the bottom and sides of the bowl. Add the vanilla bean paste and then add the eggs, one at a time, mixing well between each addition. Scrape down the bottom and sides of the bowl.

With the mixer on low speed, add a third of the flour mixture, then half of the buttermilk, and then continue to alternate between the flour and buttermilk until just combined. Take the bowl from the mixer stand and then, using a large rubber spatula, fold the batter a few times to ensure everything is well incorporated.

Add a quarter of the batter to each of the prepared pans and then divide the cinnamon-sugar ribbon mixture between the two pans, sprinkling evenly over the top of the batter. Divide the remainder of the batter evenly between the two pans and bake for 30 to 35 minutes, or until the cake springs back when gently poked.

A MESSAGE FROM THE

Cake Lady

OVERMIXING, OR THE TUNNEL OF LOVE

"Mix until just combined." "Don't overmix." This is the instruction in most every baking recipe. And it really matters. Overmixing refers specifically to mixing too long after flour is added. When flour and water interact, gluten is formed. Some gluten is good and necessary. The proteins in gluten provide structure. But there is such a thing as too much structure and when you mix a cake batter after flour and water are present (or anything that contains water, such as an egg or a milk product), you have to make sure not to produce an overabundance of gluten strands, as the end product will be tough and even chewy. At times, if you've really gone mixing crazy, the interior of the cake will have tunnels that run vertically through the cake, this is called tunneling, which is a striking visual to confirm that you have overmixed your batter. This differs from round air pockets baked into the cake, which can be easily eliminated by dropping the batter-filled cake pan from a height of 12 inches/30.5 cm onto your countertop twice to pop any bubbles. Bottom line, once flour and water meet, you want to limit the amount of time you spend mixing the batter. This is especially true when mixing using the creaming method and all-purpose flour, which contains a higher percentage of gluten versus cake flour.

DEVIL'S FOOD CAKE

MAKES THREE 8-INCH/20.5 CM OR FOUR 6-INCH/15 CM ROUND LAYERS

Devil's food cake was originally made with grated beets to contribute moisture, sweetness, and a devilish red. Modern devil's food has done away with the beets and has become a slightly less sweet and sturdier layer than a chocolate cake made with oils, a higher ratio of sugar and using the paste or "one bowl" method. This doesn't mean that it is any less chocolaty or tender. In fact, it's quite heavenly in a beautiful layer cake like my Heaven and Hell Cake (page 232).

Unsalted butter or baker's nonstick spray for pans

4 cups/480 g unbleached cake flour

1 cup/85 g natural cocoa powder

2½ teaspoons baking soda

1 teaspoon salt

2 cups/1 pound/452 g unsalted butter, at room temperature

3 cups/639 g packed light brown sugar

4 large eggs, at room temperature

2 teaspoons pure vanilla extract

3 cups/709 ml freshly brewed coffee

Preheat the oven to 350°F/180°C for conventional or 325°F/170°C convection. Butter or spray the bottom of three 8-inch/20.5 cm or four 6-inch/15 cm round cake pans and line with parchment. Attach soaked DIY cake strips to the outer sides of the pans (see page 31). Set aside.

In a large mixing bowl, whisk together the cake flour, cocoa powder, baking soda, and salt for 30 seconds. Set aside.

Place the butter and brown sugar in the bowl of a stand mixer fitted with the paddle attachment and whisk until light and fluffy, 3 to 4 minutes. Scrape down the bottom and sides of the bowl. Add the eggs, one at a time, mixing well between each addition. Scrape the bottom and sides of the bowl.

Add the vanilla and then, with the mixer on low speed, add a third of the flour mixture and then half of the coffee. Continue to alternate between the flour and coffee until just combined. Remove the bowl from the mixing stand and, using a large rubber spatula, fold the batter a few times to ensure everything is well incorporated.

Divide the batter evenly between the prepared pans and bake for 20 to 25 minutes for 8-inch/20.5 cm layers or for 25 to 30 minutes for 6-inch/15 cm layers, or until the cake springs back when gently poked.

LEMON–POPPY SEED CAKE

Traditionally, you only see the lemon–poppy seed combination in a muffin: a moist, flavorful, citrusy morsel with slightly crunchy seeds delightfully popping as you chomp away. But, I ask you, what is a muffin but a cake restrained in ruffled paper Spanx? There's no reason you can't supersize that recipe and get an even better confection out of it. In fact, I used it as one of my tiers (along with the zippiest lemon cream on earth) of Super Ray's Birthday Cake (page 269). Try it. You'll like it.

Unsalted butter or baker's nonstick
  spray for pans
2 cups/240 g bleached cake flour
1 tablespoon baking powder
1 teaspoon fine sea salt
½ cup/118 ml whole milk, at room
  temperature
4 large egg whites, at room temperature
1 large egg, at room temperature
1 teaspoon lemon extract
½ cup/1 stick/113 g unsalted butter,
  at room temperature
1 cup/198 g granulated sugar
Grated zest of 1 lemon
2 tablespoons/18 g poppy seeds

Preheat the oven to 350°F/180°C for conventional or 325°F/170°C convection. Butter or spray the bottom of two 8-inch/20.5 cm round cake pans and line with parchment. Attach soaked DIY cake strips to the outer sides of the pans (see page 31).Set aside. In a small bowl, whisk together the flour, baking powder, and salt for 30 seconds. Set aside.

In a liquid measure, combine the milk, egg whites, whole egg, and lemon extract and whisk to combine. Set aside.

Place the butter and sugar in the bowl of a stand mixer fitted with the paddle attachment and cream until light and fluffy, 3 to 4 minutes. Scrape down the bottom and sides of the bowl and the paddle.

Add a third of the flour mixture and then half of the egg white mixture on low speed and continue to alternate between the flour and egg white mixture until the batter is just combined. Scrape the bottom and sides of the bowl, along with the paddle, and mix on high speed for 1 minute more. Fold in the lemon zest and poppy seeds, using a large rubber spatula.

Divide the batter evenly between the prepared pans and bake for 25 to 30 minutes, or until the cake springs back when gently poked.

APPLESAUCE CAKE

This cake blurs the line between a supermoist and dense quick bread and a traditional, creamed cake. The applesauce packs this lovely confection with a fresh dewiness, but the creaming method keeps the cake from being merely damp. It's packed with flavor and it's as if the entire season of autumn had transformed into pastry form. I sandwich this special cake with a light, apple cider-pumpkin mousse that's studded with hidden (until you cut into this delight) chocolate (page 152) or pumpkin pastry cream-filled cream puffs in the Apple Cider Cake (page 283). Yes, please!

Baker's nonstick spray for pan
1¼ cups/150 g all-purpose flour
1 teaspoon baking powder
½ teaspoon salt
½ teaspoon ground cinnamon
¼ teaspoon freshly grated nutmeg
¼ teaspoon ground cloves
½ cup/1 stick/113 g unsalted butter, at room temperature
1 cup/213 g light brown sugar
1 large egg, at room temperature
1 teaspoon pure vanilla extract
1 cup/246 g applesauce

Preheat the oven to 350°F/180°C for conventional, 325°F/170°C convection. Spray a 9-inch/23 cm round cake pan and line the bottom with parchment. Set aside.

In a small bowl, whisk the flour, baking powder, salt, cinnamon, nutmeg, and cloves for 30 seconds to combine. Set aside.

Combine the butter and brown sugar in the bowl of a stand mixer fitted with the paddle attachment and cream until light and fluffy, about 5 minutes. Scrape down the bottom and sides of the bowl and add the egg and vanilla. Mix until incorporated. Scrape down the bottom and sides of the bowl.

With the mixer running on low speed, add half of the flour mixture, then the applesauce, and then the remaining flour. Mix until just combined. Take from the stand and fold the batter a few times with a rubber spatula to ensure everything is well incorporated.

Pour the batter into the prepared pan and bake for 25 to 30 minutes, or until the cake springs back when gently poked. Run a knife along the edges of the pan to release the cake and turn out onto a piece of parchment to cool. Once cool, transfer the cake to the freezer for 20 minutes and then torte in half. Wrap with plastic wrap until ready to assemble the cake.

BANANA CAKE

MAKES TWO 8-INCH/20.5 CM LAYERS OR 1 HALF SHEET PAN

You read that correctly. Banana *cake*, not bread. If you've been paying attention, you'll know that beating past the sad sandy mess of the early stages of butter and sugar and creaming to "light and fluffy" makes for a great cake. When you're making a banana bread, the creaming method usually isn't employed because the bread is meant to be very dense. Not so this wonderful cake that brings with it a lovely a hint of that creamy fruit and imparts a wonderful moistness to the layers that can't be beat. I love to fill these layers with a luscious Caramel Cremeux (page 144) and then coat the entire cake with a Caramel Buttercream (page 178) and a coating of chocolate Puppet Dust (page 206). It's like a bananas Foster, just better. See it in its full finished glory on page 223.

Unsalted butter or baker's nonstick spray for pans

2 cups/240 g all-purpose flour

½ teaspoon baking soda

1 teaspoon baking powder

1 teaspoon salt

½ cup/113 g whole-fat Greek yogurt

1 cup/240 g mashed ripe banana (about 3 bananas)

1 tablespoon vanilla bean paste

1½ cups/3 sticks/336 g unsalted butter, at room temperature

½ cup/99 g granulated sugar

½ cup/106 g dark brown sugar

¼ cup/85 g honey

Grated zest of 1 lemon

2 large eggs, at room temperature

Preheat the oven to 350°F/180°C for conventional or 325°F/170°C convection. Butter or spray the bottom of two 8-inch/20.5 cm round cake pans or 1 half sheet pan and line with parchment. Attach soaked DIY cake strips to the outer sides of the pans (see page 31). Set aside.

In a small bowl, combine the flour, baking soda, baking powder, and salt. Whisk for 30 seconds. Set aside.

Stir the yogurt, mashed bananas, and vanilla bean paste together in a medium bowl. Set aside.

Combine the butter, granulated sugar, and brown sugar in the bowl of a stand mixer fitted with the paddle attachment. Mix on high speed until light and fluffy, 3 to 4 minutes. Scrape down the bottom and sides of the bowl and the paddle. Add the honey and lemon zest. Mix for about 30 seconds more.

Add the eggs, one at a time, mixing between each addition until incorporated.

Scrape down the bottom and sides of the bowl and add a third of the flour mixture, mixing on low speed. Add half of the banana mixture, then a third of the flour mixture, the remainder of the banana mixture, and then the remaining flour. Mix until just combined. Take the bowl from the stand and, using a large rubber spatula, fold the batter a few times to ensure everything is well incorporated.

Divide the batter evenly between the prepared pans or on the half sheet pan and bake in the middle rack of the oven for 35 to 40 minutes, or until the cake just springs back when gently poked.

Allow to cool in the pans for 10 minutes and then run a paring knife or small offset spatula along the edge of the pans and the cake to release the cake. Turn out the cakes onto a piece of parchment and allow to cool completely.

PEANUT BUTTER CAKE

Can't decide between eating an old school PBJ or a slice of cake? Why not get the best of both worlds, with a tender and moist peanut butter cake, smeared with a sweet layer of jam and topped with a creamy peanut butter mousse? Or top with Nutella Mousse (page 149). Your peanut butter dreams are all right here, in this sweet, simple cake.

Unsalted butter or baker's nonstick
  spray for pans
3 cups/360 g all-purpose flour
1 tablespoon baking powder
1 teaspoon salt
1 cup/2 sticks/226 g unsalted butter,
  at room temperature
1 cup/198 g granulated sugar
1 cup/213 g light brown sugar
5 large eggs, at room temperature
½ cup/135 g peanut butter
1 teaspoon pure vanilla extract
1¼ cups/284 ml buttermilk

Preheat the oven to 350°F/180°C for conventional or 325°F/170°C convection. Butter or spray the bottom of two 10-inch/25.5 cm square cake pans and line with parchment. Attach soaked DIY cake strips to the outer sides of the pans (see page 31). Set aside.

In a large mixing bowl, combine the flour, baking powder, and salt. Whisk for 30 seconds to distribute the leavening. Set aside.

Place the butter, granulated sugar, and brown sugar in the bowl of a stand mixer fitted with the paddle attachment. Mix on high speed until light and fluffy, 3 to 4 minutes. Scrape down the bottom and sides of the bowl and add the eggs, one at a time, mixing well between each addition. Scrape the bottom and sides of the bowl. Add the peanut butter and vanilla. Mix until just combined.

With the mixer on low, add a third of the flour mixture. then half of the buttermilk, and continue to alternate between the two until combined. Take the bowl from the stand and, using a large rubber spatula, fold the batter a few times to ensure everything is well incorporated. Divide the batter evenly between the prepared pans and bake for 15 to 20 minutes, or until the cake springs back when gently poked.

PUMPKIN CAKE

MAKES TWO 9-INCH/23 CM BUNDT LAYERS

Sometimes, there's a baking trend that just gives me the heebie-jeebies. One such trend came about a few years ago around Thanksgiving time. It was a sweet monstrosity, meant as a tip of the hat to an equally odious savory holiday food trend, the turducken. Someone got the idea to bake a pie *inside* a cake and the resulting Frankencake was the worst of both. . . at least that's how it looked. I refuse to get near one. I mourned the loss of any flaky crispness that a pie, trapped in the wet battered coffin surrounding it on all sides, would suffer in the oven. But the idea of it wouldn't leave me because there was, in spite of the horror, something there. All the goodness of Thanksgiving called to me. The pumpkin. The pecan. And, yes, the flaky. So, I took it upon myself to make the unpalatable palatable. Maybe even great. I developed a rich pumpkin cake and baked it in a domed pan so it would take on all the aspects of a pumpkin. I baked a luscious, gooey pecan filling by itself as a layer. Then, I baked flaky, round pie layers and I assembled it all using a silken pumpkin ermine frosting to look very much like a pumpkin (see page 275). And I was happy that I had built the thing that had given me culinary nightmares to my own specifications and it was good. No. Not good. It was great.

Unsalted butter or baker's nonstick
　spray for pans
4 cups/480 g unbleached cake flour
1 teaspoon baking powder
1 teaspoon baking soda
1 teaspoon salt
1 teaspoon ground cinnamon
½ teaspoon ground ginger
¼ teaspoon freshly grated nutmeg
¼ teaspoon ground cloves
1 (15-ounce/425 g) can pure pumpkin purée
1 cup/227 ml buttermilk
1 teaspoon pure vanilla extract
1 cup/2 sticks/226 g unsalted butter, at
　room temperature
2 cups/426 g light brown sugar

4 large eggs, at room temperature
Grated zest of 1 orange

Preheat the oven to 350°F/180°C for conventional or 325°F/170°C convection. Butter or a spray a 9-inch/23 cm round Bundt pan. Set aside.

In a small bowl, combine the flour, baking powder, baking soda, salt, cinnamon, ginger, nutmeg, and cloves. Set aside.

In a liquid measure cup, stir together the pumpkin purée, buttermilk, and vanilla. Place the butter and brown sugar in the bowl of a stand mixer fitted with the paddle attachment and mix on high speed until light and fluffy, 3 to 4 minutes. Scrape the bottom and sides of the bowl. Add the eggs, one at a time, mixing well between each addition, and then add the zest. Scrape down the bottom and sides of the bowl.

With the mixer on low speed, add a third of the flour mixture, half of the pumpkin mixture, and then continue to alternate between the flour and pumpkin until just incorporated. Remove the bowl from the stand and, using a large rubber spatula, fold the mixture a few times. Add half of the batter to the prepared pan, refrigerating the remaining batter, and bake for 35 to 40 minutes, or until the cake just springs back when gently poked. Turn out the cake onto a cooling rack.

Clean the Bundt pan and butter or spray again. Spread the remaining batter evenly in the pan and bake as directed.

Sticky Toffee Pudding Cake

STICKY TOFFEE PUDDING CAKE

This might seem like such a weird cake when you read the ingredients, but it is absolutely scrumptious. The combination of rich and sweet dates, coffee, and rum make for a complex and entirely delicious layer cake. I often make it during the holidays, but it has worked its way into my monthly rotation due to its addictive flavor qualities. Layer with brown sugar buttercream and top with a caramel top and you've got one decadent cake.

Unsalted butter or baker's nonstick spray for pans

3 cups/360 g all-purpose flour

1 tablespoon baking powder

1 teaspoon salt

¼ cup/57 ml dark rum

¾ cup/170 ml freshly brewed hot coffee

1½ cups/270 g pitted and chopped dates

1 cup/2 sticks/226 g unsalted butter, at room temperature

2 cups/426 g light brown sugar

5 large eggs, at room temperature

1 teaspoon vanilla bean paste

½ cup/113 ml whole milk

Preheat the oven to 350°F/180°C for conventional or 325°F/170°C convection. Butter or spray the bottom of three 8-inch/20.5 cm round cake pans and line with parchment. Attach soaked DIY cake strips to the outer sides of the pans (see page 31). Set aside.

In a mixing bowl, combine the flour, baking powder, and salt. Whisk for 30 seconds and set aside.

In a large liquid measure cup, combine the rum and coffee. Add the dates. Set aside.

Place the butter and brown sugar in the bowl of a stand mixer fitted with the paddle attachment. Mix on high speed for 3 to 4 minutes, until light and fluffy. Scrape down the bottom and sides of the bowl. Add the eggs, one at a time, mixing well between each addition and scraping down the bowl every now and again. Add the vanilla bean paste.

With the mixer on low speed, add one third of the flour mixture, then the milk, one third more of the flour mixture, then the coffee mixture, and then the rest of the flour. Mix until just combined. Take the bowl from the stand and, using a large rubber spatula, fold the batter a few times to ensure everything is well incorporated. Divide the batter evenly between the prepared pans and bake for 25 to 30 minutes, or until the cake just springs back when gently poked.

GINGERBREAD SPICE CAKE

This is a cake made of happy. It's got the gingerbread flavor you know and love but it's wrapped in a moist cake that will have you craving gingerbread all year round. Fill the layers with a buttercream gently infused with orange, and decorate it with adorable, crisp gingerbread cookies (page 208), and you've got the one cake that can really make it a happy holiday (or wedding!).

Unsalted butter or baker's nonstick
  spray for pans
2¾ cups/330 g all-purpose flour
1 teaspoon baking powder
½ teaspoon baking soda
1 teaspoon salt
1 tablespoon ground ginger
1 teaspoon ground cinnamon
1 teaspoon freshly grated nutmeg
½ teaspoon ground cloves
1 cup/2 sticks/226 g unsalted butter,
  at room temperature
1½ cups/319 g dark brown sugar
½ cup/179 g molasses
2 large eggs, at room temperature
1 cup/227 ml freshly brewed hot coffee

Preheat the oven to 350°F/180°C conventional or 325°F/170°C convection. Butter or spray the bottom of two 8-inch/20.5 cm or three 6-inch/15 cm round cake pans and line with parchment. Attach soaked DIY cake strips to the outer sides of the pans (see page 31). Set aside.

In a large bowl, whisk together the flour, baking powder, baking soda, salt, ginger, cinnamon, nutmeg, and cloves. Set aside.

Place the butter and brown sugar in the bowl of a stand mixer fitted with the paddle attachment. Mix on high speed until light and fluffy, 3 to 4 minutes. Scrape down the bottom and sides of the bowl and scrape down the paddle. Add the molasses, then add the eggs, one at a time, mixing well between each addition. Scrape down the bowl.

With the mixer on low speed, add one third of the flour mixture, then half of the coffee, and continue to alternate between the two until you end with the flour and the mixture is just combined. Take the bowl from the stand and, using a large rubber spatula, fold the batter a few times to ensure everything is well incorporated.

Divide the batter evenly between the prepared pans and bake in the middle rack for 35 to 40 minutes for 8-inch/20.5 cm layers or 30 to 35 minutes for 6-inch/1 cm layers, or until the cake just springs back when gently poked.

COCONUT CAKE

For years I detested coconut. I couldn't smell it without bleating that I'd just *die* if I had to taste the stuff. I was a kid, so the dramatics around my protestations are understandable but, and I'm going to tell you a secret here, my dislike was based on no real experience of coconut. I just *thought* I hated it. Jiminy Christmas, I missed out on *so* much. Today, it's on my "highly approved" list of flavors. I like it on shrimp and as a sorbet. I love it as a milk and a water. I especially like it as a cake, this one in particular.

Unsalted butter or baker's nonstick
  spray for pans

1 (15-ounce/425 g) can Coco López
  cream of coconut

1 cup/236 ml buttermilk

1 tablespoon vanilla bean paste

3 cups/360 g all-purpose flour

1 tablespoon baking powder

1 teaspoon salt

1 cup/2 sticks/226 g unsalted butter,
  at room temperature

2 cups/396 g granulated sugar

5 large eggs, at room temperature

Preheat the oven to 350°F/180°C for conventional or 325°F/170°C convection. Butter or spray the bottom of two 8-inch/20.5 cm round cake pans and line with parchment. Attach soaked DIY cake strips to the outer sides of the pans (see page 31). Set aside.

In a large liquid measure cup, combine the cream of coconut, buttermilk, and vanilla bean paste. Set aside.

In a large bowl, combine the flour, baking powder, and salt and whisk for 30 seconds to distribute the leavening. Set aside.

Place the butter and sugar in the bowl of a stand mixer fitted with the paddle attachment. Mix until light and fluffy, 3 to 4 minutes. Scrape the bottom and sides of the bowl. Add the eggs, one at a time, mixing well between each addition.

Scrape down the bottom and sides of the bowl and add a third of the flour mixture, then half of the coconut mixture. Continue to alternate between the flour and coconut mixture until the batter is just combined. Take the bowl from the mixing stand and, using a large rubber spatula, fold the batter a few times to ensure that everything is fully incorporated.

Divide the batter evenly between the prepared pans and bake for 30 to 35 minutes, or until the cake springs back when gently poked.

ROYAL PURPLE VELVET CAKE

For such an iconic cake, it's pretty weird that there isn't a hard-and-fast history of the cake. American cake recipes usually come with a backstory about how a Mrs. Whosiwhatsit submitted a recipe to a popular housewife's circular and cake history was made. The red velvet cake has no such narrative. Instead, there's sketchy evidence that the cake started appearing in the 1920s and, more vaguely still, that it was served at the Waldorf Astoria. None of that is particularly intriguing. What *is* intriguing is that the original (whatever that happened to be) was frosted not with cream cheese frosting, as it most often is today, but with Ermine Frosting (page 185)—a velvety smooth and not at all tangy concoction that's almost as sexy as that siren red cake interior. But, wait, you don't *have* to make this cake red. Swap out the red for purple! The dye itself doesn't add the flavor, or the velvet, to the cake. It's the baker who brings that magic.

Unsalted butter or baker's nonstick spray for pans

5 cups/600 g unbleached cake flour

¼ cup/21 g unsweetened natural cocoa powder

1 teaspoon salt

1 teaspoon baking soda

1 teaspoon baking powder

2 cups/473 ml buttermilk

1 tablespoon cider vinegar

1 teaspoon pure vanilla extract

¾ cup/1½ sticks/170 g unsalted butter, at room temperature

3 cups/594 granulated sugar

¼ cup/51 g neutral oil, such as canola

4 large eggs, at room temperature

1 tablespoon/5 g purple gel food coloring

Preheat the oven to 350°F/180°C for conventional or 325°F/170°C convection. Butter or spray the bottom of three 8-inch/20.5 cm round cake pans and line with parchment. Attach soaked DIY cake strips to the outer sides of the pans (see page 31). Set aside.

In a large mixing bowl, whisk the flour, cocoa powder, salt, baking soda, and baking powder for 30 seconds. Set aside.

In a liquid measure cup, combine the buttermilk, vinegar, and vanilla. Set aside.

Place the butter and sugar in the bowl of a stand mixer fitted with the paddle attachment and cream until light and fluffy, 3 to 4 minutes. Add the oil and mix until combined. Scrape down the bottom and sides of the bowl. Add the eggs, one at a time, and mix well after each addition. Scrape the bottom and sides of the bowl. Add the food coloring and mix until just combined.

With the mixer running on low speed, add a third of the flour mixture, then half of the buttermilk mixture, and continue to alternate between the two until just combined. Take the bowl from the stand and, using a large rubber spatula, fold the batter a few times, scraping the bottom and sides of the bowl, to ensure everything is fully incorporated. Divide the batter evenly between the prepared pans and bake for 25 to 30 minutes, or until the cake springs back when gently poked.

CARVING CAKE/VANILLA

If you want a cake that's got a shape that isn't a cylinder or a square (sometimes oval or flowerlike, even), you'll need to take a knife to it and carve the shape you want. In those special cases, you'll need a cake that can handle being hacked and sawed, one that doesn't fall apart. That means most supermoist cakes are out of the question. Instead, what you'll need is a cake with a very tight and firm structure but that's still edible and delicious. Almost like a pound cake but lighter. This is your cake, carving people.

Unsalted butter or baker's nonstick
   spray for pans
2 cups/240 g all-purpose flour
1 teaspoon baking powder
1 teaspoon salt
1 cup/2 sticks/226 g unsalted butter, at
   room temperature
1½ cups/297 g granulated sugar
1 tablespoon vanilla bean paste
5 large eggs, at room temperature
½ cup/118 ml heavy whipping cream

Preheat the oven to 350°F/180°C for conventional or 325°F/170°C convection. Butter or spray the bottom of two 8-inch/20.5 cm round cake pans or half spheres and line with parchment. Attach soaked DIY cake strips to the outer sides of the pans (see page 31). Set aside.

In a large bowl, combine the flour, baking powder, and salt. Whisk for 30 seconds to distribute the leavening. Set aside.

Place the butter and sugar in the bowl of a stand mixer fitted with the paddle attachment and mix on high speed until light and fluffy, 3 to 4 minutes. Scrape down the bottom and sides of the bowl and add the vanilla bean paste and then the eggs, one at a time, mixing well after each addition.

Scrape down the bottom and sides of the bowl and then, with the mixer on low speed, add half of the flour, then the cream, followed by the remaining flour, mixing until just combined. Take the bowl from the mixing stand and, using a large rubber spatula, fold the batter a few times to make sure the flour is incorporated. Divide the batter evenly between the prepared pans and bake for 35 to 40 minutes, or until the cake springs back when gently poked.

CARVING CAKE/CHOCOLATE

MAKES THREE 8-INCH/20.5 CM ROUND LAYERS

Carving cake might bring to mind something that is utterly awful to eat. Not so. Think: pound cake. Rich, chocolaty, and dense, a carving cake has to be a heavy, sturdy beast to stand up to getting sawed and pummeled. A paste or high-ratio cake would never survive what it takes to undergo the manhandling a carving cake could withstand but it's still cake. It has to be delicious. This one is, *and* it can be molded into any old shape you can imagine.

Unsalted butter or baker's nonstick
  spray for pans
4 cups/480 g all-purpose flour
½ cup/42.5 g Dutched cocoa powder
1 tablespoon baking powder
1 teaspoon baking soda
1 teaspoon salt
1 cup/236 ml brewed hot coffee
8 ounces/212 g bittersweet chocolate,
  (at least 60%), finely chopped
½ cup/113 g sour cream or plain
  Greek yogurt
1 teaspoon pure vanilla extract
1½ cups/3 sticks/336 g unsalted butter,
at room temperature
3 cups/594 g granulated sugar
¾ cup/177 g neutral oil, such as canola
6 large eggs, at room temperature

Preheat the oven to 350°F/180°C for conventional or 325°F/170°C convection. Butter or spray the bottom of three 8-inch/20.5 cm round cake pans and line with parchment. Attach soaked DIY cake strips to the outer sides of the pans (see page 31). Set aside.

In a large mixing bowl, whisk the flour, cocoa powder, baking powder, baking soda, and salt for 30 seconds to combine.

In a small saucepan, combine the coffee and chocolate and stir over low heat until the chocolate is melted. Add the sour cream and vanilla and stir to combine. Set aside.

Place the butter and sugar in the bowl of a stand mixer fitted with the paddle attachment and beat until light and fluffy, 3 to 4 minutes. Scrape down the bottom and sides of the bowl and add the eggs, one at a time, scraping and mixing in between to make sure each egg is completely incorporated.

With the mixer on low speed, add one third of the flour, then half of the chocolate mixture, and then continue to alternate between the flour and chocolate until the ingredients are just combined. Take the bowl from the stand mixer and, using a large rubber spatula, fold the batter a few times, scraping the sides and bottom of the bowl, to ensure everything is well incorporated.

Divide the batter evenly among the prepared pans and bake for 25 to 30 minutes, or until the cake just springs back when gently poked.

The Foam Method

Foam cakes are leavened by eggs, sometimes with a slight addition of artificial leavening (as in a chiffon), but most often it's egg alone that does the heavy lifting. That means, the time you take to whisk the eggs is the deciding factor between a light and fluffy sponge or a flat and rubbery sponge pancake. It's easy enough to say "Whisk to quadruple in size," or "to ribbon stage," but what exactly does that look like? Well I'm so glad you asked. This is what a foam batter looks like at ribbon stage.

Adding the flour in a few additions so that the flour actually gets incorporated while still maintaining the loft of that foamy egg structure is key. But what does that folding look like? So glad you asked!

And often, when adding fats to the batter to create a suppleness to the finished cake, you'll need to combine that fat with a smaller amount of batter first instead of adding it straight in, so that it combines smoothly instead of sinking to the bottom. It just so happens that I can show you what that looks like too!

Let these visual guides help you jump into the foamy waters with confidence!

DON'T COOK THOSE YOLKS

Sugar is a special beast. You can say what you like about it, but it has magical properties. One of them is its ability to protect the vulnerable, like eggs, from heat. Sugar coats the proteins of the egg that coagulate at a relatively low temperature (read: scramble), acting as a bodyguard for all things eggy. If you're making a heated foam, it's the sugar that allows you to whisk the eggs over heat, getting them to a higher temperature than they could alone without getting a really weird (and sweet) breakfast. However, sugar isn't always an egg's best friend. If you leave that same egg yolk and sugar together in a bowl, not whisking or stirring, the sugar will start to pick the egg yolk's moisture pockets. Because not only is sugar a protector, it's a leech. Technically, it's hygroscopic, which means that it absorbs moisture from the available sources around it. If it's near a yolk and not being agitated, then it will start sucking up the water that composes 50 percent of that golden orb, leaving behind hardened bits of yellow that are like rice granules. So, be warned! Don't combine sugar and eggs until you are prepared to whisk the two together and start making your foam or other application.

GENOISE

Genoise, pronounced *jen-whaz*, is the queen of foam. It's dead simple in its makeup, just eggs, sugar, flour, and a bit of butter. And salt. Never forget the salt. Here's the thing: it's really easy to forget the butter because you don't add it until the *very* end of the process, after you've whipped the eggs and sugar and then gently folded in the flour. I can't tell you how many times I've put my genoise in the oven, patted myself on the back for being so awesome, only to be faced with a little saucer of melted butter mocking me for my premature victory dance. It might not seem like a ton of butter, either, but it makes all the difference in making what could be an otherwise dry and stiff cake more supple and tender. So: Don't. Forget. The. Butter!!! This lovely cake is used in delicate layer cakes with light, creamy fillings, such as the Princess Cakes (page 301).

Unsalted butter or baker's nonstick
  spray for pans
1²⁄₃ cups/200 g unbleached cake flour
¼ teaspoon fine sea salt
1 cup/198 g granulated sugar
5 large eggs, at room temperature
¼ cup/½ stick/56 g unsalted butter, melted
  and slightly cooled

Preheat the oven to 350°F/180°C conventional or 325°F/170°C convection. Butter or spray the bottom of two 8-inch/20.5 cm round cake pans and line with parchment. Attach soaked DIY cake strips to the outer sides of the pans (see page 31). Set aside.

In a small mixing bowl, whisk together the flour and salt. Set aside.

In the bowl of a stand mixer, combine the sugar and eggs and whisk by hand over a pot of simmering water until the sugar is melted, the mixture is hot to the touch, and an instant-read thermometer reads 150°F/65°C. Immediately transfer to the mixer and use the whisk attachment to whisk on high speed for 5 minutes, or until the mixture almost quadruples in volume, and then reduce the speed to medium and whisk for 1 minute more. This stabilizes the foam, reducing any overly large bubbles in the batter that would otherwise pop in the oven and deflate the cake. It will create a tight "micro-foam" that is more stable.

Take the bowl from the mixer stand, sift the flour mixture over the eggs, and gently fold with a large rubber spatula until no streaks of flour remain. Transfer a scant cup of the batter to the butter and stir to combine to lighten, then transfer the lightened butter back to the main bowl of batter and gently fold to incorporate.

Divide evenly between the prepared pans and bake for 20 to 25 minutes, or until the cake springs back when gently poked.

Variation: HONEY-LAVENDER GENOISE

Reduce the sugar quantity to ¾ cup/150 g and add 2½ tablespoons/50 g of honey, to be added at the same time as the sugar. Add only 2 drops of lavender extract just prior to lowering the speed of the sugar and egg mixture to medium. Proceed with the recipe to mix and bake as written.

CHOCOLATE GENOISE

My philosophy is that if you can make something delightful in a plain version, there's no reason you can't make it chocolate, too. The chocolate in this particular sponge is airy and subtle. It's also bendy and delicious. It's perfect for layering in delicate cakes and for lining dome molds effortlessly.

Unsalted butter or baker's nonstick
 spray for pans
1⅓ cups/160 g unbleached cake flour
⅓ cup/28 g Dutched cocoa powder
¼ teaspoon salt
1 cup/198 g granulated sugar
5 large eggs, at room temperature
¼ cup/½ stick/56 g unsalted butter,
 melted and slightly cooled in a bowl

Preheat the oven to 350°F/180°C for conventional or 325°F/170°C convection. Butter or spray the bottom of two 8-inch/20.5 cm round cake pans and line with parchment. Attach soaked DIY cake strips to the outer sides of the pans (see page 31). Set aside.

In a small mixing bowl, whisk together the flour, cocoa powder, and salt. Set aside.

In the bowl of a stand mixer, combine the sugar and eggs and whisk by hand over a pot of simmering water until the sugar is melted, the mixture is hot to the touch, and an instant-read thermometer reads 150°F/65°C. Immediately transfer to the mixer and using the whisk attachment, whisk on high speed for 5 minutes, or until the mixture almost quadruples in volume, and then reduce the speed to medium and whisk for 1 minute more. This stabilizes the foam, reducing any overly large bubbles in the batter that would otherwise pop in the oven and deflate the cake. It helps create a tight "micro-foam" that is more stable.

Take the bowl from the mixer stand, sift the flour mixture over the eggs, and gently fold with a large rubber spatula until no streaks of flour remain. Transfer a scant cup of the flour mixture to the butter and stir to combine, then transfer back to the main bowl of the flour mixture and gently fold to incorporate.

Divide evenly between the prepared pans and bake for 20 to 25 minutes, or until the cake springs back when gently poked.

FRAISIER SPONGE

The sponge utilized in the Fraisier Cake (page 280) is very similar to that of a traditional genoise, with its light and airy texture, but the batter makes just enough for one 9-inch/23 cm round, enough to torte and act as the base and top of the cake, sandwiching luscious strawberry mousse and fresh strawberries.

Unsalted butter or baker's nonstick
  spray for pan
½ cup/60 g unbleached cake flour
½ cup/56 g cornstarch
¼ teaspoon salt
½ cup/99 g granulated sugar
4 large eggs, at room temperature
½ teaspoon pure vanilla extract
½ teaspoon almond extract
¼ cup/ ½ stick/56 g unsalted butter, melted
  and slightly cooled in a bowl

Preheat the oven to 350°F/180°C for conventional or 325°F/170°C convection. Butter or spray the bottom of one 9-inch/23 cm round cake pan and line the bottom with parchment. Attach soaked DIY cake strips to the outer sides of the pans (see page 31). Set aside.

In a small mixing bowl, whisk together the flour, cornstarch, and salt. Set side.

In the bowl of a stand mixer, combine the sugar and eggs and whisk by hand over a pot of simmering water until the sugar is melted, the mixture is hot to the touch, and an instant-read thermometer reads 150°F/65°C. Immediately transfer to the mixer and using the whisk attachment, whisk on high speed for 5 minutes, or until the mixture almost quadruples in volume. Then reduce the speed to medium, add the vanilla and almond extract, and whisk for 1 minute more.

Take the bowl from the mixer stand and sift the flour mixture over the eggs and gently fold with a large rubber spatula until no streaks of flour remain. Transfer a scant cup of the flour mixture to the butter, stir to combine, and then transfer back to the batter and gently fold to incorporate.

Transfer the batter to the prepared pan and bake for 25 to 30 minutes, or until the cake springs back when gently poked.

MATCHA-HONEY SPONGE

Matcha powder, or green tea powder, is an earthy and ephemeral flavor. Yes, it tastes like green tea, and combined with the subtle sweetness of honey, it's a delight. Layer with a sour yuzu curd (page 123) and cherry buttercream (page 176) and you've got yourself a flavor party. It just so happens that it's darn pretty as well.

Baker's nonstick spray for pans
1¼ cups/150 g all-purpose flour
2 tablespoons/16 g matcha powder
1 teaspoon baking powder
½ teaspoon salt
6 large eggs, separated, brought to room temperature
¼ teaspoon cream of tartar
1 cup/198 g granulated sugar
⅓ cup/80 ml honey
¼ cup/60 ml neutral oil, such as canola
¼ cup/60 ml brewed green tea, cooled
½ teaspoon almond extract

Preheat the oven to 350°F/180°C for conventional or 325°F/170°C convection. Spray the bottom of two 8-inch/20.5 cm round pans or 1 angel cake pan with baker's nonstick spray, making sure not to spray the sides of the pan, and line the bottom of each pan with parchment. Attach soaked DIY cake strips to the outer sides of the pans (see page 31). Set aside.

In a large bowl, combine the flour, matcha powder, baking powder, and salt. Whisk for 30 seconds to distribute the leavening. Set aside.

Place the egg whites in the bowl of a stand mixer fitted with the whisk attachment and whisk on high speed until just foamy. Sprinkle with the cream of tartar and slowly add the sugar, whisking until the meringue holds stiff, glossy peaks. Transfer the meringue to a large bowl. Set aside.

Add the yolks, honey, oil, green tea, and almond extract to the mixing bowl that you used for the whites (you don't need to clean it). Whisk on high speed until the mixture lightens and ribbons when you lift the whisk from the yolk mixture, 3 to 4 minutes. Sift the flour mixture over the yolk mixture and whisk just until smooth. Take the bowl from the mixing stand and add a scant cup of the meringue, stir in the meringue to lighten the mixture, and then add the remaining meringue, folding gently with a large rubber spatula until no white streaks remain.

Divide the batter evenly between the prepared pans and bake for 40 to 45 minutes for the 8-inch/20.5 cm pans or 55 to 60 minutes in the angel food pan, or until the cake springs back when gently poked.

Invert the pans over a cooling rack to cool and when fully cool, run a paring knife or small offset spatula along the edge of the pans and the cake and gently rap on the bottom of each pan to release the cake from the pan.

LADYFINGER SPONGE

Ladyfingers are required in the making of a tiramisu. I have a problem with that, though. It's not that easy to find ladyfingers in any old grocery store, and when you do, you end up eating too many and then don't have enough for the recipe (and by you, I mean me). Here's the other thing about those giant unladylike fingers: you can only wrestle them into a roughly rectangular shape. I'm a fan of things round and cakelike. So, while you can pipe this batter in "fingers," I pipe the batter into circles for cake layers. Seeing the large rounds, I can keep myself from scarfing them down, leaving me enough for a gorgeous tiramisu cake (page 297).

6 large eggs, separated and brought
   to room temperature
1 cup/198 g granulated sugar, divided
1 cup/120 g all-purpose flour
¼ teaspoon salt
½ cup/56 g confectioners' sugar to finish

Preheat the oven to 350°F/180°C. Using a marker, trace two 8-inch/20.5 cm circles on 2 half sheet pan–size pieces of parchment. Flip them upside down onto two sheet pans. Set aside.

Place the egg yolks in the bowl of a stand mixer fitted with the whisk attachment and whisk on high speed until lightened in color. Slowly add ¼ cup/49 g of the sugar and continue to whisk until the mixture triples in volume and the mixture ribbons when the whisk is lifted from the batter, leaving a trail that takes a few seconds to dissolve back into the mixture. Sift the flour over the mixture and fold into the egg yolk mixture until there are no pockets of flour left.

Transfer the egg yolk mixture to a small bowl and whisk very well. Clean the mixer bowl, add the egg whites to the mixer bowl, and mix on high speed until just foamy. Add the salt and then slowly add the remaining ¾ cup/149 g of sugar, whisking on high speed until the meringue holds stiff, glossy peaks.

Transfer a scant cup of the meringue to the egg yolk mixture and fold to combine and lighten. Add the remaining whites to the egg yolk mixture and gently fold into the batter until no white streaks remain. Transfer the batter to a large pastry bag fitted with a medium open tip (Ateco 806) and pipe circles, starting in the middle and spiraling out to meet the outline. Sift an even layer of confectioners' sugar over the batter.

Bake for 20 to 25 minutes, or until the layers are golden brown and springy. Once cool, trim the layers, using an 8-inch/20.5 cm cake pan and a sharp paring knife as a guide to make the layers perfectly round.

LIGHT CHOCOLATE SPONGE CAKE
(SCHWARZWALD SPONGE)

MAKES TWO 8-INCH/20.5 CM ROUND LAYERS

This lovely cake straddles the worlds of creamed cakes and foam cakes. It's not heavy or super moist. It's not feather light, threatening collapse under the weight of a filling. This is the Goldilocks of chocolate sponges, perfect for the fairy tale cake that is the Black Forest.

Unsalted butter or baker's nonstick
  spray for pans
½ cup/60 g all-purpose flour
½ cup/56 g cornstarch
¾ cup/63 g Dutched cocoa powder
1 teaspoon baking powder
½ teaspoon salt
6 large eggs, separated and brought
  to room temperature
4 tablespoons/60 ml brewed coffee, cooled
1 cup/198 g granulated sugar, divided
2 tablespoons/28 g unsalted butter,
  melted and slightly cooled

Preheat the oven to 375°F/190°C for conventional or 350°F/180°C convection. Butter or spray the bottom of two 8-inch/20.5 cm round cake pans and line with parchment. Attach soaked DIY cake strips to the outer sides of the pans (see page 31). Set aside.

In a large mixing bowl, combine the flour, cornstarch, cocoa, baking powder, and salt. Whisk for 30 seconds. Set aside.

Place the egg yolks and coffee in the bowl of a stand mixer and whisk together to combine, and then add ⅓ cup/60 g of the sugar and whisk over a pot of simmering water until the sugar has melted and the mixture is hot to the touch. Transfer to a stand mixer fitted with the whisk attachment and mix on high speed until the mixture forms thick ribbons when you lift the whisk from the batter. Scrape the mixture into a clean mixing bowl, and thoroughly wash the stand mixer bowl and whisk.

Add the egg whites to the clean mixer bowl and whisk until foamy, then add the remaining ⅔ cup/120 g of sugar *slowly* until shiny, smooth, stiff peaks form. Fold the egg whites into the reserved egg yolks. Sieve the flour mixture over the egg mixture and gently fold together until no streaks remain.

Transfer a scant cup of the batter to the melted butter and stir to combine, then transfer back to the main batter and gently fold to incorporate. Divide the mixture evenly between the prepared pans and bake for 20 to 25 minutes, or until the cake springs back when gently poked.

CHIFFON CAKE

MAKES TWO 8-INCH/20.5 CM ROUND LAYERS

Chiffon is a sponge cake made American. That is, it's yummier (in my considered opinion) all on its own. The addition of oil makes for a super-duper tender cake that still has the spring of a genoise. You'll also notice that a leavener is included—baking powder—which, combined with the whipped egg whites, makes for lofty and spongy layers. You can make it extra flavorful by using Key lime juice. Either way, it's a beauty of a cake and delicious enough to eat on its own or layered, as it is in my "It's My Birthday and I'll Bake If I Want To Cake" (page 309).

1 cup/120 g bleached cake flour

1 cup/198 g granulated sugar, divided

½ teaspoon salt

1 teaspoon baking powder

4 large eggs, separated and brought to room temperature

½ teaspoon cream of tartar

¼ cup/60 ml neutral oil, such as canola

½ cup/118 ml water or Key lime juice

Preheat the oven to 325°F/170°C conventional or 300°F/150°C convection.

Assemble two 8-inch/20.5 cm springform pans (I use Fat Daddio's Aluminum Anodized pans. *Do not use nonstick springform pans*). Do not spray them or line them with *anything*. Do not use cake strips. Set aside. In a large mixing bowl, combine the flour, ¼ cup/49 g of the sugar, and the salt and baking powder. Whisk for 30 seconds and set aside.

Place the egg whites in the bowl of a stand mixer fitted with the whisk attachment and whisk on high speed until the whites just start to get foamy. Sprinkle in the cream of

tartar and continue to whisk while slowly adding the remaining ¾ cup/149 g of the sugar, whisking until the meringue holds a smooth, stiff peak, but don't overwhip. Transfer the meringue to a bowl.

Place the yolks, oil, and water in the stand mixer bowl and whisk on high speed for 1 to 2 minutes, until the mixture is pale and ribbons. Add the flour mixture and mix on medium speed for 2 minutes until combined and smooth. Take the bowl from the stand and gently fold the egg white mixture into the egg yolk mixture until no white streaks remain. Divide the batter evenly between the prepared pans and bake for 40 to 45 minutes, or until the cake springs back when gently poked. Flip the pans upside down over a wire rack and allow to cool upside down. Once cool, run a paring knife along the edge of the springform. Release the sides and then run a long, thin knife underneath to release from the pan and turn out the cakes onto a piece of parchment.

JOCONDE

Joconde is a sponge cake made with a large dose of delicious almond flour that can act as a regular old cake, that is, as layers *or* you can bake it into a thin layer and wrap it *around* another cake. Usually that other cake is a mousse-based cake or any cake that would benefit from a little bit of pizzazz. You might ask yourself what's so pizzazzy about a tannish cake wrapped around another cake? I'll tell you: you can pipe designs, even messages, on a sheet pan and then pour the joconde cake batter over those designs, and the design baked right into the cake. Now, I call *that* pizzazz.

1 recipe Joconde Décor Paste
  (recipe follows)
1¼ cups/120 g almond flour
¼ cup/30 g all-purpose flour
3 large eggs, at room temperature
2 large eggs, separated and brought
  to room temperature
½ cup/99 g granulated sugar, divided
½ teaspoon fine sea salt
2 tablespoons/28 g unsalted butter,
  melted and cooled
½ cup/30 g confectioners' sugar

Prepare this batter only when the décor paste is frozen and well set.

In a small bowl, whisk together the almond flour and the all-purpose flour. Set aside.

Place the 3 whole eggs, 2 egg yolks, and ¼ cup/49 g of the sugar in a stand mixer bowl, place over a pot of simmering water, and whisk vigorously until the sugar has dissolved. Transfer the bowl to the stand mixer fitted with the whisk attachment and whisk

on high speed until the bowl is cool to the touch and the mixture ribbons. Transfer the mixture to a large bowl to set aside.

Wash and dry the bowl and whisk very well (note: a bowl or whisk with any residue will not beat egg whites properly).

In the clean stand mixer bowl fitted with the clean whisk attachment, combine the 2 egg whites and salt. Whisk on high speed until frothy, then slowly add the remaining ¼ cup/50 g of sugar. Continue to whisk until the egg whites hold soft peaks. Set aside.

Transfer a spoonful of the whole egg mixture to the melted butter and stir to combine. Sift the almond flour mixture over the whole egg mixture. Using a silicone spatula, gently fold to incorporate. Fold in the beaten egg whites, followed by the melted butter mixture. Gently spread over the frozen décor paste pattern and bake for 5 to 6 minutes, or until the edges of the cake are just browning and the cake springs back when gently poked.

JOCONDE DÉCOR PASTE

Before preparing the batter as instructed on page 103, make this writing paste, pipe your pattern, and freeze the pattern solid so that it doesn't smear when covered with the batter. It's magic and fantastical. If you wish to write a message, you'll have to write backward. You can make a mirror image of a message using your computer.

½ cup/1 stick/113 g unsalted butter,
　at room temperature
1 cup/113 g confectioners' sugar
½ cup/118 ml egg whites, at room
　temperature
1 cup/120 g cake flour
Gel food coloring of your choice

Line a half sheet pan with a high-quality silicone mat (such as Silpat). Set aside.

　Place the butter and confectioners' sugar in the bowl of a stand mixer fitted with the paddle attachment and mix on medium speed until smooth. Gradually add the egg whites and mix to combine. The mixture will look broken. That's normal. Scrape the bottom and sides of the bowl and gradually add the flour and mix until a paste is formed. Divide the paste among bowls based on how many colors are desired. Add a drop or two of gel coloring to each of the bowls and stir to achieve your desired colors.

　Transfer each paste to a pastry bag fitted with a small open tip and pipe your chosen pattern on the prepared pans. Freeze the patterns until frozen solid. Once frozen solid, leave in the freezer and make the cake batter.

FOAMY IS MY MIDDLE NAME

When you whisk egg whites to create a meringue, specifically in the case of a dry, or French meringue, whereby you add sugar straight to whisked egg whites, you've probably noticed that any decent recipe will instruct you to whisk the whites until foamy and bubbly but not to the point where they've gained volume. You then slowly add the sugar until the meringue is shiny and bright white and the meringue holds stiff peaks when the whisk is lifted from it. I almost had a minor heart attack when I saw a cooking professional just dump a blob of sugar into a still lake of egg whites and *then* start up the stand mixer. Turns out, the baking world rules and science are often foreign to those in the savory part of the food world, but they make all the difference.

What happens when you start the mixer with just whites to make them foamy is crucial to a lofty meringue because that initial agitation creates a network of bubbles and stability that's activated by a protein in the whites that starts to coagulate when you start mixing. At this point, you can add a weak acid, such as cream of tartar, to further this coagulation and stability. This network of bubbles allows the sugar to take hold and form a stable foam structure, but add the sugar too fast, and you flatten the structure instead of enhancing it. Once you have *smooth*, stiff, shiny peaks, stop the mixer. French meringue isn't all that stable, even with the right precautions taken at the start of the process. If you keep mixing, the meringue will dry and get chunky, making folding it into a smooth batter near impossible without knocking all the aeration out of the meringue. Mix further still, and the entire foam/bubble structure will collapse from overmixing.

SWISS ROLL SPONGE

I have a special place for this charming cake in my heart. It's playful. It's beautiful. And it's delicious. As a matter of fact, I have a Sugar Glider Kitchen class devoted to this cake and students leave my sweet little classroom with a perfectly fluffy spiral of gorgeous cake, decorated with baked in embellishments that will bring a smile to even the grumpiest cake lover. This cake is delicious on its own, without the baked-in patterns, but then it loses a bit of its magic. So, while you can make this just as a lovely jelly-roll sponge, filled with sweet cream, I can't recommend enough the delight you'll have in piping happy patterns that reveal themselves in cake as you carefully pull back the parchment. (See the cherry template, page 313). Believe me when I tell you, this reveal is one of the great delights in baking and I don't want you to miss it. You'll thank me later.

This is also the perfect place to introduce this recipe because we're approaching the end of our journey in cake layers (there are a few more layer recipes to come, but not in the cake vein), and this cake straddles two areas: the baking of cake layers and the decorative finishing. It's the perfect two-for-one cake. All you need is a smattering of fruit and some cream filling and you're a hero.

Nonstick cooking spray

WRITING PASTE

½ cup/1 stick/113 g unsalted butter, at room temperature

1 cup/113 g confectioners' sugar

½ cup/118 ml egg whites, at room temperature

1 cup/120 g cake flour

Gel food coloring of your choice

SPONGE CAKE

8 large eggs, separated, brought to room temperature

⅔ cup/132 g granulated sugar, divided

½ cup/118 ml water, or replace fully or partially with lemon juice/orange juice/ coffee, etc., depending on flavor

⅓ cup/80 ml neutral oil, such as canola

1⅓ cups/160 g bleached cake flour

½ teaspoon cream of tartar

½ teaspoon salt

TO FINISH

¼ cup/28 g confectioners' sugar

Prepare the writing paste: Line a half sheet pan with parchment and spray with a very light layer of nonstick cooking spray. Set aside.

Place the butter and confectioners' sugar in the bowl of a stand mixer fitted with the paddle attachment and mix until smooth. Add the egg whites slowly and then add the flour and mix until a paste is formed. Divide the batter into small bowls, depending on the number of colors you choose to use, and add a drop or two of gel coloring to each of the bowls. Stir to combine.

Transfer the paste to a pastry bag fitted with a small open tip and pipe your chosen pattern on the prepared parchment. Freeze the patterns until frozen solid. Once frozen solid, leave in the freezer and make the cake batter.

Prepare the sponge cake: Preheat the oven to 350°F/180°C. Place the frozen pattern on a half sheet pan and then place a sheet of parchment on top of the pattern only, spraying lightly with nonstick cooking spray. Set aside.

Place the yolks and ⅓ cup/66 g of the sugar in the bowl of a mixer fitted with the paddle or whisk attachment. Beat until light and tripled in volume. Scrape down the bowl and add the water and oil. Mix until combined. Sift in the cake flour and mix on low speed until just combined and then beat on high speed for 2 minutes. Set aside in a separate bowl, and clean the mixer bowl and whisk attachment thoroughly.

Place the egg whites in the clean bowl of the stand mixer fitted with the whisk attachment. Whisk on high speed until foamy. Add the cream of tartar and salt. Whisk again until combined. Slowly add the remaining ⅓ cup/66 g of the granulated sugar and continue to whisk on high speed until the meringue achieves medium-stiff peaks. Don't overmix the meringue so that it becomes "dry."

Gently fold the egg whites into the egg yolk batter.

Spread the batter over the frozen writing paste pattern and bake for 15 to 20 minutes, or until the cake springs back when gently poked. Immediately score the edges of the cake to release it from the pan. Using a sieve, sprinkle a layer of confectioners' sugar over the surface of the cake. Place a kitchen towel over the cake and place a sheet pan over the towel, then flip the cake over. Remove the parchment from the bottom of the cake. Place another towel over the cake and flip it over again. Roll up the cake in the towel while still warm.

YOU FLAKE

There are times where a well-placed layer of flake will make a cake. A layer of flake is ess-entially flaky pie dough made into a cake layer either standing in for all the cake layers or added as a lovely counterpoint, as it's used in the Giant Pumpkin Cake (page 275). The method of making the dough takes a page out of French laminated techniques and results in a fabulously tender and buttery pastry that you can use as a standard pie dough as well as a cake layer.

¼ cup plus 2 tablespoons/88 ml
   ice cold water
1 teaspoon freshly squeezed lemon juice
2 cups/240 g all-purpose flour
1 teaspoon fine sea salt
1 cup/2 sticks/226 g unsalted butter,
   slightly cooler than room temperature

Combine the water and lemon juice in a small cup. Set aside.

Place the flour and salt in a large mixing bowl. Whisk to combine. Cut the butter into tablespoon-size chunks and toss in the flour mixture to coat. Gently flatten the pieces of butter with your fingers; be careful not to knead—you are simply flattening them. Once you've made your way through all the pieces of butter, break the pieces apart a bit more so that they range from ½ to 1 inch/1.3 to 2.5 cm in diameter but are uniformly flat.

Pour the lemon water over the flour mix-ture and gently stir with a wooden spoon to distribute the water and then use your hands to gently massage the mixture between your fingers to break apart any large clumps of moisture. If the mixture is still very dry and doesn't hold together when you pinch the dough, sprinkle up to the remaining 2 table-spoons of lemon water over the dough and continue working.

Toss the mixture again, making sure to root out any dry patches and incorporate them into the mixture, and then gently compact the dough, using your palm or your knuckles, to gently "smear" the dough so that the butter streaks in the dough. Be careful not to heat up the dough too much. You don't want the butter to melt; it should stay independent.

Turn out the dough onto your work surface and fold it over a few times to make sure there aren't any obvious dry patches. Roll the dough into an 8 x 12-inch/20.5 x 30.5 cm rectangle and then fold that into a trifold, like a business letter (this is also called a single or letter fold). Fold the dough in half again, then cover with plastic wrap and refrigerate for at least 20 minutes to rest. During the resting period, preheat the oven to 375°F/190°C.

Once it has rested, cut the dough in half and roll out each piece into a rough 8½- to 9-inch/21.5 to 23 cm round. Place on a parchment-lined sheet pan, cover with plastic wrap, and allow to rest in the fridge to 20 minutes. Using an 8-inch/20.5 cm cake pan as a guide, use a sharp paring knife to trim the dough into an 8-inch/20.5 cm round. Dock the dough (prick it all over with a fork) and cover the rounds with a piece of parchment and then another sheet pan, to slightly weigh the dough down so the layers rise evenly. Bake for 15 minutes with the sheet pan on top of the dough and then remove the top sheet pan and parchment and continue to bake for 15 to 20 minutes more, or until the pastry is puffed and uniformly golden brown. Remove from the oven and allow to cool completely.

EGG WHITES OF EUROPE

There are three types of meringue: French (also known as dry), Swiss, and Italian. And no, this isn't the start of a dirty joke, although I'm inclined to make one up now that I think about it. Anyway, each type of meringue is used in different applications. French meringue is most often used in making meringue cookies. It's the process most people are familiar with: whisking egg whites and then slowly adding the sugar until the stiff peaks form. It's pillowy, fabulous, and airy as all get out. The stuff *grows* in the bowl but you can't get hypnotized by the wonder of it all because you can overwhip French meringue to the point that it's dry and chunky, or even until it falls completely, which helps no one. French meringue is also used quite often in foam cakes because it lightens and aerates the batter beautifully.

With Swiss meringue, you combine the sugar and egg whites and whisk them in the top of a double boiler, heating the two together to form a lovely, stable bond. This helps melt the sugar and somewhat stabilize the whites. Most recipes ask that you whisk over the heat until the mixture reaches 140°F/60°C and then whisk with a mixer until stiff peaks form, which makes for a really luscious, almost marshmallowy meringue. I prefer to keep whisking over the heat until the mixture reaches 175° to 180°F/80° to 82°C, so that I know that the whites are "cooked" to the point that they'll be incredibly stable when whipped *and* you won't kill anyone with the raw eggs. That's a win-win, in my book.

The other option is the Italian meringue, whereby you pour in a hot sugar syrup that's been heated to at least 234°F/112°C (I tend to heat to 245°F/118°C for the same reasons as I heat my Swiss meringue to a higher temperature: more stability/no unintentional murder). I use both Swiss and Italian meringues in my buttercreams and for piping on tarts. I also use both as the *best* fluffy frosting. You'll see all these types used throughout the book and now you'll be able to put the name to the meringue!

NUT DACQUOISE (MACARON)

MAKES TWO 10-INCH/25.5 CM ROUNDS AND
6 SMALL MACARON SHELLS OR 36 SMALL MACARON SHELLS

Let's just cut to chase. *Dacquoise* is just a schmancy (and French) name for a type of meringue. Specifically, it's a nut meringue and it's used as a cake layer in some incredibly delicious cakes. Some cakes just use the layers alone, no other type of cake. When used alone, unless you fill the layers with something like an ermine frosting, which uses flour as a thickening agent, the cake will be gluten-free. In other cases, the meringue layers are used as a counterpoint to more spongy layers in a type of cake called *entremet* which is a very precisely layered beauty that makes sure to combine not only precision in the thickness of each layer, but in texture. *Entremet* combines a balance of flavor and textures to make each bite perfection. A *dacquoise* layer gives you a slight chew and crispness that a sponge layer just can't deliver. But there's more! This same batter can be piped into small rounds for *macarons* to adorn the tops and sides of your layer cakes as well. It's a win-win!

1½ cups/168 g confectioners' sugar

1½ cups/150 g almond flour, or ¾ cup/
  75 g almond flour and ¾ cup/75 g
  hazelnut flour combined

1 teaspoon Speculoos spice mix (optional)

4 aged egg whites, divided (totaling
  110 g; see note)

Pinch of salt

1 scant teaspoon/4 g gel coloring (optional)

¼ cup/60 ml water

A few drops of freshly squeezed lemon juice

¾ cup/150 g granulated sugar

On a piece of parchment, trace two 8-inch/20.5 cm circles with a dark marker. Turn the parchment upside down on a half sheet pan. Line a second half sheet pan with parchment. Make sure you can see the circles through the first piece of parchment. Set both aside.

Sift together the confectioners' sugar, almond flour, and Speculoos spice mix (if using) into a large mixing bowl.

Place all but about a tablespoon of the aged egg whites in a stand mixer bowl first, along with the salt. Give a quick stir.

Add the remaining tablespoon of the egg whites and the food coloring to the almond flour mixture but do not stir. Set the almond mixture aside.

Place the water, lemon juice, and then the granulated sugar in a small saucepan. Stir gently over medium heat, using a damp pastry brush to brush down any sugar granules that are clinging to the side of the pot, until the sugar has completely melted. Stop agitating when the sugar has melted, and continue to heat the syrup. When the sugar syrup reaches 235° to 240°F/113° to 116°C, start the mixer on high speed to whisk the egg whites to make them foamy and continue to heat the syrup to 245°F/118°C. When the sugar syrup reaches that final temperature, as you continue to whisk to make sure the egg whites are nice and foamy, carefully pour the sugar syrup down the *side* of the bowl as close to the egg whites as possible, taking care not to pour it onto the moving whisk (DANGER!). Whisk on high speed until the whites are bright white, shiny, but are not yet holding a stiff peak (*bec d'oiseau*).

Transfer the meringue to the almond flour mixture and fold together until the batter is smooth, reaches the flowing consistency of ketchup, and is shiny. This batter now has a brand new name: *macaronage*.

Transfer the macaronage to a pastry bag fitted with a medium-size open tip (Ateco 805). Starting at the middle of the traced 8-inch/20.5 cm circle, pipe a spiral up to the edge of the outline. Do the same with the second 8-inch/20.5 cm guide and set the sheet pan aside on a countertop to dry for 30 minutes, but no more. Fifteen minutes into the drying time, preheat your oven to 350°F/180°C. Once the macaron layers have dried, lower the oven temperature to 275°F/140°C, place the macaron layers in

the oven, and bake for 25 minutes. Remove from the oven and allow to cool completely before layering in a sophisticated beauty, such as the Linzer Macaron Cake (page 290). Meanwhile, leave the oven on.

Use any remaining batter to pipe 1-inch/2.5 cm-diameter dollops on the second lined sheet pan. Once piped, each macaron should settle without peaks after a few minutes. Slam and shimmy the sheet pan 3 to 4 times to help settle the macarons. Allow to sit at room temperature for 20 to 30 minutes to form a skin, but for no longer. Bake the macarons for 15 to 20 minutes, opening the oven door during the baking *very* quickly once or twice if it's very humid, to allow moisture to escape. Remove from the oven and allow the shells to cool completely before filling.

Note: How (and why) to age egg whites: To age an egg white, you need to separate your eggs 3 to 5 days ahead of baking your macaron. Place your egg whites in a very clean, oil-free container. I keep glass jars around for just this purpose. Cover the jar with plastic wrap and poke holes in the wrap. Leave in a cool dry place for 24 hours and then refrigerate for up to 3 to 5 days. The purpose of aging is to evaporate extraneous moisture while still keeping the protein power of the egg white for a more stable meringue, a must for macaron.

COCONUT DACQUOISE

MAKES FOUR 8-INCH/20.5 CM ROUNDS OR
TWO 18 X 12-INCH/45.5 X 30.5 CM RECTANGLES

When encountering an "everything is soft with this cake" cake, something crispy can make things just right. When I made my Joconde Décor Key Lime Cake (page 309), I incorporated some of these crispy layers to keep things exciting and keep things from getting, well, soft.

1 cup/85 g fine sweetened flake coconut, lightly toasted and cooled

¼ cup/24 g almond flour

½ teaspoon salt

4 egg whites, at room temperature (totaling 120 g)

½ teaspoon cream of tartar

1 cup/198 g granulated sugar

Preheat the oven to 300°F/150°C.

On two pieces of parchment, both the size of half sheet pans, trace two 8-inch/20.5 cm circles with a dark marker on each. Turn the parchments upside down onto half sheet pans. Make sure you can see the circles through the first piece of parchment. Set both aside.

In a large bowl, whisk together the coconut, almond flour, and salt. Set aside.

Place the egg whites in the bowl of a stand mixer fitted with the whisk attachment. Whisk on high speed until just foamy. Add the cream of tartar and then slowly add the sugar, a tablespoon at a time, until all the sugar is added and the meringue holds stiff, glossy peaks.

Gently fold the meringue into the coconut mixture and transfer the coconut meringue to a pastry bag fitted with a medium open tip (Ateco 805). Starting at the middle of a traced 8-inch/20.5 cm circle, pipe a spiral up to the edge of the outline. Do the same with the remaining three 8-inch/20.5 cm guides. Lower the oven temperature to 200°F/90°C, place the meringues in the oven, and bake for about 1 hour, or until dry to the touch. Turn off the oven and open the door, allowing the meringues to cool in the oven.

PAVLOVA-STYLE MERINGUE

MAKES FOUR 8-INCH/20.5 CM MERINGUE ROUNDS

Anna Pavlova was a ballerina, a world-famous Russian ballerina visiting either Australia or New Zealand—it's not clear which—on a world tour when this dessert was created in her honor. There's a long-running argument between the two countries as to where the confection came to be. This recipe is for the meringue portion of the confection. Traditionally, a single layer of meringue is gently swept into a circle and then baked until just set. It's topped with stiff whipped cream and berries. I prefer to pipe the meringue into neat disks, as I do with *dacquoise*, so I can use the light meringue as multiple layers filled with something tangy, such as a smooth lemon curd, and then coated with a shiny, almost marshmallowy Swiss meringue, as I do with the Pavlova Cake (page 294), so that it's as pretty as a ballerina in a tutu.

1¼ cups/247 g granulated sugar, divided

2 tablespoons cornstarch

4 large egg whites, at room temperature (totaling 120 g)

¼ teaspoon salt

¼ teaspoon cream of tartar

Preheat the oven to 300°F/150°C.

Line two half sheet pans with parchment. Use a dark marker to draw two 8-inch/20.5 cm circles on each and flip the parchments over. Make sure you can see the circles through the first piece of parchment. Set aside.

In a small bowl, whisk together ¼ cup/49 g of the sugar and the cornstarch. Set aside.

Place the egg whites in the bowl of a stand mixer fitted with the whisk attachment and mix on high speed until just foamy. Sprinkle with the salt and cream of tartar and continue to mix until the whites just begin to gain volume. Slowly add the remaining cup/198 g of sugar and then slowly add the cornstarch mixture, whisking until the meringue holds a stiff, glossy peak.

Transfer the meringue to a pastry bag fitted with a medium open tip (Ateco 805). Starting at the middle of a traced 8-inch/20.5 cm circle, pipe a spiral up to the edge of the outline. Do the same with the remaining three 8-inch/20.5 cm guides. Lower the oven temperature to 200°F/90°C, place the meringues in the oven, and bake for about 1 hour, or until dry to the touch. Turn off the oven and open the door, allowing the meringues to cool in the oven.

MÜRBERTEIG: A GERMAN TOUCH

To move an assembled layer cake around, if you don't assemble it on the serving dish where it's going to live and be presented, it's best to start assembly on a cardboard cake round that's the same size as the layers. You use these rounds beneath all sizes of cake and even when they are stacked. Especially when they are stacked as tiers. But I have a secret. In Germany, many cakes use a thin cookie base called *Mürberteig* to serve as an edible base. It's sturdy...and delicious. It also lends a lovely crispness to the entire cake that's usually lacking in most cakes. I use this base for my Black Forest Cake (page 286) but you can use it beneath any old cake you like. I make a larger batch and roll out a portion for a cake and freeze the rest. You can thaw the dough overnight in the fridge for your next project. You can also use it as a sweet pie or tart crust or as a crumble on top of pies and cakes. It's the sweetest tool in my pastry toolbox.

6 tablespoons/ ¾ stick/85 g unsalted butter, at room temperature

½ cup/56 g confectioners' sugar

1 large egg yolk, at room temperature

½ teaspoon pure vanilla extract

1 tablespoon Kirschwasser (optional)

1 cup/120 g all-purpose flour

Use a dark marker to draw an 8-inch/20.5 cm circle on a half sheet of parchment and flip the parchment upside down on a sheet pan. Make sure you can see the circles through the first piece of parchment. Set aside.

Place the butter and confectioners' sugar in the bowl of a stand mixer fitted with the paddle attachment. Mix on medium speed until smooth. Scrape down the bottom and sides of the bowl. Add the yolk, vanilla, and Kirschwasser (if using). Mix on low speed until just combined. Scrape the bottom and sides of the bowl and add the flour, all at once, mixing on low speed until just combined.

Transfer the dough to a sheet of plastic wrap. If there are dry bits of flour, fold the dough over a few times to incorporate but do not knead. Press the dough into a disk, wrap tightly, and refrigerate for about 20 minutes. While the dough is resting, preheat the oven to 350°F/180°C.

Roll the dough into a slightly larger circle than drawn on the prepared parchment and then trim the edges to form a clean 8-inch/20.5 cm round, using a cake pan as a guide. Bake for 10 to 15 minutes, or until baked through and golden brown along the edges of the "cookie."

TORTING AND FREEZING LAYERS

Once you've baked and cooled a cake, you could go ahead and jump in and fill it, even put a finished coat of icing on it. However, I prefer to take it a bit more slowly. I like to relish in the finishing of a cake, so I plan the baking part of my beauties at least a few days, even a week, ahead of time. In that case, I wrap my cooled cake in a light layer of plastic wrap and place in the freezer for 45 minutes to an hour. I make sure that the cake gets properly cold and firm but doesn't freeze through.

Torting is just a fancy word for slicing a layer of cake into multiple layers. Place the chilled layer on a cake turntable and using a ruler, find the halfway mark on the layer and gently mark the middle of the layer by resting a long, thin serrated knife (a thin bread knife works perfectly for this) on the side of the cake while spinning the turntable. Using the mark as a guide, gently press the serrated knife into the cake while keeping your other hand firmly pressed on top of the cake to keep the cake steady and to spin the turntable slowly. Keep the knife perfectly horizontal and the pressure on the cake even, only slightly sawing as you spin the cake. Continue until you've sliced all the way through.

By really chilling the cake, you tighten the crumb structure of the layers, making cutting much cleaner and easier. If you've ever sliced a cake in half after it's just cooled, you'll likely have had chunks of cake shedding from the cut layers. By properly chilling the cake all the way through, this won't happen. But be careful that the cake isn't frozen through. This makes cutting near impossible and, frankly, dangerous. Make sure to put constant pressure on the knife and turn the cake turntable steadily.

Wrap each layer really well in plastic wrap but be careful not to wrap too tightly, otherwise the layers could distort. Wrap again in aluminum foil and freeze for up to a month. The cake will be just as delicious and moist as if you'd filled and coated the day you baked the layers, just as long as you properly wrap the cake so that not a bit of it is exposed. I promise it will be perfect and you'll be able to enjoy the filling and finishing process that much more.

Part Two
FILLING

If cake layers are the foundation of good cake, the filling is the heart. Sometimes it's the kind of heart you wear on your sleeve for all to see. That's when you use the filling to both coat *and* fill the layers of your cake. No surprises. It's all hanging out there. But then there are the fillings that are truly the secret soul of the cake, the kind that vary in taste *and* texture from everything else that's visible from the outside. And at their best, they also bring a visual *pop* to the proceedings, such as a sunshiny lemon curd hidden inside the confines of a white buttercream–coated cake. Suddenly, the slice appears and that luscious layer of bright yellow makes you smile.

Other times, a combination of fillings that are entirely different from the outside coating win the day, such as a thin layer of caramelized puffed rice topped by rich, chocolate *cremeux* sandwiched between moist chocolate cake layers and coated with coffee buttercream. Sometimes that's the only way to go, as it was with Dan's 50th Birthday Cake (page 228). The delight on people's face when they get a bite of tender cake *and* crispy, sweet caramel nuggets *and* melt-in-your-mouth chocolate is a pleasure to behold . . . and to eat. When a filling can successfully play both roles of filling and coating, it's a beautiful thing and something of a time saver. But when you want to really play with the things that are both beautiful and sublimely delicious, hiding a delicious surprise inside the cake will make a great cake fantastical.

THAT BLOOMIN' GELATIN

Gelatin is quite an intimidating ingredient. It's a great setting agent but more often than not, when you use it, it clumps unattractively, leaving ugly knobs of hard Jell-O in something that should have been creamy and smooth. Other times, it simply doesn't set *or* it sets too much. Heavy sigh. But the very first thing you have to do is soften the gelatin, and that means that you saturate it so that it can be heated and melted and incorporated into the ingredient that needs a little help.

With powdered gelatin, the most common kind found in US grocery stores, you need to sprinkle the gelatin over cool water. I use ¼ cup/56 ml of water per 7 g packet or scant tablespoon. When you sprinkle, first make sure you get a pretty wide bowl so that the water spreads out, sprinkle the gelatin in a very even layer so it saturates evenly, and just let it sit until it looks like wet sand. Then, before incorporating into the element that needs setting, you must heat and melt the gelatin. You can do this in a double boiler or in a microwave in 10-second blasts at about 70% power, swirling between blasts until the gelatin is melted. Be careful when doing this step, as it is possible to overheat gelatin. If you allow it to boil, it can lose its efficacy. Bad gelatin! Once melted, you can carefully introduce the gelatin to the cream or other element you are stabilizing.

To saturate leaf gelatin (1 sheet = 2.5 g; 3 sheets silver leaf are the equivalent of one 7 g packet of powdered gelatin in setting power), you submerge the leaves in ice cold water. I usually use a large, shallow bowl, put about 3 cups/710 ml of ice water into it, and submerge my gelatin one leaf at a time, crisscrossing them to make sure that each leaf gets softened. I leave the leaf gelatin in the ice water for 5 minutes but no longer than 10 minutes. The gelatin will absorb a limited amount of water, always the same amount, so the amount of water it's submerged in doesn't have to be exact. You just need to make sure that the gelatin is indeed submerged, that the water is *cold*, and that you don't leave the leaves in the water for too long, so they don't dissolve. When ready, take the leaf gelatin out of the water and *squeeze* the water from the leaves. You can then add the softened leaves straight into a heated base to melt it completely. It melts seamlessly and sets beautifully when done right.

Fruity

I'm a big fan of fruit fillings. I wasn't when I was a kid. I liked it chocolate. Sometimes caramel. Never fruit. Thank goodness we grow up and mature. Perhaps I haven't matured in a lot of ways, but certainly when it comes to my taste buds, I've matured. What's fabulous about fruity fillings, whether berry or citrus or tropical, is that they provide not only gorgeous and fresh flavor but, very often, gorgeous color. That's something I love in a great filling: flavor and a blast of delightful color when you slice into a cake. In this way, fruit will rarely fail you. Thank goodness for growing up, so we can enjoy *all* the wonderful things.

—— SIMPLE IS SOMETIMES THE WAY ——

Some of my favorite cakes are my patterned Swiss rolls. I pipe fruity patterns and they transfer to the light and fluffy cakes. Not only are they adorable little treats but they actually advertise what's hiding inside. Kiwi, strawberry, cherry, banana: the fruity world is your so-called oyster. What I like almost as much as my jaunty and edible cake cartoons, is how simple it all is. I slather the rolls with a slightly tart and sweet whipped cream and then stud the cream with fresh fruit. I don't heat the fruit; I don't sweeten it. Sometimes I cut it into reasonable, bite-size nibbles but otherwise, it's the real deal without any embellishment and it couldn't be more delicious.

Jam is another fabulous option for a simple filling. You can find some of the loveliest fruits in jam form that you rarely find fresh, such as blood orange, lingonberry, and black currant. Never underestimate the flavor power of a modest sweep of jam over a tender layer of cake.

It's also worth exploring juice and international aisles of your grocery store for inspiration and surprise. Mango, passion fruit, guava, papaya, tamarind, even soursop (soursop! what the heck?), are all there for you to experiment with. Why not make a soursop curd? Call me when you find out what a soursop is, by the way (it's actually a spiny green fruit that tastes of strawberry and pineapple, with a few citrusy notes . . . or so it says on the Goya juice can). Once you realize that you can use these infinitely available, utterly fantastical juices in curds or reduce the juices to the consistency of a thick purée to add to mousses or pastry creams, a world of flavor opens up to you. Don't be afraid to try things you'd never thought of in cake; you might invent something utterly delectable.

MACERATED STRAWBERRY

MAKES 1 CUP/400 G, ENOUGH TO FILL
ONE 8-INCH/20.5 CM LAYER

Sometimes fruit is enough. And sometimes it's better with a little sugar. I'm thinking specifically of strawberries. One of my all-time favorite fillings was from my mother's strawberry cream cake. She'd make it every summer when strawberries were at their freshest and sweetest. The cake was simplicity itself: A simple sponge cake, sandwiching layers of lightly sweetened whipped cream and, the star of the show, sliced, juicy strawberries. I macerate my strawberries in a bit of sugar to draw out the juice, creating a soaking syrup for the sponge cake.

1 pint/340 g fresh strawberries, hulled
  and cut in half
¼ cup/50 g granulated sugar
1 tablespoon freshly squeezed lemon juice
½ teaspoon vanilla bean paste

In a small bowl, toss together the strawberries, sugar, lemon juice, and vanilla bean paste. Allow to sit for at least 10 to 15 minutes, so the sugar has time to draw out the juices from the strawberries and dissolves. If not using immediately, cover with plastic wrap and refrigerate.

STOVETOP MANGO CURD

**MAKES ENOUGH TO FILL
ONE 12 X 8-INCH/30.5 X 20.5 CM CAKE**

Curd takes *forever*. I can't lie about it because everyone else does. It's just like caramelizing onions. Every recipe says, "About five to ten minutes," and twenty minutes later, you're all, *"Whaa?"* The lovely thing about this curd, however, is that it does come together more quickly than most. It's made directly on the stovetop, no double boiler necessary. I stir together the sugar, butter, juice, and eggs *beforehand*, so that the eggs are well coated in the extra fat and sugar, two ingredients that help delicate eggs reach a higher temperature than they can on their own without setting into tart and sweet scrambled eggs. Just remember not to leave the stove. Keep stirring constantly until you get the right texture and you'll be rewarded with the curd of your cake dreams.

½ cup/1 stick/113 g unsalted butter,
   very soft but not melted

1¼ cups/250 g granulated sugar

2 large eggs, at room temperature

3 large egg yolks, at room temperature

1 cup/236 ml mango or citrus juice,
   such as lemon, lime, Key lime, yuzu,
   Meyer lemon, grapefruit

Generous pinch of salt

1 (7 g) packet powdered gelatin or
   3 sheets silver gelatin (optional),
   softened (see page 120)

Place the butter and sugar in a large saucepan. Mix with a wooden spoon until the mixture resembles wet sand. Add the eggs and egg yolks and continue stirring until combined, about 2 minutes. Add the juice and stir to combine. The mixture will appear curdled; do not worry. Place the pan over medium heat, add the salt, and continue to stir until the mixture thickens and coats the back of a wooden spoon and the temperature reads 180°F/82°C on a candy thermometer.

Remove the pan from the heat and immediately add the softened gelatin, stirring until it's melted. Transfer to a large bowl and cover the surface of the curd with plastic wrap to prevent a skin from forming. Refrigerate until cool, about 2 hours or overnight.

MICROWAVE CITRUS CURD

MAKES ENOUGH TO FILL ONE 9-INCH/23 CM BUNDT CAKE

My mother, Helga, refused to get a microwave. To her mind, it was a thing of evil and weird science-fiction devilry. It was a device so forbidden in my childhood that I don't have one in my own residential kitchen. However, I've always kept one in my bakery for three things and three things only: emergency butter softening, gentle chocolate melting, and gelatin melting. Once in a while I've broken my rule and used it to get sugar to temperature for Italian meringue or test a microwave sponge cake. And then I was teaching a tart class and I needed just *one* more batch of curd to fill a tart and I needed it fast: Helga's nemesis to the rescue. And it works!

1 cup/198 g granulated sugar

1 cup/236 ml citrus juice, such as lemon, yuzu, lime or Key lime juice, freshly squeezed or bottled

Grated zest of 1 lemon

2 large eggs, at room temperature

½ cup/1 stick/113 g unsalted butter, melted

¼ teaspoon salt

½ (7 g) packet powdered gelatin or 1½ sheets silver gelatin (optional), softened (see page 120)

In a large microwave-safe bowl, whisk together all the ingredients well, except the gelatin, if using. Microwave on full power for 3 minutes. Stir the curd. Microwave for 3 minutes more. Stir again. Microwave for 2 minutes, stir, and check to see whether the curd coats the back of a wooden spoon and has thickened in the bowl and the temperature reads 170°F/77°C on an instant-read thermometer. If not, zap again, a minute at a time, until you reach the right consistency. This should not take longer than 10 minutes. If using, immediately stir in the gelatin and continue to stir until melted and incorporated. Place a sheet of plastic wrap onto the surface of the curd and refrigerate until cool, about 2 hours to overnight.

LEMON CREAM

If you like lemon curd, you'll *love* lemon cream. And as with curd, you can translate it into other citrus languages, such as grapefruit or yuzu or lime. If you're asking yourself, "What's the difference between a curd and a cream?" well, the name says it all. Curd is ever so slightly gelatinous, in the loveliest of ways. A citrus cream is, well, creamy while keeping every scintilla of citrusy tartness and flavor. It's pretty much a pastry miracle and whenever I introduce it to my students, they marvel at how they've lived without it. It's just that good.

1 cup/198 g granulated sugar

Grated zest of 3 lemons

4 large eggs, at room temperature, whisked together

¾ cup/177 ml freshly squeezed lemon juice

Generous pinch of fine sea salt

1 (7 g) packet powdered gelatin or 3 sheets silver gelatin (optional), softened (see page 120)

1¼ cups/2½ sticks/283 g unsalted butter, at room temperature, cut into cubes

Stir together the sugar and zest. Set aside for 10 minutes.

In a large metal bowl, combine the sugar mixture, eggs, lemon juice, and salt. Place the bowl over a pot of simmering water and whisk until the mixture thickens and the temperature reaches 180°F/82°C. Add the gelatin, if using, and stir. Strain the mixture through a sieve into a blender and allow to cool to 140°F/60°C.

Turn on the blender and add the pieces of butter, one at a time, until combined. Transfer to a large clean bowl, cover with plastic wrap, and allow to cool.

SCHWARZWALD CHERRY FILLING

MAKES ENOUGH FOR ONE 8-INCH/20.5 CM CAKE

I typically use this lovely filling in my Black Forest Cake (page 286, along with a luscious whipped cream filling) but you can feel free to use it as a filling in any cake you like. Just off the top of my head, I can see slathering it on a cherry-festooned Swiss Roll Cake (page 298) or smoothing it out in a food processor and running through a sieve to add an extra-tart cherry punch to my Cherry Blossom Cake (page 225). I bet you'll cook up plenty of other ways to use this delicious filling but don't discount how delicious it is just by the spoonful.

1 (10-ounce/283 g) jar pitted sour cherries

¼ cup/49 g granulated sugar

Pinch of ground cinnamon

¼ teaspoon salt

2 tablespoons cornstarch

⅓ cup/78 ml Kirschwasser or concentrated cherry juice

Pour the jarred cherries into a sieve set over a large bowl to collect the juice. Reserve 1 cup/236 ml of the juice for the next step of the filling (setting aside the remainder of the juice for use as a cake syrup).

Place the cup/236 ml of cherry juice in a saucepan, along with the sugar, cinnamon and salt. Stir over low heat until the sugar has melted. Transfer about one quarter of the juice mixture to a small bowl, add the cornstarch, and stir to make a paste. Transfer the paste back to the saucepan and stir over low heat until the mixture thickens and just starts to bubble. Add the drained cherries and the Kirschwasser. Stir to combine and transfer to a large bowl. Cover with plastic wrap and refrigerate until cool, about 1 hour.

QUICK RASPBERRY JAM

MAKES ENOUGH FOR TWO 10-INCH/25.5 CM SANDWICH CAKES

This jam is perfect for cake fillings. You get beautiful, homemade fresh berry flavor with very little work and you don't need to go through the rigmarole of canning. You can use any berry you like, but raspberries and strawberries in season are my all-time favorite and work perfectly in my Princess Cakes (page 301) or my PBJ Cake (page 238).

2 pints/680 g raspberries
   (about 1½ pounds), hulled and
   cut into quarters
1 cup/198 g granulated sugar
Grated zest of 1 lemon
1 teaspoon freshly squeezed
   lemon juice
Pinch of salt

In a large saucepan, combine all the ingredients and allow to sit for about 10 minutes, until the raspberries release their juice (macerate). Place over medium-low heat and stir occasionally until the raspberries break down and the juices start to thicken and coat the back of a wooden spoon, 15 to 20 minutes. The jam will thicken further once it has cooled. For a chunkier jam, transfer to a jar and allow to cool in the refrigerator, about 2 hours. For a smoother jam, pulse until smooth in a food processor and then transfer to a jar.

MIXED BERRY FILLING

This berry bonanza of a filling is my way of having my pie *and* cake and eating them both, too. In this case, I cook the berries until they're thick enough to act as a stable filling rather than baking them in a pie shell in the oven. Layer them in the soft vanilla sponge of a patterned Swiss Roll (page 298) for a perfect summer treat.

½ cup/99 g granulated sugar

¼ cup/28 g cornstarch

⅛ teaspoon fine sea salt

¼ cup/56 ml water

Grated zest and juice of 1 lemon

1 cup/125 g fresh raspberries

1 cup/155 g fresh cherries, pitted and cut in half

1 teaspoon pure vanilla extract or vanilla bean paste

1 cup/145 g hulled and quartered small strawberries

2 tablespoons/28 g unsalted butter

In a small bowl, whisk together the sugar, cornstarch, and salt.

Place the sugar mixture, water, and lemon juice and zest in a large saucepan. Stir to combine. Add the raspberries and cherries and cook over medium-low heat until the mixture begins to bubble and thicken, then allow to continue simmering for about a minute. Add the vanilla, strawberries, and butter, and gently stir until the butter has melted.

Transfer to a bowl and chill in the refrigerator until set and cold, 2 hours to overnight.

Creamy

Heavy cream. Whipping cream. What the heck is the difference? Well, a few things. But first, just know you can use both to make whipped cream. Heavy cream is indeed heavy . . . with fat, that is. Heavy cream has to include at least 36 percent fat to be considered a "heavy" cream and my local dairy's cream boasts 39 percent in its heavy cream (and boy, is it delicious). A whipping cream must have at least 30 percent fat and will almost always include added "whipping agents," such as carrageenan. Either can be used in cream sauces, which require at least 25 percent fat to keep acidic ingredients from curdling the cream, and both are great for making whipped cream. I prefer my local dairy's high-fat heavy cream for whipping because the flavor is phenomenal, but you use what you prefer or what you can find. With both types of cream, if you accidentally overwhip either just a bit (not so much that it's already turning into butter), you can add a healthy ¼ cup/56 ml of unwhipped cream and gently whip it into the slightly curdled cream by hand to smooth out.

STABILIZED SWEET WHIPPED CREAM

MAKES ABOUT 4 CUPS/946 ML WHIPPED CREAM

No, your whipped cream doesn't need to get on meds. Well, not the pharmaceutical kind. While a whipped cream made with only two ingredients, sugar and heavy cream, is perfectly lovely and acceptable, there are times (and that time is always when you use it in a layer cake) when those two ingredients need a little help to keep themselves perky. Think of stabilization as Spanx for whipped cream. And what is "it"? It can be any number of things. Mascarpone is a beautiful stabilizer, adding a bit of structure to the proceedings. Gelatin is also very good but since whipped cream is meant to be cold and gelatin seizes when chilled too quickly, it causes some people difficulties, creating weird little lumps of hard gel amid luscious cream. I choose to use an interesting ingredient most often used in pie making but ends up being the perfect and fail-safe stabilizer: Instant ClearJel. Trust me on this one. It's a wonder ingredient.

¼ cup/28 g confectioners' sugar

1 tablespoon Instant ClearJel

2 cups/472 ml very cold heavy cream (see sidebar)

1 teaspoon extract or flavoring (such as Kirschwasser for Black Forest Cake, page 286)

Place the confectioners' sugar and Instant ClearJel in a small bowl and whisk together to combine. Note: If you add the Instant ClearJel straight to the cream, without whisking it into the sugar first, it can clump.

Place the cream in the bowl of a stand mixer fitted with the whisk attachment (or simply use a large bowl, a whisk, and your muscles) and then the confectioners' sugar mixture. Whisk on low speed to combine. If using, add your extract at this time, and then slowly raise the speed so that you don't splatter yourself and your kitchen with cream as it thickens. Whisk until it just reaches medium peaks and then continue to whisk by hand until you reach firm, stiff peaks.

Variation: COCOA CREAM

Add 1 tablespoon of Dutched cocoa along with the confectioners' sugar.

TIRAMISU CREAM

Tiramisu cream starts with a zabaglione, a thin custard of egg yolks, sugar, and marsala wine. Some people enjoy it as a drink (and before you go all "Blech," just think: eggnog). Traditionally, it was made with raw egg yolks, but I just can't go there with the Rocky Balboa raw egg shake, even with the addition of the wine. Here's the good news: I whisk the ingredients over heat. By warming the three over a double boiler, you not only get rid of any cooties that may be hanging out in the yolks, you'll also thicken and stabilize the custard that you then fold together with mascarpone cheese (one of my *favorite* things ever) and whipped cream. This combination of zabaglione, mascarpone, and heavy cream are the tent poles of tiramisu flavor for me, but you don't have to go the usual route and layer it with ladyfingers soaked in coffee. You can use the cream in a filling in a light almond cake or in a moist chocolate cake. There's a reason this is the most famous of Italian desserts, so why not play around with the thing that makes it so delicious?

7 large egg yolks, at room temperature

½ cup/99 g granulated sugar

⅓ cup/78 ml sweet Marsala wine

Pinch of salt

1 (7 g) packet powdered gelatin or 3 sheets silver gelatin (optional), softened (see page 120)

2 cups/472 ml heavy whipping cream, very cold

8 ounces/226 g mascarpone cheese, very cold

Place the yolks, sugar, wine, and salt in a heat-safe bowl. Whisk to combine and place over a pot of simmering water. Make sure the water does not touch the bottom of the bowl, otherwise you could scorch the eggs.

Whisk constantly until the sugar has completely melted and the mixture thickens to the point that it coats the back of a wooden spoon and a candy thermometer reads 170°F/77°C. Remove from the heat and, if using, add the gelatin and stir to melt, and then and allow to cool to room temperature.

Place the cream and mascarpone in the bowl of a stand mixer and whisk until you get stiff peaks. Transfer a large spoonful of the whipped cream mixture to the zabaglione and whisk to combine and lighten, then carefully fold the lightened zabaglione into the remaining whipped cream mixture, making sure that the mixture remains stiff enough to pipe.

Cake Lady

CRÈME DE LA CRÈME

One of the most intimidating elements of baking and pastry is the language. You might think that it's just the baking part itself but I swear, it's the language that can really make people turn tail and run. Most often, that language is simply French that, had it been translated, you'd be all, "Oh. That's it?" For instance, *crème Chantilly* is just sweetened whipped cream. Honestly. That's all. *Crème patissière* is pastry cream. Pastry cream is really just a very nice pudding. *Crème legère* is pastry cream (pudding) with whipped cream folded in to lighten it. Bavarian cream is just *crème legère* with gelatin thrown in to stabilize it. You've likely made some, most, or even all of these without knowing you made them and by now you've likely said, "Oh. That's it?" Yeah! That's it! I'm not saying you can't screw up any one of these. Plenty of people have overwhipped a whipped cream to the point of curdle, an easy task easily screwed up if you don't pay attention. But if you pay attention, you'll be the crème de la crème.

CARAMEL CREAM

MAKES ENOUGH TO FILL ONE 8-INCH/20.5 CM CAKE

Oh my goodness. I'm so proud of myself for sitting here and writing this when I have a bowl of caramel cream sitting in the fridge, only half eaten. To be fair, I'm really distracted. It's calling to me. And now it occurs to me that even though I made it to incorporate into a yummy cake, I could go ahead and eat the rest and then make another quick batch without too much trouble. That's settled. I'm going to leave you guys with this recipe so you can experience the joy yourself. I've got a bowl of caramel cream to finish.

1 cup/198 g granulated sugar

½ teaspoon freshly squeezed lemon juice

½ cup/118 ml hot water

¼ teaspoon fine sea salt

1¾ cups/414 ml heavy whipping cream

¼ cup/56 ml water

½ (7 g) packet powdered gelatin (see directions for when and how to soften)

Place the sugar in an even layer in a large, stainless-steel skillet and then sprinkle with the lemon juice. Stir gently over low heat to melt the sugar and then continue to cook until the color is a light amber brown (I always think of it as the color of a brand-new penny). Take the caramel from the heat and slowly add the hot water, and then the salt, stirring to melt any clumps of caramel that may have seized. Allow the caramel mixture to cool. Once cool, the caramel should be syrupy enough to be easy to incorporate into the cream.

Place the cream in a stand mixer bowl fitted with the whisk attachment and whisk to medium-soft peaks. Take a generous dollop of the cream and stir it into the cooled caramel. Pour the cream mixture back into the stand mixer bowl and whisk until medium peaks form.

Place the water in a heat-safe bowl and sprinkle the gelatin in an even layer over the water, then place over a pot of gently simmering water to melt. Remove from the heat and add a large dollop of the cream mixture to the gelatin and stir to combine to temper. Gently but very quickly fold the gelatin mixture into the cream.

Vanilla Bean Pastry Cream

This is a wonderful base pastry cream. You can add a variety of flavors to it to get your dream filling flavor. But I've got to say, "plain" vanilla is terribly yummy and isn't so plain at all. If you use a healthy dollop of vanilla bean paste, which is a thick emulsion of vanilla and vanilla beans, your pastry cream will sing to the high heavens of delicious vanilla.

¼ cup/50 g granulated sugar

2 tablespoons cornstarch

½ cup/118 g heavy whipping cream

½ cup/118 g whole milk

3 large egg yolks, at room temperature

1 teaspoon vanilla bean paste

¼ teaspoon fine sea salt

Place the sugar and cornstarch in a saucepan. Whisk to combine. Add the cream, milk, yolks, vanilla bean paste, and salt and whisk to combine. Continue to whisk over medium heat until the mixture thickens to the consistency of mayonnaise and just starts to bubble. Transfer to a clean bowl and cover with plastic wrap, making sure to touch any exposed cream to keep a skin from forming. Refrigerate until cool, about an hour.

A MESSAGE FROM THE

Cake Lady

PASTRY CREAM

Pastry cream, a.k.a. or *crème patissière* (or PC as we pastry chefs are wont to call it) is a recipe that freaks some home bakers out. It seems like such a, well, *scary* thing. It has "pastry" right there in the title, so it must be hard and then if you say it in French? Forget about it. But what if I said "pudding" instead? Would that make you feel more at ease about making this glorious stuff? Because that's what pastry cream is: the best, creamiest pudding *ever*. You can just eat it with a spoon if you like and then whip up another batch in no time for your cake.

SALTED CARAMEL PASTRY CREAM

MAKES ENOUGH TO FILL AN 8-INCH/20.5 CM CAKE

Oh, are you in for a treat. This pastry cream is all good things about caramel and pastry cream. It's smooth and rich, as a pastry cream should be. It's also full of luscious caramel flavor and a slight hint of salt. This is the filling I always teach in my éclair class because there's this moment, when my students make their own caramel and then transform it into a world-class pastry cream, the classroom gets incredibly quiet and the requests for spoons get called out. I always make sure they don't eat it all. They still need some to fill éclairs. But the utter joy they take in tasting something they thought they'd only taste in a world-class pastry shop in the heart of Paris makes my heart swell.

1 cup/198 g granulated sugar

⅓ cup/79 ml water

Splash of freshly squeezed lemon juice or distilled white vinegar

1 cup/236 ml heavy whipping cream

1 cup/236 ml whole milk

6 large egg yolks, at room temperature

¼ cup/28 g cornstarch

½ teaspoon salt

1 tablespoon pure vanilla extract

Combine the sugar, water, and lemon juice in a heavy-bottomed saucepan. Stir gently over low heat until the sugar has completely melted. If you see sugar granules, wipe them down with a damp pastry brush. Stop stirring once the sugar has completely melted and continue to cook for 2 to 3 minutes, until it's medium amber. Remove from the heat and immediately add the cream and milk (carefully). Put the caramel back on the heat and stir until the hardened caramel has completely melted.

In a small bowl, whisk together the yolks, cornstarch, salt, and vanilla. Slowly drizzle about ½ cup/118 ml of the hot caramel mixture into the yolk mixture, whisking constantly until incorporated to temper. Slowly add the tempered yolks back to the remaining caramel, again whisking constantly, and then return to medium-low heat and whisk until the mixture thickens to the consistency of mayonnaise. Immediately remove from the heat and spread over a parchment-lined sheet pan in an even layer, then lay a piece of plastic wrap directly onto the pastry cream and chill until completely cool.

Cake Lady

À LA MINUTE

There are many things in this book that are perfect for making ahead. Cake layers that can be frozen. Lemon cream that can be frozen. Lemon curd that can be stored in the fridge in decorative jars. However, pastry cream isn't one of those things. First, because of the composition of pastry cream—lots of dairy and eggs—it's recommended for food safety reasons that pastry cream be enjoyed at within two days after making it. And the pastry cream will tell you so: it starts to get watery and weird, so you won't want to eat it anyway. "So, I'll freeze it," you're saying. Not so fast, buster. Doing so really messes with the texture of pastry cream, making it grainy and weird. Again, weird isn't good when it comes to pastry.

But the thing with pastry cream is that it comes together incredibly quickly, compared to some other things (curd and creams) and you *can* quickly cool it so that you can use it within minutes of its coming together. I line a sheet pan with parchment and when my pastry cream comes to the perfect thickness, I spread it in a thin layer over the parchment and cover the exposed cream with plastic wrap and then I put it in the freezer. "But you said I can't freeze it!" you're thinking to yourself. Well, you can't freeze it, but you can use your freezer to get the cream cooled off quickly, within 5 to 10 minutes. I recommend you set a timer, though. If you forget the stuff, it will freeze and then—wait for it—it gets weird.

PUMPKIN PASTRY CREAM

I've never understood why pumpkin is almost exclusively baked in a pie shell using a recipe from the back of a can of pumpkin purée. I'm not going to lie, I love pumpkin pie made this way, but it's not the *only* way that pumpkin can be used in a delicious dessert. In fact, my all-time favorite way to use pumpkin purée is in a pastry cream that's light and airy, not heavy and dense.

½ cup/99 g granulated sugar

¼ cup/28 g cornstarch

2 cups/473 ml half-and-half (or 1 cup heavy whipping cream plus 1 cup whole milk)

¼ teaspoon ground cinnamon

Pinch of freshly grated nutmeg

1 teaspoon pure vanilla extract

Generous pinch of salt

5 large egg yolks, at room temperature

½ cup/113 g pure pumpkin purée

Place the sugar and cornstarch in a saucepan. Whisk to combine. Add the half-and-half, cinnamon, nutmeg, vanilla, salt, yolks, and pumpkin. Whisk to combine. Lower the heat to low and whisk until the mixture bubbles and thickens. If using in the Giant Pumpkin Cake, immediately add to the cooled piecrust and then cover with plastic wrap and refrigerate until cool. For other uses, transfer to a heatproof jar or bowl, cover with plastic wrap and press down directly on the surface, and refrigerate until cool.

Cake Lady

CHOCOLATE

Boy, has the world of chocolate changed since I was a kid. At least in America. In Germany, where my mother's from and where I spent a good deal of my childhood, quality dark chocolate was a common thing. You could get it anywhere. In fact, my grandmother always kept a bar of Lindt bittersweet chocolate in her purse and savored bits during forays into town to run errands. Back in the Arlington, Virginia, of my childhood, you could only find milk chocolate of the Hershey variety or the semisweet of the Toll House variety, and while these are both yummy and bring with them a heavy dose of sentimentality, they aren't the best ingredients for baking. Thankfully, you can now find really nice chocolate suitable for both noshing *and* baking in any grocery store. But now that you can find great chocolate, what does all that stuff on the packaging mean?

First, look for a type of chocolate that is called for in your recipe. If the ingredients list just says "bittersweet chocolate," look for that on the packaging. If the chocolate only gives you percentages, which stand for the cacao content percentage, you must first know that the higher the number, the more cacao and less sugar: 100% is all cacao, no sugar, what is traditionally known as "baker's" chocolate. Bittersweet chocolate is the next level, with the highest amount of cacao versus sugar. Semisweet and bittersweet must have at least 35% cacao content to be categorized as such, but most of the chocolates I use and consider "bittersweet" are at least 60% for optimal flavor and balance of sugars. One other thing that's really important: tasting chocolate. Like coffee and wine, chocolates are made with different varieties of cacao from different regions. I know it's asking a lot of you, a true sacrifice, but I suggest you take some time and buy a ton of chocolate to decide what *you* like best. Someone's got to do it.

CHOCOLATE PASTRY CREAM

MAKES ENOUGH FOR 2 PRINCESS CAKES
OR 12 CREAM PUFFS

This pastry cream is a chocolate lover's dream. It's creamy, chocolaty, and smooooth. What's even more fabulous is that the chocolate adds an extra stability to it, making it the perfect firmness for a filling that's both creamy and perfect for sandwiching between cake layers.

¼ cup/50 g granulated sugar

2 tablespoons cornstarch

½ cup/118 ml heavy whipping cream

1 cup/118 ml whole milk

3 large egg yolks, at room temperature

1 teaspoon vanilla bean paste

¼ teaspoon fine sea salt

1 ounce/28 g bittersweet chocolate, finely chopped

Place the sugar and cornstarch in a saucepan. Whisk to combine. Add the cream, milk, yolks, vanilla bean paste, and salt and whisk to combine. Continue to whisk over medium heat until the mixture thickens to the consistency of mayonnaise and just starts to bubble.

Remove from the heat and add the chocolate. Stir until the chocolate is melted and combined. Transfer to a clean bowl and cover with plastic wrap, making sure to touch any exposed cream to keep a skin from forming. Refrigerate until cool, about an hour.

HONEY-PEAR-LAVENDER CREMEUX

When I think of bees, I think of the vegetation that flourishes when they are around. Before bears decided to decimate my hives, I spent a few glorious summers marveling at how everything on our property thrived in their presence. My strawberries were legion. My fruit trees were bent double from the bountiful fruit. My flowers bloomed and bloomed, some I never even knew existed on our property. It only follows that any dessert with honey would also have flavors from vegetation that benefits from the busy life of bees. I can think of no better beneficiaries than lavender and pear, two delicious plants that were never happier here on my little farm in Vermont than when their bee friends were everywhere.

4 egg yolks, at room temperature

½ cup/118 ml pear juice

¼ cup/50 g granulated sugar

2 tablespoons/42 g honey

Pinch of salt

¼ cup/28 g cornstarch

½ (7 g) packet powdered gelatin or 1½ sheets silver gelatin, softened (see page 120)

½ cup/1 stick/113 g unsalted butter, at room temperature

1 teaspoon pure vanilla extract

1 drop lavender extract

Place the yolks in a medium mixing bowl and cover with plastic wrap. Set aside.

Combine the pear juice, sugar, honey, and salt in a small saucepan and stir, over low heat, until the sugar has melted.

Remove the plastic from the yolk bowl, whisk the cornstarch into the yolks, and then continue to whisk the yolks while drizzling in about a quarter of the juice mixture to temper. Continue to whisk until completely combined. Transfer the egg mixture to the saucepan of the remaining juice mixture and whisk over low heat until the mixture reads 180°F/82°C on a candy thermometer. Pour the mixture through a sieve into a medium bowl and immediately add the gelatin, butter, vanilla, and lavender, stirring until the gelatin and butter are melted and everything is well incorporated. Cover with plastic wrap and refrigerate until cool, about 2 hours.

CHOCOLATE CREMEUX

MAKES ENOUGH TO FILL ONE 8-INCH/20.5 CM CAKE

I made a cake for our friend Dan's 50th birthday. We were invited to spend the weekend at his family's camp in Maine to celebrate and I asked whether it was okay if I made the cake. Even if you're a fancy, professional baker, you can *never* assume that there isn't another baker in your friend's life who's always made the cake and knows a lot better than you what the birthday girl or boy likes. Luckily, I got an enthusiastic *"Yes!"* I was given my debriefing as to Dan's favorite flavors: coffee and chocolate. I knew immediately how I wanted to build the cake: inky black, superfudgy chocolate cake with thin layers of espresso Italian buttercream and elegantly soft chocolate *cremeux* in between. Ray drove and I fretted in the back the entire three-hour drive, making sure the giant cake I'd made stayed upright. It survived beautifully and it's since become one of my all-time favorite celebration cakes. In fact you can see it for yourself on page 228.

10 ounces/283 g bittersweet chocolate, 60%, finely chopped

7 large egg yolks at room temperature

½ cup plus 1 tablespoon/125 ml whole milk

1 cup plus 2 tablespoons/250 ml heavy whipping cream

⅓ cup plus 2 tablespoons/75 g granulated sugar

¼ teaspoon salt

1 scant teaspoon/2.3 g powdered gelatin or 1 sheet silver gelatin, softened (see page 120)

Place the chocolate in a heatproof bowl and set over a pot of slightly simmering water to melt, stirring now and again with a rubber spatula.

Place the yolks in a medium mixing bowl and cover with plastic wrap. Set aside.

In a separate saucepan, combine the milk, cream, sugar, and salt and heat over low heat until the sugar has completely melted. While whisking the yolks, slowly drizzle in about 1 cup/235 ml of the hot milk mixture to temper the eggs (i.e., to keep from scrambling them). Whisk well until combined and then add the tempered egg mixture to the saucepan of the remaining milk mixture, stirring constantly until the mixture reads 170°F/77°C on a sugar thermometer.

Pour the hot milk mixture through a sieve over the melted chocolate, immediately add the softened gelatin, and whisk to combine completely. Cover with plastic wrap and refrigerate until cool and set, about 2 hours.

Cake Lady

CREMEUX

Stop! Don't run away! It's just a weird, French word that means "creamy." It's pronounced "kray-Meyoo." You can just call it Cray Cray, if you want. I don't care, as long as you try it! It's the perfect word for what I'm about to introduce you to. I don't know why it isn't a common filling in everyday layer cakes because it's pure magic. It's a texture that was made in the pastry kitchens of heaven and it's easy. It's soft and creamy yet stable and spreadable. You can make it chocolate, caramel, or fruity. It's softer than a ganache and creamier than a mousse. Every time I serve a cake with a cremeux, people will ask "What's this, right there?" and they'll be scraping their fork into the cake, digging out that layer of cremeux and shoving it into their mouth. You want this in your life.

CARAMEL CREMEUX

Sometimes I make an element of a cake and end up eating all of it before I realize what I've done. I've done that with caramel *cremeux*. More than once. The last time I did it, I walked around the house with the bowl and a spoon in my hand murmuring, "You're soooooooo good." I have absolutely no shame in admitting this. I'm pretty sure it's how everyone and anyone who's ever tried this behaves when they take a bite.

1 cup/200 g finely chopped white chocolate
8 large egg yolks, at room temperature
½ cup/99 g granulated sugar
¼ teaspoon salt
1½ cups/340 ml heavy whipping cream, warmed
½ (7 g) packet powdered gelatin or 1½ sheet silver gelatin, softened

Place the white chocolate in a heatproof bowl and melt over a pot partially filled with simmering water, stirring occasionally.

Place the yolks in a medium mixing bowl and cover with plastic wrap. Set aside.

Sprinkle the sugar and salt in an even layer into a large, stainless-steel skillet and melt over low heat until medium amber, stirring only occasionally to make sure it caramelizes evenly. Remove from the heat and carefully pour in about a third of the cream. The mixture will bubble vigorously at first and then calm. Add the rest of the cream and stir over low heat until the caramel melts (it often seizes into hard shards when you pour in the cream).

Remove the plastic wrap from the yolk bowl and whisk the yolks a bit, then slowly drizzle about a quarter of the caramel mixture into the yolks while whisking constantly. Continue to whisk until completely combined and then transfer the yolk mixture to the remaining caramel mixture in the skillet and whisk constantly over low heat until the mixture reads 180°F/82°C on a sugar thermometer. Pour the mixture through a sieve into the melted milk chocolate. Add the gelatin and whisk until the mixture is smooth and combined. Cover with plastic wrap and refrigerate until cool, about 2 hours.

Cake Lady

WET AND DRY CARAMEL

Caramel is a scary beast, the *least* scary element of it is that it can burn like a Mother Hubbard when it's at temperature. The *most* scary element is that it can come out wrong. For a traditional eating caramel, that means it hasn't set or it's set too hard. For a simple caramel, it can burn or crystallize. The not-setting outcome can be fixed with a perfectly calibrated sugar thermometer. The most common solution to keeping a simple caramel from burning is by adding water, or making a *wet* caramel. Adding water, usually about 1 part water to 3 parts sugar, makes the caramelization process go more slowly, allowing you to control the amber.

But you invite another problem by adding water, the possibility of crystallization, wherein the sugar decides it wants to rebel and build an Elsa-like white crystal fortress in your pan that is decidedly *not* caramel and will refuse to ever budge from said pan (just do a Google search for crystallized caramel. It's not pretty). That's why many simple caramel recipes include a small dose of acid, such as lemon juice or vinegar, to split the sucrose molecule to make it harder to gang up on you, and others use corn syrup or glucose to essentially "coat" the crystals in a sweet straitjacket so they can't cause problems. These are both called interfering agents—ingredients that come between the sugar crystals so they can't ruin your caramel.

On the other hand, you can more easily avoid the crystallization problem by making a dry caramel, whereby you simply heat sugar all by itself until it caramelizes. It's awfully easy to burn caramel using the dry method, so you have to be Joanna or Johnny on the Spot and agitate the sugar just enough that it melts and colors evenly. Either way, make sure you keep your fingers well away from the hot stuff. It burns!

FRUIT CREMEUX

Fruit seems very general, doesn't it? But that's the beauty of this recipe: if you have a favorite fruit juice, you can make a fabulous fruit filling for your cakes. From tropical to simple orange or apple, this recipe allows you to transform what would usually be in a sippy cup to a confection that could be found in the best Parisian patisserie. But before you start, please check the sidebar "Bromelain and You."

4 large egg yolks, at room temperature

⅔ cup/160 ml fruit juice

½ cup/99 g granulated sugar

Generous pinch of salt

¼ cup/28 g cornstarch

½ (7 g) packet powdered gelatin
or 1½ sheets silver gelatin, softened
(see page 120)

½ cup/1 stick/113 g unsalted butter,
at room temperature

1 teaspoon pure vanilla extract

Place the yolks in a medium mixing bowl and cover with plastic wrap. Set aside.

Combine the fruit juice, sugar, and salt in a small saucepan and stir, over low heat, until the sugar has melted.

Remove the plastic from the yolk bowl, whisk in the cornstarch, and then continue to whisk the yolks while drizzling in about a quarter of the juice mixture. Continue to whisk until completely combined. Transfer the egg mixture to the saucepan of the remaining juice mixture and whisk over low heat until the mixture reads 180°F/82°C on a candy thermometer. Pour the mixture through a sieve into a medium bowl and immediately add the gelatin, butter, and vanilla, stirring until both are melted and completely combined. Cover with plastic wrap and refrigerate until cool, about 2 hours.

BROMELAIN AND YOU

If you look at the back of a Jell-O box, it will tell you *not* to use certain fruits in the jiggly mixture. Fruits on the verboten list include pineapple, papaya, mango, guava, figs, and ginger. These fruits all carry an enzyme that messes with collagen proteins in the gelatin. Pineapple has bromelain. Papaya has papains. Either way, they are both proteases (enzymes that are gelatin bullies) and both do the same thing: they act as jelly disruptors and keep the stuff from setting. So, if you want to make a fruit mousse with pineapple that actually sets, you'll want to do something about that pesky enzyme. Luckily, it's quite easy. You need only heat the fruit or the juice to make sure the enzyme is neutralized. So, if your tastes leans toward the tropical, make sure you heat any of the fruit juices you use in *cremeux*.

FRESH AND EASY STRAWBERRY MOUSSE

MAKES ENOUGH TO FILL ONE 9-INCH/23 CM CAKE

This mousse is as fresh and fruity as an early summer day and incredibly simple. I use this as a filling in my Fraisier, or Strawberry Cake. In a traditional Fraisier, a fresh farmer cheese is used in the filling but I find that particular ingredient is pretty hard to come by in the States. Cream cheese is a great and similar stand-in. The cream cheese also adds a lovely tartness to the fruity sweetness and also gives the mousse stability. To see this mousse in action, see page 280.

2 tablespoons/30 ml water

2 tablespoons/30 ml freshly squeezed lemon juice

½ (7 g) packet powdered gelatin or 1½ sheets silver gelatin, softened (see page 120)

4 ounces/113 g cream cheese, at room temperature

½ cup/118 ml strawberry purée, at room temperature

½ cup/57 g confectioners' sugar

Pinch of salt

1½ cups/355 ml heavy whipping cream

Combine the water and lemon juice in a small bowl. Sprinkle the gelatin over the liquid in an even layer and allow to sit until the gelatin is saturated and looks like wet sand. Microwave in 30-second bursts at 40%, swirling the bowl between bursts, until the gelatin is melted.

Place the cream cheese, strawberry purée, confectioners' sugar, and salt in the bowl of a stand mixer fitted with the whisk attachment and whisk together until smooth. Add the cream and whisk until you achieve stiff peaks. Transfer about ⅓ cup/80 ml of the mixture to the gelatin mixture and whisk to combine. Transfer back to the stand mixer bowl and whisk on high speed until incorporated and cream mixture is stiff.

NUTELLA MOUSSE

When I was a kid living in the Dark Ages, Nutella wasn't available in the United States. The only time I could get my hot little hands on it was in Germany, where it was everywhere. I had it with breakfast, lunch, and dinner. Once in a while, my aunt would ship over a treats package with gummi bears (also not available in the United States. Dark Ages, indeed), marzipan, and Nutella. My mother would tuck the goods into some secret compartment, but I have always had a sixth sense for sugar and I found her hidey-hole in no time. Just because I was smart enough to *find* the stuff doesn't mean I had the sense to dig into it with some moderation so my tracks were covered. Before I knew it, I'd eaten half the jar and I had no way of refilling the empty space I'd left in the smooth hazelnut and chocolate goodness. I was well and truly screwed. I've recovered from Helga's wrath, just barely, and I've come out of it with my love of Nutella still intact.

1 cup/290 g Nutella spread, or similar chocolate-hazelnut product
2 cups/454 ml heavy whipping cream
Pinch of salt

Place the Nutella in the bowl of a stand mixer fitted with the whisk attachment and mix on low speed until smooth. Add the cream and salt with the mixer on low speed and continue to mix on low speed until the Nutella and cream are combined. Increase the speed to high and whisk until the mixture holds medium stiff peaks. Transfer to a bowl, cover with plastic wrap, and refrigerate to set, about two hours.

PEANUT BUTTER MOUSSE

I'm that person who can't buy Halloween candy until the day of because I. Will. Eat. All. The. Candy. And then, when I do buy that bulk bag of danger, I try to steer clear from anything resembling a peanut butter cup because if those get near me, I'll go underground and won't see sunlight again until I've eaten every last one. This damn mousse does me no favors when it comes to the "eat it all in one sitting" problem I've got with all things peanut butter.

1½ cups/354 ml heavy whipping cream

8 ounces/227 g cream cheese, at room temperature

1 cup/270 g creamy peanut butter

2 cups/227 g confectioners' sugar

¼ cup/½ stick/57 g unsalted butter, soft

¼ cup/57 ml whole milk

½ teaspoon fine sea salt

In the bowl of a stand mixer fitted with the whisk attachment, whisk the cream to stiff peaks. Transfer to a mixing bowl and refrigerate.

Place the cream cheese, peanut butter, confectioners' sugar, butter, milk, and salt in the same bowl of the stand mixer fitted with the paddle attachment (no need to wash it first). Mix until smooth. Fold in the whipped cream.

APPLE CIDER—PUMPKIN MOUSSE

MAKES ENOUGH FOR ONE 10-INCH/25.5 CM CAKE

Every fall, we harvest the apples from our ancient trees, so ancient not even our Vermont elder farmers can make out the variety. We run them through an equally ancient apple mill and press to make cider and then we fight over who gets the first sip from the juice running from the press. It just so happens that when we get around to pressing (usually later than anyone else because we get a little lazy), my pie pumpkins are perfectly ripe. And since the two lovely fruits of our land are ready at the same time, I like to combine the two to celebrate all the yumminess of the season in one perfect mousse.

1 (15-ounces/425 g) can pure pumpkin purée, divided

2 cups/454 ml heavy whipping cream, divided

5 large egg yolks, at room temperature

½ cup/106 ml light brown sugar

¼ cup/28 g cornstarch

1 teaspoon ground cinnamon

½ teaspoon freshly grated nutmeg

½ teaspoon ground cloves

1 teaspoon vanilla bean paste

Pinch of salt

1 cup/236 ml apple cider

1 (7 g) packet powdered gelatin or 3 sheets silver gelatin, softened (see page 120)

Place half the pumpkin purée and 1 cup/227 ml of cream in the bowl of a stand mixer fitted with the whisk attachment and whisk until stiff peaks form. Transfer to a bowl and refrigerate until needed.

In the same stand mixer bowl, combine the remaining pumpkin purée, yolks, brown sugar, cornstarch, cinnamon, nutmeg, cloves, vanilla bean paste, and salt. Whisk until smooth. While whisking, bring the remaining 1 cup/227 ml of cream and the apple cider to a simmer in a large saucepan.

With the mixer on low speed, slowly pour in the heated apple cider mixture and whisk until combined. Scrape the bottom and sides of the bowl and transfer the pumpkin mixture to the saucepan. Whisk over medium-low heat until it thickens to the consistency of mayonnaise and a few bubbles form. Remove from the heat and immediately add the softened gelatin. Whisk to combine. Transfer the mixture to a clean bowl and cover with plastic wrap, making sure the plastic wrap touches the pastry cream, to keep a skin from forming. Cool completely in the refrigerator, about 45 minutes.

Once cool, whisk the mixture to loosen and, using a large rubber spatula, gently fold in the reserved cold pumpkin whipped cream.

FRUIT MOUSSE

The options for fruit mousse are only limited to the number of fruits you can get your hot little hands on (please see my warning on page 147 about some tricky fruits that can mess with gelatin setting). There's one base for the mousse. One. Then you just have to get the purée down. Yay! The world is your fruity oyster. In fact, you can go a little too crazy with all the options you've got but there are worse ways to go crazy. If you can't get your hands on purée or the fruit you'd like to use for the purée, you can reduce fruit juice over low heat until it becomes thick and concentrated.

1 cup/240 ml fruit purée (recipe follows)
1 (7 g) packet powdered gelatin or 3 sheets silver gelatin, softened (see page 120)
⅓ cup/79 ml water
½ teaspoon freshly squeezed lemon juice
1 cup/200 g granulated sugar
5 large egg whites, at room temperature
Generous pinch of salt
1½ cups/360 ml heavy whipping cream
½ cup/115 g mascarpone cheese

In a medium saucepan, gently heat the purée and stir in the gelatin to melt. Set aside.

Place the water and lemon juice in a heavy-bottomed saucepan and then carefully pour the sugar into the middle of the pan. Stir very gently over medium-low heat until the sugar has completely dissolved. Take a damp pastry brush and knock down any sugar granules that are clinging to the sides of the pot. Clip on a candy thermometer, stop stirring, and heat the syrup to 243°F/117°C.

While the sugar heats, place the egg whites and salt in the bowl of a stand mixer and whisk until just foamy. When the sugar reaches temperature, lower the speed of the mixer and carefully pour the syrup into the meringue, taking care not to pour the syrup on the whisk (you'll just spin syrup onto the side of the bowl and into your face, not into the egg whites). Try to aim the syrup just where the egg whites start hitting the side of the bowl. Once the syrup has been added, increase the speed to high and whisk until the meringue holds stiff, shiny peaks. Transfer the meringue to a metal bowl and set aside.

Using the same mixing bowl (you don't have to clean it), combine the cream and mascarpone. Whip until the cream holds medium stiff peaks.

Gently fold together the meringue into the cream mixture. Add ½ cup/118 ml of the meringue mixture to the purée and whisk to lighten. Quickly add the lightened purée mixture to the remainder of the meringue and gently fold until no white streaks remain. Two things are very important here: On the one hand, the purée mixture can't be too warm, otherwise it will melt and deflate the cream/meringue mixture. On the other hand, the purée mixture can't be so cool that it has set. It's a balancing act, but you can do it! Pour the mousse into the specified mold to set.

SIMPLE FRUIT PURÉE

MAKES 2 CUPS/472 ML PURÉE

I keep fruit purée in my freezer, just in case I need to make a zippy, fruit-laced butter cream or a batch of *pâte de fruit* or even to use as thin a thin layer over tender yellow cake. It's a great way to use up fruit that would otherwise go bad in the fridge and here, in Vermont, when the berries are going gangbusters, I often make large batches of purée to freeze instead of making jam because I have more room in my freezer than I have in the pantry. And it's so much easier than canning (which is still great fun and worth doing, by the way). Using homemade purée from superfresh fruit is a fabulous way to bring a furiously fresh punch of flavor to any cake.

1 pound/454 g fresh or frozen fruit
½ cup/100 g granulated sugar
1 tablespoon freshly squeezed lemon juice

If using frozen fruit, thaw it in a colander in a sink, so that some of the moisture drains. Transfer the fruit to a large saucepan and stir in the sugar and lemon juice. Stir over low heat until the sugar has melted, the fruit has broken down, and the purée has thickened to the point that the juice coat the back of a wooden spoon.

Transfer the mixture to a food processer or blender and process until smooth. For a seedless and extra-smooth purée, run the mixture through a fine sieve. You can freeze any extra purée you aren't using in a recipe.

COCONUT MOUSSE

When people love coconut they really *love* coconut. I like it well enough, but I'm not one for a full-throttle evening of it. This subtle, light, and creamy mousse is a perfect balance of coconut flavor. It will please coconut extremists and the coconut fence sitters alike. For those cuckoo for coconut, I pair it with my coconut cake and coat it all with coconut buttercream, but you can tone it down and use a chocolate cake and a vanilla buttercream as well. There are options for everyone on the coconut spectrum.

1 cup/240 ml coconut cream

1 (7 g) packet powdered gelatin or 3 sheets silver gelatin, softened (see page 120)

⅓ cup/79 ml water

½ teaspoon freshly squeezed lemon juice

1 cup/200 g granulated sugar

5 large egg whites, at room temperature

Generous pinch of salt

1 teaspoon coconut extract

1½ cups/360 ml heavy whipping cream

½ cup/115 g mascarpone cheese

In a medium saucepan, gently heat the coconut cream to a bare simmer and stir in the gelatin to melt. Set aside.

Place the water and lemon juice in a heavy saucepan and then carefully pour the sugar into the middle of the pan. Stir very gently over medium-low heat until the sugar has completely dissolved. Take a damp pastry brush and knock down any sugar granules that are clinging to the sides of the pot. Clip on a candy thermometer, stop stirring, and heat the syrup to 243°F/117°C.

While the sugar heats, place the egg whites and salt in the bowl of a stand mixer and whisk until just foamy. When the sugar reaches temperature, lower the speed of the mixer and carefully pour the syrup into the meringue, taking care not to pour the syrup on the whisk (you'll just spin syrup onto the side of the bowl and into your face, not into the egg whites). Try to aim the syrup just where the egg whites start hitting the side of the bowl.

Once the syrup has been added, add the coconut extract, increase the speed to high, and whisk until the meringue holds stiff, shiny peaks. Transfer the meringue to a metal bowl and set aside.

Place the cream and mascarpone in the same mixing bowl (you don't have to clean it). Whip until the cream holds medium stiff peaks.

Gently fold together the meringue into the cream mixture. Add ½ cup/118 ml of the meringue mixture to the coconut cream mixture and whisk to lighten. Quickly add the lightened coconut mixture to the remainder of the meringue and gently fold until no white streaks remain. Two things are very important here: On the one hand, the coconut cream mixture can't be too warm, otherwise it will melt and deflate the meringue mixture. On the other hand, the coconut cream mixture can't be so cool that it has set. Room temperature is best. It's a balancing act, but you can do it!

DEEP DARK CHOCOLATE MOUSSE

MAKES ENOUGH TO FILL ONE 8-INCH/20.5 CM CAKE

Good golly, I love this mousse. And yes, I love all things fruity but this mousse tells me exactly why I was all in on chocolate when I was a kid. *Because it's the best!* And this chocolate mousse, it's the best chocolate mousse. It's exactly what a mousse should be: Light, airy, yet creamy and substantial. Substantially chocolaty, that is.

1 cup/2 sticks/225 g unsalted butter, melted

8 large eggs, separated and brought to room temperature

4 cups/960 ml heavy whipping cream, divided

½ cup/100 g granulated sugar, divided

1 tablespoon/15 ml vanilla bean paste

¼ teaspoon fine sea salt

1 pound/455 g bittersweet chocolate (60%), finely chopped

In a large, heatproof mixing bowl, combine the melted butter, egg yolks, 2 cups/480 ml of the cream, ¼ cup/50 g of the sugar, the vanilla bean paste, and the salt. Place the bowl over a pot of simmering water to create a double boiler and whisk constantly until the mixture thickens, coats the back of a spoon, and the temperature of the mixture reads at least 180°F/82°C. The mixture may appear to break but continue on: keep whisking until it does thicken.

Take the custard mixture from the heat and immediately add the chocolate, making sure all the chocolate is coated with hot custard. Let the chocolate rest for a few minutes to melt and then whisk with a clean whisk until the chocolate is completely melted and incorporated into the custard. If you have unmelted pieces of chocolate, place the bowl atop the simmering water again until fully melted. Set aside. Keep the water in the saucepan gently simmering.

Place the remaining 2 cups/480 ml of cream in a clean mixing bowl and whisk until it holds *almost* stiff peaks. Transfer the cream to a clean bowl and refrigerate until needed. Carefully clean the stand mixer bowl and whisk so they're spotless!

In the clean bowl of a stand mixer, combine the egg whites and remaining ¼ cup/ 50 g of sugar. Place the bowl over the simmering water to create a double boiler and whisk constantly until the sugar has completely melted and the mixture reads 180°F/82°C on a sugar thermometer.

Immediately transfer the mixture to the stand mixer and whisk on high speed until the meringue holds stiff, glossy peaks. Be careful not to overmix to the point that the meringue dries and becomes lumpy. It must be smooth to incorporate beautifully into the remaining ingredients. If it's lumpy, you'll have to work too hard to incorporate the whites and you'll end up deflating the mousse.

With a rubber spatula, transfer about one quarter of the beaten egg whites into the chocolate custard and stir vigorously to combine the two. Transfer the remaining egg whites to the custard and gently fold the two together until just combined.

Gently fold the reserved whipped cream into the custard mixture until there are no white streaks of either egg white or whipped cream. Transfer the mousse to the mold indicated in the cake recipe.

PUMPKIN PIE FILLING

MAKES TWO 8-INCH/20.5 CM ROUND FILLING LAYERS

I have a *big* problem with Frankensteining food, like that abomination the turducken. What did that turkey, duck, and chicken ever do to you to be treated in such a manner? But while this amalgamation offended me, deeply, I kept my opinions to myself. Well, not entirely, but for me, I was pretty quiet about my disapproval. But then came the pie-cake. A pumpkin pie, baked *inside* a cake. *How dare they?!* Whoever created this horror story clearly had no respect for cake and most definitely had some deep-seeded resentment toward the beauty of a pie, where crust is queen and should be crispy and seen, not embedded in the goopy confines of cake batter and then baked to oblivion, losing all its personality and goodness. But as a lover of dessert, I saw hope in all that sogginess. I saw a way of making it right and that meant treating each element of both the pie and cake as special and worthy of shining and to do that, you have to bake them not in a swamp heap together, but alone and *then* assemble them so you get the best of tender cake layers, custardy pumpkin filling, and crisp and flaky piecrust accents. Now that's a Frankenstein I can get on board with.

½ cup/106 g light brown sugar

1 tablespoon all-purpose flour

1½ teaspoons ground cinnamon

1 teaspoon ground ginger

½ teaspoon ground cardamom

¼ teaspoon freshly grated nutmeg

¼ teaspoon ground cloves

½ teaspoon salt

Nonstick cooking spray for pans

½ cup/156 g pure maple syrup, preferably dark amber

3 large eggs, at room temperature

1 (15-ounce/425 g) can pure pumpkin purée

1¼ cups/284 g heavy whipping cream or eggnog

1 tablespoon pure vanilla extract

In a small mixing bowl, whisk together the brown sugar, flour, cinnamon, ginger, cardamom, nutmeg, cloves, and salt.

Preheat the oven to 425°F/220°C. Line the bottom of two 8-inch/20.5 cm round cake pans with parchment and spray the cake pans with nonstick cooking spray. Set aside.

In a large mixing bowl, whisk together the maple syrup, eggs, pumpkin purée, cream, and vanilla. Add the flour mixture to the pumpkin mixture and whisk to combine.

Divide the filling evenly between the two prepared pans, lower the baking temperature to 350°F/180°C, and bake for 30 to 35 minutes, or until the filling just barely shimmies in the middle. Turn off the oven and open the oven door, to allow the filling to cool slowly in the cooling oven. Using a paring knife, release the filling from the sides of each pan. Line a sheet pan with parchment and turn out the filling onto the parchment. Freeze for 20 to 30 minutes, to firm up before assembling in a cake, such as the Giant Pumpkin Cake (page 275).

A MESSAGE FROM THE

Cake Lady

TEMPER, TEMPER

You've likely heard of tempering chocolate. It's a method of melting chocolate to use as a coating and bringing it to a constant temperature so that it maintains shine and that lovely *snap* you get when you bite off the head of a fine-quality chocolate Easter bunny. But tempering also refers to introducing two disparate ingredients together, usually one that is hot and one that isn't too happy when it's combined with something hot. Eggs are such a finicky ingredient. If you add them too quickly to something hot, you can probably guess what'll happen. They scramble. I can't think of a single dessert where that's a good thing. That's where tempering comes into play; think of the old-fashioned rules of courtship wherein a young lady wouldn't dream of speaking to a young man until they had been introduced by an intermediary. So, think of tempering as a dessert courtship, whereby you add a small amount of the hot liquid to eggs while whisking them constantly to introduce the two. Once they are tempered in this manner, you can add the egg mixture to the main body of hot stuff without it scrambling. A happy marriage indeed.

PECAN PIE FILLING

MAKES ONE 8-INCH/20.5 CM ROUND LAYER

I don't know why pecan pie is relegated to such a very short season in our lives. I think it's worth eating all year, don't you? The filling is so wonderfully smooth and almost like candy. And it's soft, easy to cut through but it still holds its shape. All of this has made it pretty hard for me to resist turning that scrumminess into a filling for a cake. And why bother resisting?

Nonstick cooking spray for pan
4 large eggs, at room temperature
½ cup/1 stick/113 g unsalted butter
1½ cups/320 g light brown sugar
½ cup/156 g corn syrup
¼ cup/78 g pure maple syrup
1 tablespoon pure vanilla extract
¼ teaspoon fine sea salt
2 cups/250 g lightly toasted pecans, chopped

Preheat the oven to 350°F/180°C. Line the bottom of one 8-inch/20.5 cm round cake pan with parchment and spray with nonstick cooking spray. Attach soaked DIY cake strips to the outer sides of the pans (see page 31). Set aside.

In a mixing bowl, whisk the eggs. Set aside.

In a saucepan, melt the butter over low heat. Add the brown sugar and continue to heat until the sugar melts. Remove from the heat and stir in the corn syrup, maple syrup, vanilla, and salt. Slowly pour ¼ cup/59 ml of the butter mixture into the eggs while whisking constantly. Once tempered, continue to whisk while pouring in the remaining butter mixture. Stir in the pecans and pour into the prepared pan. Bake for 15 to 20 minutes or until the middle of the filling just barely jiggles.

Remove from the oven and allow the filling to cool in the pan, then, using a paring knife, release the sides of the pecan filling. Line a sheet pan with parchment and turn out the pecan filling onto the lined pan. Freeze until very firm before assembling the cake.

KEY LIME CHEESECAKE

MAKES ENOUGH TO FILL ONE 8-INCH/20.5 CM CAKE

You know, it's not just for the factory. You can actually use cheesecake as a filling. In fact, whenever I see a recipe for no-bake cheesecake, I think, "That's not a *real* cheesecake, that's just a filling for a cake." Did I say that out loud? I'm such a cheesecake snob. But what a filling! It's rich and tart, like a good cheesecake, but it's slightly softer and more spreadable, like a cake frosting. And it's zippy! I particularly like Key lime as a flavor, but you can choose just about any juice you can think of to flavor this lovely filling. This is especially lovely with more tropical flavors, such as in the fruity version of my "It's My Birthday and I'll Bake If I Want To Cake" (page 309).

¼ cup/28 g confectioners' sugar

1 tablespoon Instant ClearJel

1 cup/236 ml heavy whipping cream

2 (8-ounce/227 g) packages cream cheese, at room temperature

1 (14-ounce/397 g) can sweetened condensed milk

¼ cup/59 ml Key lime juice

1 teaspoon vanilla extract

¼ teaspoon salt

In a small bowl, whisk together the confectioners' sugar and Instant ClearJel. Place the cream and confectioners' sugar mixture in the bowl of a stand mixer, fitted with the whisk attachment. Whisk until stiff peaks form. Transfer the whipped cream to a bowl. Place the cream cheese in the same stand mixer bowl you just used (you don't have to clean it) and whisk until smooth. Add the sweetened condensed milk and continue to whisk until combined and smooth. Add the lime juice, vanilla, and salt. Continue to whisk until smooth, light, and fluffy. Fold in the whipped cream. Keep refrigerated until ready to use.

Works Well with Others

There are some fillings that, while they are lovely all on their own, they are even happier when they have a companion. Some are nubby and crunchy, such as caramelized rice puffs and Schoko Crossies, and they need a little creamy element, such as a simple *cremeux* (perhaps not so simple to say but truly simple to make) to keep them in place and to complement their crispy nature. Others are a thin coating of flavor and texture, such as caramel filling, and are better off when they have a topper of buttercream or ganache to balance the flavors.

In fact, it's these kinds of fillings (I like to call them secret pastry agents) that are the hallmark of the best Parisian pastries. These are the little-known heroes of the baking world that bring delight to anyone that has the pleasure of encountering them in a single bite from an *entremet*. That's a lot of fancy French there, isn't it? What is it with all the French and fancy trickery? I'll tell you, it's exactly what I say it is. Secret pastry agents that are kept hidden from you to keep you in the dark about how fancy pastry shops create cakes with dimensions of flavor and texture that you are meant to believe are impossible to create at home, let alone pronounce. I'm here to expose these undercover tasties as the simple additions to cakes that can elevate *any* cake to new heights.

ENTREMET

Entremet. Pronounced *ehn-trah-MAY*. It's French. It literally means "between servings," which is confusing because pastry chefs know it as one thing: a superfancy and perfectly composed layer cake. Sometimes, in fact quite often, the *entremet* is small. Individual size. Sometimes it's sharing size, but it's always composed in very precise layers with very precise flavor and textural compositions. When you cut into one, it's freakin' intimidating because the layers inside are *perfect* and the coating that surrounds the top and sides is *perfect*. Everything is expertly plumb. Each layer is exactly the same depth and each layer is easily distinguishable from the next in color and texture. *Entremets* are built in rings that allow for precision. My guess is you don't have rings. That's okay. Because I've got a secret for you, you can take the top *and* bottom off cans for individual sizes, and you can take the lid and bottom off a big ol' Crisco tub and use it as a ring for larger sizes.

You can (and should) take a few lessons from the French and incorporate a couple *entremet* tricks into your everyday layer cakes, from adding textures, such as crispy caramelized rice, to learning a simple filling called a *cremeux* which lands on the creamy side of mousse but is, quite frankly, much easier to make (and is my #1 favorite filling in the whole wide world), to learning to make *pâte de fruit*, which is simply a type of firmly set jelly that brings an excellent punch of flavor and a lovely, fruity chew to a filling. Many of these things you can make ahead, such as the crispy elements, and then add them on a whim to your filling. Others, such as *cremeux*, should be used once cooled but are so delicious and easy to make and can be frozen in an assembled cake. It should be no surprise by now that when I make my own birthday cake, and of course I do, no one else gets to have all the fun, I layer my cakes in the manner of an *entremet*. You'll see this technique in my "It's My Birthday and I'll Bake If I Want To Cake" cake (page 309).

CRISPY CARAMELIZED RICE PUFFS

MAKES 1 CUP/150 G CARAMELIZED RICE PUFFS

You might think that rice cereal is only good in desserts when it's surrounded by melted marshmallow. And while you'd be correct in thinking a Rice Krispie Treat is a thing of beauty and divine goodness, I'm here to share the secret pastry chefs have been hiding from you: there's another way of revering that puffy kernel of yummy. You can caramelize the rice cereal and use it to add a sweet snap, crackle, and pop to the inside or outside of layers. It's most often hidden, so you only really know there's something delightful when you start chewing and the ordinary nature of the thing is kept a mystery. You are left thinking you just experienced an unknowable exclusive ingredient, when in fact it's the same rice cereal you can find in family packs in the grocery store, just coated in caramelized sugar. Not only is it simple *and* delicious, you can make it ahead and store in an airtight container to add to layers (I especially like to comingle the stuff with ganache), to sprinkle on top of cakes (or ice cream), or to adhere to the sides of cakes. Or just to snack on. If you want to know one of *my* pastry secrets, I caramelize a box of rice cereal and use it in my Rice Krispie Treats. Sometimes, I'll even use them as a layer inside a cake. I'm crazy that way, but that's no secret.

½ cup/99 g granulated sugar
Pinch of salt
1 cup/40 g puffed rice cereal, such as Rice Krispies

Line a half sheet pan with parchment. Set aside.

Sprinkle the sugar and salt in an even layer onto a large, flat, stainless-steel skillet (you won't get as good a read on the caramel color in a nonstick or darker pan). Stir occasionally over low heat until the sugar has melted and turns a light amber. Immediately add the rice cereal and stir to coat. Transfer to the prepared sheet pan and allow to cool.

FEUILLETINE

MAKES 1 CUP/225 G FEUILLETINE

I've done it again, asked you to indulge me with these weird names and ingredients I keep bandying about. But fear not because like many French-named ingredients, this one is as simple as it is delicious. *Feuilletine* is essentially paper-thin, crêpelike sweet crispity crunchities that you want in your life, now. But please trust me on this (and all things sweet, quite frankly), the stuff is wonderful and easy to make. *Feuilletine* is an ingredient professional pastry chefs use to add a sweet, crispy, caramel/praline magic to cakes and they are *hiding them from you*! There's no reason at all you shouldn't have it in your life. You can use it inside layers or to coat the outside of a cake. It's insanely delicious. In fact, it's dangerous. But if you can keep your paws off it long enough to use in a cake, you'll experience a dimension of delicious in your cakes that you'll be speaking of to your grandchildren and great-grandchildren in the years to come.

½ cup/1 stick/113 g unsalted butter,
  at room temperature
½ cup/99 g granulated sugar
1 large egg white, at room temperature
½ teaspoon pure vanilla extract
Generous pinch of salt
½ cup/60 g all-purpose flour

Preheat the oven to 375°F/190°C. Line a sheet pan with parchment. Set aside.

Place the butter and sugar in the bowl of a stand mixer fitted with the paddle attachment. Mix until light and fluffy. Scrape down the bottom and sides of the bowl and then add the egg white, vanilla, and salt. Mix to combine. It will look curdled and broken. That's okay. Scrape the bottom and sides of the bowl again, add the flour, and mix until smooth.

Transfer the batter to the prepared parchment and smooth it into a *very* thin layer. Paper thin, in fact. Bake for 5 minutes, or until the mixture is golden brown. Remove from the oven and allow to cool on the sheet pan, then break the thin "cookie" into small shards. This is *feuilletine*. Take a nibble, but just a nibble, because you'll end up eating it all if you aren't careful. If you aren't going to use your new best friend in a culinary creation just yet, you can store the flakes in a resealable plastic bag for weeks on end. You can freeze the stuff for months, too.

SCHOKO CROSSIES À LA GESINE

MAKES 2½ CUPS/400 G

Schoko Crossies are a German candy, chocolate-coated, frosted flake and toasted almond clusters that dominated my childhood due to their tastiness and my ability to get my hands on them in abundance. During the school year in Virginia, Mom would be on full "vegan/healthy food only" patrol, while I was in full stealth candy mode, consuming sugar on the sly wherever I could find it. However, when we visited Germany in the summer, the world of German sweets was at my fingertips. My grandmother, Omi, and my aunt, Tante Christel, slipped me pocket money and I had relative freedom, so no one could stop me from loading up a shopping cart with all my favorites in the well-stocked candy aisle and ripping into them in plain view of my mother. Invariably, she'd grab a handful of Schoko Crossies. Even she couldn't resist them. If you think you're sensing a trend here, you'd be right. I never miss an opportunity to incorporate my childhood favorites into my adult dream desserts, especially when it's a treat that adds magic to cake, such as my birthday cake (page 309). My take on Schoko Crossies does just that.

1 cup/198 g granulated sugar

1 cup/25 g cornflakes

1 cup/86 g sliced almonds, lightly toasted

4 ounces/113 g bittersweet chocolate, 60%, finely chopped

1 teaspoon neutral oil or shortening

Line a half sheet pan with parchment. Set aside.

Sprinkle the sugar in an even layer onto a large, flat, stainless-steel skillet (you won't get as good a read on the caramel color in a nonstick or darker pan). Stir occasionally over low heat until the sugar has melted and turns a light amber. Immediately add the cornflakes and almonds and stir to coat. Transfer to the sheet pan and spread with a spoon. Allow to cool.

Once cool, place the chocolate and oil in a heatproof bowl and gently melt over a pot of simmering water. Drizzle over the cornflakes and almond slices and allow to set, about 2 hours. Break apart into small pieces and store in an airtight container.

GERMAN CHOCOLATE CAKE FILLING

German chocolate cake isn't German. Well, it's German to the degree that the gentleman who owned a chocolate company in Texas that bore his name was named "German." So when you hear, "German chocolate cake" it's probably more apt to add an "'s" to it, so it reads "German's chocolate cake," because that's what it is. It was a recipe created to sell his eponymous, unsweetened chocolate and contained some very un-German (in the sense of the country) ingredients, such as Texas pecans and tropical shredded coconut. It's no wonder that it became incredibly popular because it's so damn delicious, but it's time we give credit where credit is due: Mr. German and his home state of Texas. But since that's, like, never going to happen, I give this filling a true German spin and I use it as a filling in my Maple Sticky Bun Cake (page 72). You see, sticky buns *are* of German origin (originally called *Schnecken*). The added coconut might not be terribly on point, in terms of German-ness, but it sure is yummy! Mr. German would approve (and so would Germans).

3 large egg yolks, at room temperature

1 cup/213 g light brown sugar

1 (12-ounce/340 g) can evaporated milk

½ cup/1 stick/113 g unsalted butter, at room temperature

1 teaspoon pure vanilla extract

¼ teaspoon fine sea salt

2½ cups/282 g coconut flakes, very lightly toasted

1½ cups/189 g pecans, chopped and lightly toasted

Place the yolks in a small bowl and whisk to combine. Set aside.

Combine the brown sugar, evaporated milk, butter, vanilla, and sea salt in a saucepan. Heat over low heat, stirring, until the brown sugar and butter have melted. Carefully pour ½ cup/118 ml of the sugar mixture into the yolks, whisking constantly, to temper. Transfer the tempered yolk mixture back to the remaining sugar mixture, stirring constantly. Continue to stir over low heat until the mixture thickens and the temperature reads 170°F/77°C on a candy thermometer. Remove from the heat and stir in the coconut and pecans. Allow to cool to room temperature before using in assembling the cake.

COCONUT CARAMEL FILLING

Kinda like a German chocolate cake filling but actually closer to a Samoa topping (no pecans…loads of caramel), this filling is dense, perfectly chewy, and downright delicious, and this is coming from someone who used to despise coconut in all its forms. This treat, however, I can eat by the bucketful. It's a wonderful, hidden, addition to the snowy perfection that is the Coconut Snowball Cake (page 241).

Nonstick cooking spray for pan
½ cup/156 g pure maple syrup
½ cup/107 g light brown sugar
½ cup/114 g heavy whipping cream
¼ cup/78 g sweetened condensed milk
¼ cup/78 g corn syrup
½ teaspoon salt
2 tablespoons/28 g unsalted butter
3 cups/336 g shredded coconut, gently toasted and cooled

Line the bottom of three 8-inch/20.5 cm cake pans with parchment and spray with nonstick cooking spray. Set aside.

Combine the maple syrup, brown sugar, cream, sweetened condensed milk, corn syrup, and salt in a large saucepan. Stir over medium heat until the mixture reaches 240°F/116°C. Remove from the heat and stir in the butter and coconut.

Immediately divide the filling evenly among the three prepared pans, gently pressing the mixture into an even layer. Set aside until needed.

PÂTE À CHOUX

"Whaa?" If you know what *pâte à choux* is, you're asking that. If you don't know what *pâte à choux* is, you're asking that. So that everyone's on the same page, *pâte à choux* is a type of paste from which you make cream puff or éclair shells. It's not the typical kind of thing you'd use in the *filling* of a cake but in Germany, it kinda is. You see, what they do is make a cream puff: they bake some *choux* paste, cool it, and then fill it with pastry cream. Now a normal baker would just stop there and serve the yummy stuff. But Germans aren't normal bakers. They are *genius* bakers because they then take those filled cream puffs and submerge them in a mousse filling so the filled cream puffs become a part of the filling. Sandwich the mousse with the hidden bombs of yummy with cake and you've got something marvelous.

½ cup/118 ml water

½ cup/118 ml milk

½ cup/1 stick/113 g unsalted butter,
  cut into small pieces

1 tablespoon granulated sugar

1 teaspoon salt

1 cup/120 g all-purpose flour
  (I like King Arthur)

4 to 5 large eggs, at room temperature

Preheat the oven to 425°F/220°C.

Combine the water, milk, butter, sugar, and salt in a saucepan and stir over low heat until the sugar, butter, and salt have melted. Increase the heat to medium and allow to simmer.

Remove from the heat, immediately add the flour, and stir with a wooden spoon until thickened, smooth, and no flour lumps remain. Once the flour is added, the

mixture is called a *panade* and only becomes a *choux* paste when you add the eggs. Return the saucepan to the heat and stir until a film forms on the bottom of the pan. Continue to stir, being careful not to scrape up the film, for a minute or two more.

Transfer the *panade*, being careful not to scrape off the film on the bottom of the pan, to a stand mixer fitted with the paddle attachment. Mix for a minute to dissipate the heat.

Whisk 3 of the eggs together and slowly add to the mixer while it runs on low speed. Scrape the bottom and sides of the bowl. Whisk and add the fourth egg slowly, as you may not need it all. If the paste is shiny and slowly falls from the paddle when lifted from the paste, it's ready. If the mixture is chunky, looks dry and doesn't fall at all from the paddle, whisk the fifth egg and add just a bit at a time until you've reached proper consistency.

Transfer the *choux* paste to a pastry bag fitted with a large, open top (Ateco 808) and pipe walnut-size dollops on a parchment-lined sheet pan, spaced 2 inches/5 cm apart. Place the *choux* puffs in the oven and immediately reduce the heat to 375°F/190°C and bake for 20 minutes before you even *think* of opening the oven and then, make sure the puffs have browned well. Rotate the pan and bake for 5 to 10 minutes more, or until the shells feel very firm. Allow to cool completely before filling.

Goes Both Ways

There are some fillings that can also act as icing and some icings that can act as fillings, they are great on the inside and outside of the cake. There are moments when it's lovely to have a contrast between what's hidden inside and what's exposed for the world to see, but there are times when just the one thing is just perfect. Right now I'm thinking about my yellow cake and how it's so damn happy to be filled and coated by my Fudgy Chocolate Frosting. Anything else in the middle would muddy the already perfect waters. What's important, though, isn't what I think. It's what you think. So, while I get to pick and choose what I put together in this book, it's your house and your rules. You get to pick exactly what goes on the inside and the outside, whether they are the same or many different things.

Cake Lady

"THAT'S NOT REAL BUTTERCREAM."

Different people have different feelings about what a "real" buttercream is. I think I'm pretty vocal about it, but I'm nothing compared to my mother, Helga, and her utter disdain for anything other than what she deemed a "true" buttercream. And that meant that it had to be made in one of two methods: with a hot meringue (either Swiss or Italian) or in the French method, with a *pâte à bombe* base that relies on yolks instead of meringue for its base. Either way, she could taste whether it was or wasn't made with her approved methods. In hindsight, I'm almost certain that my mother had what is called a superpalate. She could taste anything and everything in food. Famously, she would describe elements she disapproved of on her plate as "unclean" and she had no trouble asking for the chef to visit our table so she could tell her/him to her/his face. Tough crowd, that Helga. So, it happens that when we went on a search for the maker of my wedding cake, I took her to what was then known as the premier cake maker in Los Angeles. I'd decided to give myself a break and not make my own. However, when we sat down for the tasting, my mother declared, quite loudly, that there was not a single cake that contained a lick of "real buttercream." And I had to agree with her. None of it was, even to my mind, the real deal.

SWISS BUTTERCREAM

MAKES ENOUGH TO FILL OR COVER
AN 8-INCH/20.5 CM CAKE

This is a beautiful buttercream. It makes life better, just knowing you can make this at the drop of the hat. One of the tricks is getting your meringue to a pretty high temperature, 180°F/82°C, for two reasons: (1) to heat it so that you pasteurize the egg whites, making them food safe and "cooked" without it scrambling them, and (2) by heating the egg whites pretty high, you stabilize the meringue, making it possible to add less butter than most recipes for the buttercream to come together. Why's that important? Because one problem people have with (real) buttercreams is that they can be either too buttery or two sweet. This one is neither. It's just perfect. And you can flavor it in any number of ways to make it exactly the buttercream you love.

Note: This recipe says 1 pound/453 g of butter (that's four sticks) but if you do every-thing right, you'll only need ¾ pound/340 g (three sticks). That extra stick is like carrying an umbrella so that it doesn't rain. If you get the initial sugar–egg white mixture to the right temperature, you'll find you'll only need the three.

5 large egg whites, at room temperature

1 cup plus 2 tablespoons/233 g granulated sugar

Generous pinch of salt

1 teaspoon extract of choice (don't use oil-based extract)

1 pound/453 g unsalted butter, at room temperature

Place the egg whites, sugar, and salt in the bowl of a stand mixer. Whisk together and place over a pot of simmering water to make a double boiler. Whisk constantly until the sugar has completely melted and the mixture is hot to the touch and reaches 170°F/77°C on a candy thermometer.

Immediately transfer the bowl to a stand mixer fitted with the whisk attachment. Whisk on high speed until the meringue holds stiff peaks and the bowl is cool to the touch. Do not add any butter until the bowl is cool. Repeat after me. No. Butter. Until. The. Bowl. Is. Cool. At this stage, you can add the extract.

Add the butter, a few tablespoons at a time. Wait about 10 seconds between each addition. This kind of patience is important, especially as you get close to the last few tablespoons of the third stick of butter. The mixture may look as if it's starting to curdle a bit toward the end. This is fine.

It's not ruined. I call this stage the "puberty" of buttercream. Just let it ride and add a few more tablespoons of butter and leave it alone, just as you would a preteen. The buttercream will smooth out, thicken, and become spreadable. If after you add the last bit of the third stick of butter the buttercream doesn't come together after a minute of mixing, slowly start adding a tablespoon of butter at a time from the last stick of butter. But remember: be patient between each addition and it will come together. Once the buttercream has thickened and smoothed, continue whisking it on high for about two to three more minutes for optimal texture.

It's best to use buttercream immediately. Once refrigerated, it will set. You can get it spreadable again by putting in a mixer and whisking it, but getting it to the right consistency takes longer than it does to make a batch from the very beginning. On the other hand, if you make too much, you can freeze buttercream in a resealable plastic bag, thaw it in the fridge, and then whisk it (takes forever), but it does work when you have extra. But when it comes to making something ahead for the sake of making something ahead, buttercream isn't the best choice.

Variations:

TART CHERRY SWISS MERINGUE: Add ¼ cup/ 60 ml concentrated tart cherry juice to the meringue prior to adding the butter. I use Cherry Bay Orchards' 100% Tart Montmorency Tart Cherry Concentrate.

SWISS MERINGUE TOPPING: Whip the meringue to stiff peaks and forget the butter! Once the bowl is cool, you can frost your cake.

ITALIAN BUTTERCREAM

Italian buttercream is made with a base of Italian meringue. Sometimes I make it with espresso, to make it super Italian. But there are plenty of other versions of this buttercream. What's lovely about my Italian Buttercream is that I heat the sugar syrup higher than most recipes, which allows me to use less butter for the frosting to come together. One of the complaints cake eaters have with some meringue buttercreams is that they are too buttery. This solves that problem allowing the wonderful marshmallowy nature of the meringue to come through.

5 large egg whites, at room temperature

⅛ teaspoon fine sea salt

½ cup/118 ml water

½ teaspoon freshly squeezed lemon juice

1 cup plus 2 tablespoons/233 g
  granulated sugar

1½ cups/3 sticks/340 g unsalted butter,
  slightly cooler than room temperature,
  with ½ cup/1 stick/113 g more on reserve

Combine the egg whites and salt in the bowl of a stand mixer fitted with the whisk attachment.

Combine ½ cup/118 ml of water and the lemon juice in a saucepan and add the sugar. Stir gently over low heat until the sugar is melted. Using a damp pastry brush, knock any sugar crystals on the side of the pan back into the melting sugar. Heat the sugar syrup until it reads 245°F/118°C on a candy thermometer. When the syrup first reaches 235°F/113°C, start your mixer and begin whisking the egg white mixture. Once the syrup reaches final temperature, take it from the heat and care-fully pour it into the egg white mixture while the mixer is still running, being careful not to hit the whisk while it's moving. Continue to whisk until the meringue holds stiff, shiny peaks and the bowl is completely cool to the touch, about 5 minutes.

Add the butter, a few tablespoons at a time. Count to 10 between each addition. After the last tablespoon of the third stick is added, the mixture should thicken and become a shiny, smooth spreadable frosting. If, after 1 minute of whisking after the last bit of the third stick is added, the buttercream is still loose, start adding a tablespoon at a time of the reserve stick of butter.

Variations:

ESPRESSO BUTTERCREAM: Add 1 table-spoon/7 g espresso powder (I use Medaglia D'Oro Instant Espresso Coffee) to the egg whites and salt at the beginning of the recipe.

EXTRACT-FLAVORED ITALIAN BUTTERCREAM:
Add 1 teaspoon of extract to the buttercream once it has come together. If using oil flavors, use only a drop or two as oils tend to be highly concentrated.

HONEY BUTTERCREAM:
Replace ½ cup/99 g sugar with ½ cup/170 grams honey.

CARAMEL BUTTERCREAM:
To the finished Italian buttercream, add ½ cup cooled gourmet caramel sauce (I like Trader Joe's Fleur de Sel Caramel Sauce) and whisk to combine.

RED CURRANT GERMAN BUTTERCREAM

MAKES ENOUGH TO FILL 1 LARGE DACQUOISE

German buttercream is a custard-based, instead of a meringue-based, frosting and also goes by the moniker *crème mousseline*. This makes it creamier (not the name, *mousseline*, just the way it's made), denser, richer. It is unbelievably delicious and it's truly perfect when combined with tarter fruits, such as red currants or cranberries. The combination of the rich base frosting and the tart fruit is delicate and delightful. I pair this buttercream with a spiced meringue layer for my Linzer Macaron Cake (page 290), but you can use it to top cupcakes or as the filling in a yellow cake.

¼ cup/50 g granulated sugar

2 tablespoons cornstarch

⅛ teaspoon salt

3 large egg yolks, at room temperature

⅓ cup/103 g smooth red currant jam (such as Hero brand)

½ cup/118 ml heavy whipping cream

½ cup/118 ml whole milk

½ cup/1 stick/113 g unsalted butter, at room temperature

Place the sugar, cornstarch, and salt in a large saucepan. Whisk to combine. Add the yolks, jam, cream, and milk. Whisk over medium-low heat until the mixture thickens to the consistency of mayonnaise and starts to bubble, about 5 minutes.

Transfer to the bowl of a stand mixer fitted with the whisk attachment. Whisk on low speed to dissipate the heat, until the bowl is cool to the touch. Increase the mixer speed to high and add chunks of butter, a tablespoon at a time, until the mixture thickens and transforms into a spreadable frosting.

HELGA'S CHOCOLATE BUTTERCREAM

This frosting was famous in the Washington, DC, area in the 1980s. My opera singer mother paired this delicate and decadent frosting with her pecan nut cake layers and a legend of a cake was born. At least among the professional opera set. And while I was happy to eat the chocolate frosting *with* the pecan layers, I was even happier to forgo the cake layers all together and just nosh on the luscious frosting.

12 ounces/340 g bittersweet chocolate, (60%), finely chopped

8 large egg yolks, at room temperature

2 teaspoons vanilla bean paste

¼ teaspoon salt

½ cup/118 ml boiling hot brewed coffee

1 cup/2 sticks/226 g unsalted butter, at room temperature

Place the chocolate, yolks, vanilla bean paste, and salt in a food processor. Pulse a few times to get the chocolate very fine (this can be incredibly loud). With the processor running, add the *hot* coffee in a steady stream. Once added, add the butter, a tablespoon at a time, and run the processor until all the butter is added and the frosting is smooth. If it's too soft to spread, refrigerate until it firms a bit, 20 to 30 minutes.

ZIPPY DARK CHOCOLATE GANACHE

MAKES ENOUGH TO COVER ONE 8-INCH/20.5 CM CAKE

Ganache couldn't be simpler. It's just chocolate and cream and in this ratio (for a thinner saucelike ganache, you'd add more cream). You can double and triple and quadruple this recipe without any trouble. I add a pinch of salt to round it out. I add a touch of extract, such as peppermint or orange, to add some fun to the cocoa partay. And sometimes, I add some kick, such as a touch of lime oil, like I do in my Skull Cake (page 248). Some people add a knob of butter for creaminess at the end or a splash of corn syrup for shine. For all that simplicity, things can go wrong. It's possible that when you add the cream, the chocolate doesn't melt completely. In that case, you can gently heat the chocolate in a double boiler to get the ganache smooth. In that case, you can go wrong again. You can overheat the ganache to the point that it breaks, the fat separating. If that happens, have some low-fat milk on hand. Slowly add it, a tablespoon at a time, whisking all the while until it comes together. Either way, ganache can be fixed.

8 ounces/226 g bittersweet chocolate (at least 60% but no more than 70%), very finely chopped
½ cup/118 ml heavy whipping cream
Slight pinch of salt
¼ teaspoon lime oil (optional, or your extract of choice)

Place the chocolate in a wide-bottomed heatproof bowl. Set aside.

Combine the cream and salt in a small saucepan. Bring to a steady simmer over low heat. Make sure the cream comes to a simmer. Immediately pour the hot cream over the chocolate and add the lime oil. Shimmy the bowl to make sure all the chocolate is submerged in the hot cream and allow to sit for 2 to 3 minutes to allow the chocolate to melt completely. Whisk until smooth.

WHITE CHOCOLATE PUMPKIN GANACHE

This stuff is magical in its pumpkin-ness without being all soft and mushy, and isn't that exactly what we expect from pumpkin desserts? I use this particular ganache to help sandwich the layers in the Giant Pumpkin Cake (page 275). It slips in between the layers of pecan (or pumpkin) pie filling, flaky pie layers, and moist pumpkin Bundt cake. It works as glue and as a taste sensation. Not bad for a little ol' ganache.

2 tablespoons/28 g unsalted butter
⅓ cup/80 ml heavy whipping cream
1 tablespoon corn syrup
⅓ cup/76 g pure pumpkin purée
½ teaspoon salt
5½ ounces/156 g white chocolate, finely chopped

Place the butter, cream, corn syrup, pumpkin purée, and salt in a saucepan. Stir over medium heat to combine and allow to come to a gentle simmer. Remove from the heat and immediately add the white chocolate. Shimmy the pan to make sure the chocolate is completely covered in the hot pumpkin mixture. Allow to sit 2 minutes, undisturbed, to allow the chocolate to melt, and then whisk to combine the ingredients until the mixture is completely smooth.

Transfer the ganache to a small, clean bowl and cover with plastic wrap. Allow to cool at room temperature (do not refrigerate) until thickened and spreadable but not set, 15 to 20 minutes.

WHEN BUTTERCREAM HITS PUBERTY

Just as in life, there's a moment for buttercream when things could potentially go horribly wrong. At least it seems that way at the time, when your gorgeous frosting is reaching perfection and then—*blammo*—it suddenly looks curdled and in need of some pastry Clearasil. It's something that can happen if your ingredient temperatures are a little out of whack with each other, kind of like a teenager's hormones. Many inexperienced bakers believe that all is lost when they experience this little change in texture, and that it's time to dump the ugly stuff and start over.

Not so fast! Continue whisking, add one more pat of butter, and leave it alone for a few minutes. In time, the buttercream will thicken and smooth out. If the buttercream looks curdled *and* pretty soupy, put the mixer bowl in the freezer for 5 to 10 minutes and then continue whisking. If the mixture looks curdled *and* there are obvious pea-sized chunks of butter that are swimming around in the mix, you can heat the mixing bowl gently with a blow dryer to get things smoothed out and perfect.

CHOCOLATE TRUFFLE FILLING

If you've ever had ganache, you know how delightfully rich and decadent it is. Well, meet Chocolate Truffle Filling. This will blow the beans out of a traditional ganache. It's silky, dense, and insanely flavorful. I'm in love with the stuff and you will be, too. I add a touch of cinnamon oil and just a splash of cayenne to turn this decadent filling into a world-class party for my Skull Cake (page 248). It balances beautifully with the zippy chocolate ganache that coats the cake.

1 pound/453 g bittersweet chocolate (60%), finely chopped

2 cups/473 ml heavy whipping cream

4 large egg yolks, at room temperature

2 tablespoons plus 1 teaspoon/28 g granulated sugar

¼ cup/85 g honey

⅓ cup/79 ml brewed coffee, cooled

1 drop cinnamon oil (optional)

¼ teaspoon cayenne pepper (optional)

¼ teaspoon salt

Place the finely chopped chocolate in a heatproof bowl and set over a pot of simmering water to melt. Stir occasionally. Set the bowl aside when the chocolate melts, but leave the water simmering.

In the bowl of a stand mixer fitted with the whisk attachment, whip the cream to soft peaks. Transfer it to a clean bowl and set aside.

Place the yolks, sugar, honey, coffee, cinnamon oil, and cayenne pepper (if using), and salt in the bowl of the stand mixer and set over the simmering water. Whisk until the mixture thickens to the point that it coats the back of a spoon and the temperature reaches 180°F/82°C on a candy thermometer.

Transfer the bowl to a stand mixer fitted with the whisk attachment and whisk until the mixture ribbons and the bowl is cool to the touch. Add a large dollop of the thickened egg yolk mixture to the melted chocolate and stir to combine and then add the lightened chocolate to the yolk mixture and gently fold the two together. Fold in the whipped cream until well combined.

RAY HATES CHOCOLATE

At our little baking school in Vermont, my husband, Ray, and I keep things very simple. I set up the classroom and *mise* out everything for my demos and for the students. When the students arrive, Ray checks in to see whether he can make anyone a cappuccino with a hint of our home-sugared maple syrup. It's rare that anyone refuses his famous espresso drinks. Once he delivers the steaming goodness, he leaves to attend to his own work, but he always keeps an ear out for a little bell that tinkles away near his studio door. It's a doorbell system he set up for me so I can alert him to when I need him to start washing dishes. He comes trotting down and he asks, "What's the priority?" I tell him. And as he makes his way to the dirty dish trolley, he invariably turns back with a look of dread and asks, "How much chocolate are we talking about here?" Washing chocolate-coated dishes is the bane of any hardened dishwasher and Ray has dealt with his fair share of chocolate-coated dishes. But there's something you can do for the one you love who gets stuck scrubbing the brown stuff from your baking mess: a bowl scraper. It's a flat plastic tool, about 6 x 4 inches/15 x 10 cm, rounded on one end and flat on the other. It is a superior tool for scraping every last bit of melted chocolate or frosting or batter from a bowl, which is great for your cake and even better for the poor soul stuck with the dishes.

ERMINE FROSTING

If you've never, ever heard of ermine frosting, it's probably because you've heard it called by its other name: boiled milk frosting. You can see why I prefer the former moniker. "Boiled milk frosting" just doesn't sound all that delicious when, in fact, this stuff is crazy delicious. It's also a lovely, soft frosting that's very easy to work with and perfect for making swirls in the finished cake. Just make sure to cook the milk and flour mixture long enough that it thickens, for two reasons: First, for the frosting to come together when you start adding the butter, it needs to have thickened enough to form a decent structure for the butter to do its work. The second reason is that you need to cook out the raw flour taste. It takes a while, but you know what I'm going to say. *Be patient!*

⅓ cup/40 g all-purpose flour
1¼ cups/250 g granulated sugar
Pinch of salt
1¼ cups/295 g whole milk
½ cup/118 ml heavy whipping cream
½ cup/113 g pumpkin purée (optional)
1 teaspoon pure vanilla extract
1½ cups/3 sticks/340 g unsalted butter,
at room temperature

Whisk together the flour, sugar, and salt in a heavy saucepan. Add the milk and cream (and pumpkin, if using) and whisk over medium heat until bubbling and thickened. This can take 5 to 10 minutes. Be patient.

Transfer the mixture to the bowl of a stand mixer fitted with the whisk attachment. Beat until the bowl feels cool. Add the vanilla and then the butter, a few tablespoons at a time, beating until the mixture is light and fluffy.

FUDGY CHOCOLATE FROSTING

This simple, fudgy chocolate frosting is not only delicious, it's a dream to pipe. I pair it with yellow cake for Agnes's Birthday Cake (page 234) for a delicious take on America's favorite birthday cake. As with anything chocolate, using the *best* chocolate and cocoa you can find makes this frosting sing and turns a childhood staple into a pastry dream.

2 cups/227 g confectioners' sugar

1 cup/85 g Dutched cocoa powder
  (I use Cacao Barry's Extra Brute)

¼ teaspoon salt

10 ounces/280 g bittersweet chocolate
  (at least 60%)

2½ cups/1 pound plus 1 stick/567 g
unsalted butter, very soft

½ cup/114 g plain, whole-fat Greek yogurt

2 teaspoons vanilla bean paste

½ cup/118 ml freshly brewed hot coffee

In a mixing bowl, whisk together the confectioners' sugar, cocoa powder, and the salt. Set aside.

Place the chocolate in a heat-safe bowl and place over simmering water to melt. Set aside.

Place the butter in the bowl of a stand mixer fitted with the paddle attachment and mix until light and fluffy, 3 to 4 minutes. Scrape down the bottom and sides of the bowl. Add the confectioners' sugar mixture and turn the mixer speed to low to combine. Add the yogurt and vanilla bean paste and then slowly add the coffee. Mix to combine and then add the melted chocolate and mix on high speed until smooth and combined.

PASSION FRUIT FRENCH BUTTERCREAM

The base of French buttercream is a hot sugar concoction delightfully named *pâte à bombe*. It really is the bombe. It's also a great way to use some of those egg yolks you've got hanging around after making so much meringue. It's also a technique that may be familiar to you by now. As with Italian buttercream, you pour a hot sugar syrup into whisking egg yolks and sugar to form a thick and creamy mixture that, once cool, is ready for you to add copious amounts of butter to create a rich and, with the addition of passion fruit, tangy buttercream.

⅓ cup/79 ml water

1 teaspoon freshly squeezed lemon juice

1 cup/198 g granulated sugar

10 large egg yolks, at room temperature

½ cup/118 ml passion fruit purée

Generous pinch of salt

2 cups/1 pound/453 g unsalted butter, at room temperature

Combine the water and lemon juice in a large saucepan and then add the sugar. Stir gently over medium-low heat until the sugar has completely melted, wiping any sugar crystals from the side of the pot with a damp pastry brush. Once melted, stop stirring the sugar mixture and heat the syrup. When its temperature reaches 240°F/116°C, place the yolks, passion fruit purée, and salt in the bowl of a stand mixer and whisk on high speed until the syrup reaches 230°F/110°C. With the mixer running, slowly pour the syrup as close to the egg yolks mixture as you can without hitting the whisk. Continue to whisk until the mixture thickens and completely cools. You've just made *pâte à bombe*!

With the mixer running on medium speed, add the butter, a few tablespoons at a time, to the *pâte à bombe* until the mixture thickens and becomes a spreadable frosting.

AMERICAN CRUSTING BUTTERCREAM

This stuff is for kids. Quite literally. It's the frosting you'll find on *every* grocery store *Frozen-* or *Star Wars*–themed birthday sheet cake. My mother hated the stuff. As a matter of fact, most schmancy bakers, including home bakers, do too. I'm of two minds about it, myself. The kid in me loves the stuff. It's pure sugar and naughty. It's also overly sweet and can be greasy if made with shortening alone. That's why, when I use it, and there are applications where it's the only way to go, such as when I make buttercream transfers as I do in my World Cake (page 277). Whether you use it or not in any other application is up to you. And I won't judge if, even after making the perfect "real" buttercream with meringue and all butter, you still prefer the American stuff. My inner child approves.

1 cup/2 sticks/226 g unsalted butter, at
   room temperature
1½ cups/297 g shortening (I use Crisco)
1 (2-pound) bag/907 g confectioners' sugar
Pinch of salt
¼ cup/59 ml whole milk

Place the butter in the bowl of a stand mixer fitted with the paddle attachment and mix until very smooth. Scrape down the bottom and sides of the bowl and add the shortening, confectioners' sugar, and salt. Mix on low speed until just combined and then continue to mix on high speed until smooth. Slow down the mixer and add the milk slowly and continue to mix until smooth.

CREAM CHEESE FROSTING

Someone I love to bits likes cake just fine, but if you're going to give her a sweet treat for her birthday, just give her a bowl of cream cheese frosting. I'm pretty sure that quite a few readers would agree that cream cheese frosting is all that and a bag of chips. And it is. The one problem that comes with it, if you aren't just eating it from the bowl, is that it doesn't set firm and it never gets completely smooth in the manner that a buttercream would. But for something so delicious, aren't those setbacks worth it? I think so. But I've create a recipe that's still as delicious as the best cream cheese frosting with just a bit more stability. Now *that's* all that!

3 cups/340 g confectioners' sugar

1 tablespoon Instant ClearJel

¼ teaspoon salt

1 cup/2 sticks/226 g unsalted butter, very soft

8 ounces/226 g cream cheese, at room temperature

¼ cup/59 ml heavy whipping cream

1 teaspoon pure vanilla extract

In a small bowl, whisk together the confectioners' sugar, Instant ClearJel, and salt. Set aside.

Place the butter in the bowl of a stand mixer fitted with the paddle attachment and mix until smooth. Add the cream cheese and continue to mix on high speed until combined and smooth. Scrape down the bottom and sides of the bowl and add the confectioners' sugar mixture. Mix on low speed until just combined. Slowly add the cream and vanilla and when incorporated, mix on high speed until very smooth and light and fluffy.

Variations:

MAPLE ESPRESSO CREAM CHEESE FROSTING:

Replace 1 cup/113 g of the confectioners' sugar with 1 cup/156 g of maple sugar. Add 1 tablespoon of espresso powder (I use King Arthur Flour Espresso Powder) to the milk and stir to combine before adding.

MAPLE BROWNED BUTTER PECAN CREAM CHEESE FROSTING:

Brown the butter called for in the recipe by melting the butter over low heat until it starts to brown. Carefully pour the melted butter into a bowl, leaving the majority of the dark bits in the pan, and allow to come to room temperature before using in the recipe. Replace 1 cup/113 g of the confectioners' sugar with 1 cup/156 g of maple sugar. Fold in ½ cup/55 g of finely chopped, lightly toasted, and cooled pecans once the frosting comes together.

SIMPLE CHOCOLATE COATING

MAKES 1 CUP/236 ML

I use this truly simple chocolate coating to make sure crispy elements hidden in cakes actually stay crispy. The coating sets firmly, coating but not sogging up the works.

8 ounces/225 g bittersweet chocolate (I use Guittard's 60%)

2 teaspoons vegetable shortening, such as Crisco

Place the chocolate and shortening in a heatproof bowl over a pot of gently simmering water, making sure the water doesn't touch the bottom of the bowl. Stir the chocolate until the mixture is melted and smooth.

A MESSAGE FROM THE

SPRUCE IT UP!

Beauty is on the inside. We all know this to be true. But even if you aren't Angelina Jolie–gorgeous, doesn't it just make you feel better when you spruce yourself up?

Pulling yourself together means different things at different times. Sometimes, you're feeling fancy-free and running around the house in the buff. There's a naked cake for that! When the layers are so pretty, it feels a shame to cover them up. Sometimes, you're feeling fit and fancy-free but want just a few strategic strips of fabric to leave something to the imagination. There's a seminaked cake for that! There are times when everything's looking pretty great but you need to throw on a baseball hat to tame your hair. There's a thing called puppet dust for that. And when you want to pull out all the stops, the full head-to-toe sparkle treatment, there's everything from mirror glaze to ombré cakes to strategically placed embossed fondant for that...and so much more. Sprucing up a cake is the final step to making your cake just right, but there are so many ways to get there. You get to decide which one is right for you (and your cake).

MARZIPAN/ALMOND PASTE

MAKES ENOUGH TO COVER 1 PRINCESS CAKE

In this book, I use almond paste *in* cakes, as an ingredient along with butter, sugar, and flour, as I do with the Almond Cake (page 63). I also use it to cover cakes, as I do with the Princess Cakes (page 301). I also use it for optimal cuteness (an official decorating term), by molding it into an adorable bunny to top my Carrot Cake (page 265). It's obvious that it's versatile. It's also delicious. So, be careful when you make it not to eat so much of it that you run out of what you need for the recipe. I tell you this from personal experience and I don't regret it for a moment.

2 large egg whites

½ teaspoon almond extract

2½ cups/240 g almond flour

2½ cups/284 g confectioners' sugar, plus ¼ cup/30 g to finish

¼ teaspoon salt

2 tablespoons Dutched cocoa powder (optional)

Gel dye color of your choice (optional)

In a small bowl, stir together the egg whites and almond extract. Set aside.

Place the almond flour, 2½ cups/284 g of confectioners' sugar, and the salt in the bowl of a food processor. If using the cocoa powder, as you would for the cocoa Princess Cake, add the cocoa powder. Pulse a few times to combine. Slowly add the egg white mixture, continuing to pulse until the mixture just comes together. Do not overmix, other-wise the almonds could start expressing too much oil and the mixture could get greasy.

Turn out the marzipan onto a clean work surface sprinkled with the extra confectioners' sugar and knead until smooth. For the traditional green Princess Cake, remove a quarter-size piece of marzipan before dyeing the remainder of the marzipan green. Dip a toothpick into pink dye and scrape a small amount of the dye onto the quarter-sized piece and knead until the dye is evenly distributed. Then, add a small drop of Americolor Leaf Green to the main portion of marzipan (or use Americolor Soft Pink for the pink Princess Cake) and knead the color into the marzipan until no streaks remain. If not using immediately, cover the marzipan with plastic wrap and seal in a resealable plastic bag.

Cake Lady

MAKING A MARZIPAN ROSE

Divide a quarter-size round of marzipan into 6 pieces. Roll each piece of marzipan into a ball. Keep one piece round and flatten the rest with your palm, cut in half, and pinch the edges to thin them. Wrap one flattened piece around the marzipan ball and continue adding pieces, overlapping them, and gently flaring out the tops of the "petals."

MIRROR GLAZE

**MAKES ENOUGH TO GLAZE ONE 10-INCH/25.5 CM
CAKE OR A TALL 8-INCH/20.5 CM CAKE**

Mirror glaze is all the rage these days. You know you've watched and rewatched those videos that stream on Facebook of some disembodied hand pouring shiny magic onto a patiently waiting cake and turn it into a gleaming cake orb that you thought could only be found in dreams or at Hogwarts. A few things you should know about this enchanting stuff: (1) professional pastry shops buy mirror glaze in buckets; they don't make their own. (2) It's best to pour it on a domed or curved cake, not one with sharp edges, so that the glaze coats evenly. (3) The underlying cakes are chilled, most often mousses which are so cold and smooth that the glaze sets quickly (the cold does that) and smoothly (the mousse does that). (4) You can make your own at home in a snap and be the talk of the town! Does this recipe make a boatload of mirror glaze? Yes. But on your first go-round, it's fabulous to have lots and lots so you can mess up and have plenty more to get it right. You can also halve the recipe, but if you make it all, even if you don't use it all, you can save any extra and store it in the fridge for another occasion. Just reheat a bit and away you go!

23 ounces/ 650 g white chocolate,
  finely chopped

1½ cups/390 ml water

3 cups/600 g granulated sugar

2 cups/600 g glucose syrup (available at
  cake supply stores) or light corn syrup

21 ounces/595 g sweetened condensed milk

4 (7 g) packets powdered gelatin or
  12 sheets silver gelatin, softened
  (see page 120)

Gel color of choice

Put the white chocolate into a large, heat-proof bowl. Set aside.

In a saucepan, combine the water, sugar, syrup, and sweetened condensed milk.

Place over medium heat and heat, stirring occasionally, until the sugar has completely melted and the mixture is hot.

Remove the mixture from the heat, immediately stir in the gelatin, and then pour over the white chocolate, shimmying the bowl slightly to make sure the chocolate is completely covered in the hot liquid. Allow to sit for about 5 minutes to melt the chocolate and then whisk until smooth (you can also use an immersion blender to combine, if you have one). Add 4 to 5 hearty drops of gel dye and whisk to combine, adding more gel dye as needed. Pour the mixture through a sieve into a clean bowl and allow to cool to between 90° and 94°F/30° and 34.5°C. This is the optimal temperature and thickness for coating cakes. To shorten the cooling time, place the bowl of glaze over a bowl of ice and stir occasionally. To store the glaze, place in a sealed jar and refrigerate. To reheat, transfer the cooled glaze to a large, heatproof bowl and gently warm over a pot of boiling water until the optimal temperature is reached.

FRUIT GLAZE TOPPING

MAKES ENOUGH TO TOP 1 FRAISIER CAKE

There are cakes where just a bit of glaze will do, where you don't (and shouldn't) cover the entire cake with the shiny stuff and use it instead as an accent. That's the exactly the case with a Fraisier Cake (page 280), where the glorious carousel of strawberries along the perimeter of the cake would be swallowed up with a full coating but a lovely partial topping of the stuff sets off the jewel tones of the berries delightfully.

¼ cup/60 ml water

¼ cup/50 g granulated sugar

¼ cup/59 ml Simple Fruit Purée, prepared with strawberries (page 155)

1 (7 g) packet powdered gelatin or 3 sheets silver gelatin, softened (see page 120)

In a small saucepan, combine the water and sugar. Stir over low heat until the sugar has melted and then add the purée. Remove from the heat and add the softened gelatin, stirring until the gelatin has completely melted. Allow to sit until the gelatin has slightly cooled and thickened but still flows, 15 to 20 minutes.

CHOCOLATE "BLACK OUT" MIRROR GLAZE

Mirror, Mirror, on the wall, who's the fairest glaze of all? Chocolate glaze, of course! Goodness gracious, there really isn't anything so pretty as a shiny chocolate cake. Sure, those brightly hued glazed cakes of red and blue bring forth squeals of glee, high-pitched "oh, cool!"—it's the NSYNC of finishes. But that doesn't compare to the low growl, the deepthroated "hubba hubbas" that a chocolate glaze inspires. It definitely brings sexy back.

1 cup/198 g granulated sugar

½ cup/42 g Dutched cocoa powder (for an almost black appearance to the glaze, choose a "black" cocoa; e.g., King Arthur Flour's Black Cocoa)

½ cup/118 ml water

⅓ cup/79 ml heavy whipping cream

2 ounces/56 g bittersweet chocolate (at least 60%), finely chopped

1 (7 g) packet gelatin or 3 sheets silver gelatin, softened (see page 120)

In a heavy-bottomed saucepan, combine the sugar and cocoa powder and whisk to combine. Add the water and cream. Whisk over low heat until the sugar has completely melted.

Bring the mixture to a boil and immediately add the chocolate, stirring constantly until it's melted. Remove the mixture from the heat and add the gelatin. Whisk to combine and pour through a sieve into a container. Before using, you must cool the mixture to 105° to 100°F/40.5° to 38°C for optimal coating.

To store the glaze, place in a sealed jar and refrigerate. To reheat, transfer the cooled glaze to a large, heatproof bowl and gently warm over a pot of boiling water until the optimal temperature is reached.

FONDANT

Is it easier to just buy fondant? Yes. Do people like to eat store-bought fondant? No. And there's the rub. I can't think of a single person who is crazy about that gummy layer over the cake. Sure, it looks smooth and perfect (if done right), but it's no one's favorite part of the cake. It's not even anyone's third-favorite thing about a piece of cake. The exception is homemade fondant that uses a base of marshmallows to make it quite tasty. If you are in the market for a white or lightly colored *yummy* fondant, this recipe is for you. However, if you are going for a fondant coating that's very dark in color, especially one that's deep green or blue, I highly recommend buying a ready-made fondant in a hue very close to the color you're going for. Dark dyes bring out a very bitter taste but professionally manufactured fondants manage to mitigate that bitterness. My favorite store-bought brand is Fondarific. It is wonderful to work with, it is better tasting than most, and it comes in a wide variety of colors.

1 (7 g) packet powdered gelatin or 3 sheets silver gelatin, softened (see page 120)

½ cup/170 g glucose syrup (available at cake supply stores)

1 tablespoon glycerin (available at cake supply stores)

2 tablespoons shortening, plus more for your hands (I use Crisco)

8 cups/880 g confectioners' sugar, divided

Melt the gelatin over a double boiler by placing either the softened powdered or the softened and drained leaf gelatin in a heatproof bowl. Place the bowl over a pot of gently simmering water, making sure that the water isn't touching the base of the bowl. Once melted, add the glucose and glycerin and stir to combine. Add the 2 tablespoons of shortening and remove from the heat. The residual heat will continue melting and softening the shortening.

Place 4 cups/440 g of the confectioners' sugar in the bowl of a stand mixer fitted with the paddle attachment. With the mixer on low speed, slowly add the warm gelatin mixture, continuing to mix until smooth. Slowly add the remaining 4 cups/440 g of confectioners' sugar and mix until just combined. Transfer the mixture to a clean work surface. Rub a dime-size bit of shortening into your hands and continue to knead the fondant until it is smooth and no longer sticks to your hands or the work surface. If the mixture looks dry, add more shortening to your hands, a bit at a time, until the fondant is smooth and shiny. If it's too sticky, sprinkle a bit of confectioners' sugar on your work surface, as you knead until it's smooth and no longer sticky. If not using immediately, wrap well in plastic wrap and place in a large, resealable plastic bag. Store in a cool, dry place but do not refrigerate.

GUM PASTE

MAKES 2 CUPS/ABOUT 400 G GUM PASTE OR
ENOUGH FOR A GARDEN OF FLOWERS OF DIFFERENT SIZES

Gum paste, like fondant, can be bought premade. Both are readily available at craft and cake stores. While I'm happy to buy store-bought fondant (Fondarific is my choice), I really prefer to make gum paste. I find the store-bought stuff gets too hard to work with, and when I make a batch of gum paste, I divide it up and dye it with gel paste dye immediately. That way, I have a rainbow of colors with which to work, such as in the skull of my Skull Cake (page 248). Gum paste, once molded, gets rock solid if left out in the open air, making it perfect for making decorations way ahead of time.

3 cups/340 g confectioners' sugar, sifted
Pinch of salt
2 large egg whites
4 teaspoons Tylose powder (I use Wilton's Gum-Tex Tylose Powder)
1 to 2 tablespoons shortening for your hands
Gel food coloring (optional)

Place the confectioners' sugar and salt in the bowl of a stand mixer fitted with the whisk attachment and whisk briefly to combine. Make a well in the middle of the mixture and add the egg whites. Mix on low speed until just incorporated and then mix on high speed until very smooth and shiny. Stop the mixer, sprinkle in the Tylose powder, and continue to mix until the mixture starts to clump into pieces. Transfer the paste to a work surface. Rub a dime-size bit of shortening in your hands and knead the gum paste until smooth, adding more shortening to your hands as needed to keep it pliable.

If dyeing the gum paste, divide the paste and, using a toothpick, wipe a dab of the color onto the gum paste and knead until smooth and combined. Add only a small dab of dye at a time to make sure you don't start out too dark!

Wrap the gum paste really well in plastic wrap and then place in a resealable plastic bag. Too much time spent in the open air will dry out the paste, so work quickly.

FRENCH MERINGUES

MAKES 24 LARGE MERINGUE TREES

If you've been paying attention, you know that there are three kinds of meringue. Swiss and Italian meringues have already been covered. Both Swiss and Italian require sugar and egg whites to be heated outside of the oven to add stability (and health safety!) to the meringue. French (or dry) meringues, however, live on the edge. You add the sugar to the egg whites, whisking constantly, without heating either the sugar or egg whites during the process, and then you pipe and bake it in the oven (or broil if you're topping a lemon meringue pie with the stuff). In fact, you've probably made this kind of meringue already! I love to use meringues on top of cakes to add a little visual interest and a sweet little crunch. You can make them big and treelike, as I do in the cake on the book cover, or petite, as I do in the Cherry Blossom Cake (page 225).

5 large egg whites, at room temperature
1 cup/198 g superfine (baker's) sugar (see note)
Pinch of salt

Preheat the oven to 175°F/80°C. Line 2 sheet pans with parchment. Set aside.

Place the egg whites and salt in the bowl of a stand mixer fitted with the whisk attachment and whisk on high speed until just foamy. Slowly add the sugar: to make sure you are adding it slowly enough, sprinkle it in, 1 tablespoon at a time, counting to 10 as you do it. Whisk until the meringue is shiny, white, has quadrupled in volume, and holds a stiff peak. Transfer the meringue to a pastry bag fitted with a medium plain round tip (Ateco 805) for tiny little "kisses," or a large star tip (Ateco 823) for large trees. For small kisses, place the tip on the parchment and apply a

small amount of pressure, slightly lifting the tip as a small dollop of meringue comes out. Stop applying pressure and lift the pastry bag straight up. For the trees, place the piping tip just above the parchment and apply slight pressure. When a quarter-size dollop of meringue is out, press down and then turn the pastry bag a quarter turn to the right and then lift a bit, apply pressure to allow a smaller amount of meringue out, press down gently, and turn the tip to the left. Do this one or two more times, allowing less and less meringue to come out and then lift the pastry bag straight up to create a sweet little peak.

Note: If you can't find superfine sugar, you can make regular granulated sugar a bit finer by pulsing it in a food processor.

FIRM CARAMEL COATING

This is the caramel of my dreams. When it sets, you can roll it out to cover cakes entirely or just enough that when you pull gently at the edges, it dips down as if it was an elegant, amber curtain. Yes, you can pour the hot caramel syrup straight from the pot into a caramel mold, let them cool, and then cut them to create caramel bites, but there's magic in the making when you let the caramel cool in a thin layer and enrobe a cake with its deliciously chewy goodness.

Nonstick cooking spray
½ cup/156 g pure maple syrup
½ cup/106.5 g brown sugar
½ cup/118 ml heavy whipping cream
¼ cup/78 g sweetened condensed milk
¼ cup/78 g light corn syrup
½ teaspoon salt
2 tablespoons unsalted butter

Line a half sheet pan with parchment and lightly spray with nonstick cooking spray. Set aside. On a second sheet pan, set the cake that will be covered with the caramel.

Combine the maple syrup, brown sugar, cream, condensed milk, corn syrup, and salt in a saucepan. Stir over medium heat until the mixture reaches 240°F/115°C. Remove from the heat and stir in the butter. Immediately pour into the lined sheet pan and allow to cool and set, about 1 hour.

Once cooled, transfer the caramel to the cake by overturning and centering the parchment over the top of the cake. Once it is centered, peel off the parchment and gently pull down on the sides of the caramel to stretch it to cover the entire cake. Trim with a sharp paring knife.

HARD CARAMEL COATING (FOR CREAM PUFFS)

At my pastry shop, Gesine Confectionary, we made vats of hard coating caramel. When we wouldn't use it all, we'd allow it to harden in the pot, cover it, and in the morning, usually 3:30 a.m., we'd set it over very low heat, stir occasionally, check on it periodically, and bring it back to fluid so we could get to coating consistency once our cream puffs were ready. The problem was, more often than not, we'd forget the stir-and-check-on-it parts. Like clockwork, one of us would ask the other, "What is that smell?" and lo, it would be the caramel smoking and burning. In the winter, we had a mountain of snow in the back we called Vesuvius because we'd pour molten burned caramel down the middle of it and, by springtime, it looked like a volcanic disaster area. This is all to say that hard coating cara-mel is delicious and incredibly easy to make, but it's just as easy to forget that it's cooking on the stovetop. So, don't forget to check on it!

⅓ cup/79 ml water
1 teaspoon fresh lemon juice
1 cup/198 g granulated sugar

Fill a large bowl halfway with ice. Set aside.

Combine the water and lemon juice in a heavy-bottomed saucepan and swirl to disperse the lemon juice. Carefully add the sugar so it stays right in the middle of the water. Place over medium heat and stir gently with a wooden spoon until the sugar has completely melted. If you notice small granules of sugar clinging to the side of the pan and not in the water, brush the crystals back into the sugar syrup with a damp pastry brush. Once all the sugar has melted, stop stirring and watch the syrup carefully until it turns a medium amber brown (a color similar to that of a new penny). Immediately place the pot on top of the ice in the bowl to stop it from cooking and from turning darker, and allow it to thicken slightly. Once it has thick-ened to the consistency of honey, take from the ice and immediately (and carefully) dip the tops of cream puffs into the caramel and transfer them, caramel-side up, to a piece of parchment. Set them aside until set, 15 to 20 minutes.

PUPPET DUST

Puppet Dust isn't made from puppets. The finish, especially if it's very orange or blue, just reminds me of certain Muppets (Elmo! Cookie Monster!). Puppet Dust also isn't a recipe as much as it is cake "upcycling," but it's brilliant to have on hand when you want to finish a cake fast and with panache. So, you must be wondering, *what is Puppet Dust and how do you make it?*

Puppet Dust is made from leftover cake that hasn't been frosted. Sometimes your cake domes and you cut off the offending bit to make it flat and stackable. Sometimes you make a sheet pan of cake and you stamp out rounds and have odds and ends left over. I don't look at those bits as snacks or trash. I see them as Sprucing Up gold! I break up the bits of cake, trimming off any parts that are overly browned in a nonchocolate cake, and I spread them out on a sheet pan in an even layer. You can expect roughly 1 cup/140 g of Puppet Dust from every 5 ounces/140 g of cake trimmings, but your mileage may vary. You can line the pan with parchment or not. The main point is that you want an even layer of cake that doesn't overlap and you want to make the pieces small, about quarter size. Bake in a very low-temperature oven, about 200°F/93°C so that the cake gets dry but it doesn't brown. When the cake feels very dry, 20 to 30 minutes, remove from the oven and let the bits come to room temperature. Put the cooled cake bits (they should feel rock solid, without any give) in a food processor and pulse them until the mixture looks like very fine sand . . . or dust.

To store, transfer the Puppet Dust into a resealable plastic bag and label the bag with the date it was made and the flavor of the cake. Then freeze until needed.

A great use of Puppet Dust is when you have just enough frosting left over to make a smooth coat over a cake but not so much that it's perfectly coated; that is, you can see some of the cake underneath in patches. In that case, I cut bits of parchment to create a pattern on the cake. Smooth the parchment onto the cake where it's looking good. It sticks beautifully. Gently press the Puppet Dust over the cake so that it sticks to those areas that need a little concealer and then carefully remove the parchment. Voilà! A beautiful and colorful pattern remains on a cake. You'd never know that it looked a bit patchy before.

ROYAL ICING

Originally, royal icing was just called egg white icing. That's a bummer of a name. But things took a turn for the fancy when Queen Victoria's cake maker (the queen is credited for starting the elaborate wedding cake craze), used the icing to coat and decorate a 300-pound/136 kg cake with the stuff. Since so much of it was used, it was only fair to change the name to "royal." Today, it's quite rare for a cake to be covered in royal icing; it was supplanted by the invention of rolled fondant. It's the most common icing for decorating cookies because it holds its shape when piped (when made to the right consistency) and becomes brick hard when set. Perfect for cookies that are made to adorn a cake.

4 cups/450 g sifted confectioners' sugar
3 tablespoons meringue powder
(I use Wilton brand meringue powder)
5 to 8 tablespoons lukewarm water

Place the confectioners' sugar and meringue powder in the bowl of a stand mixer fitted with the whisk attachment. Whisk to combine. With the mixer running on low speed, slowly add the water, a tablespoon at a time, until the mixture is smooth and just loose enough to pipe. If not using immediately, transfer to a bowl and cover with plastic wrap to keep it from forming a skin. Keep at room temperature.

GINGERBREAD COOKIES

These gingerbread cookies are delicious. Feel free to use this recipe when you want a few zingy cookies around or if you want to build a gingerbread house or two. The other option, of course, is to bake off enough of these little gems to decorate a cake. I use them in a holiday-inspired tiered Gingerbread Cake (page 256) and in Rudy's Rootin' Tootin' First Birthday Cake (page 260). If you don't use all the dough, you can wrap it in plastic wrap and freeze for up to a month (or more . . . I don't judge).

3 cups/360 g all-purpose flour,
  plus more for dusting

1½ tablespoons ground ginger

1 tablespoon ground cinnamon

1 teaspoon ground white pepper

1 teaspoon salt

½ teaspoon baking soda

½ teaspoon freshly grated nutmeg

½ teaspoon ground cloves

¾ cup/160 g dark brown sugar

1 cup/2 sticks/226 g unsalted butter,
  at room temperature

½ cup/170 g molasses

1 large egg, at room temperature

1 teaspoon pure vanilla extract

In a large bowl, whisk together the flour, ginger, cinnamon, white pepper, salt, baking soda, nutmeg, and cloves. Set aside.

Combine the brown sugar and butter in the bowl of a stand mixer fitted with the paddle attachment. Mix until smooth. Scrape down the bottom and sides of the bowl and add the molasses. Mix until smooth. Scrape down the bottom and sides of the bowl. Add the egg and vanilla and mix until incorporated. Scrape down the bottom and sides of the bowl again.

Slowly add the dry ingredients to the wet with the mixer on low speed until just combined. Turn out the dough onto a large piece of plastic wrap and turn over a few times to make sure all the flour is incorporated. Gently pat into a rectangle and cover well with plastic wrap. Refrigerate for at least 30 minutes.

While the dough chills, preheat the oven to 350°F/180°C. Line 2 sheet pans with parchment. Set aside.

On a lightly floured work surface, roll out the dough to ¼ inch/6 mm thick. Using cookie cutters (see note), stamp out your preferred shapes and place on the prepared sheet pans, spacing the cookies 1 inch/2.5 cm apart. Place the sheet pan in the freezer for about 5 minutes to set the shape of the cookies.

Bake for 10 to 15 minutes, or until the cookies are just browning at the edges. Allow to cool completely before icing with Royal Icing (page 207).

Note: For my Gingerbread Cake (page 256), I used R&M International's Gingerbread House Bake Set that includes cutters for a house, of which I used just the front of the house, a gingerbread man cutter, tree cutter, heart cutter, and a candy cane cutter. I also used a larger (2-inch/5 cm) heart cutter.

Part Three
THE CAKES

THE "BIRTHDAY SUIT" CAKE

Naked cakes are, as a rule, naked on the outside. In most cases, they are simply cakes that have been baked in a cake pan, per usual, and then filled and topped with frosting, with the sides left clean. That makes for a perfectly fine naked cake. But, to my mind, if you're going to go naked, make it really count. By that I mean, make sure the sides of the cake are perfect. You can get nice sides in a cake pan, but you get perfect sides by stamping out the cake from a sheet pan so that there's absolutely no hint of browning at all. This effect is pure, unadulterated confetti delight.

YOU'LL NEED

1 recipe White Party Cake (page 52), made with the rainbow jimmies, baked in a half sheet pan and completely cooled, then cut into four 6-inch/15 cm rounds

1 recipe Swiss Buttercream (page 175), made with 1 teaspoon lemon extract

EQUIPMENT

Pastry bag

Medium-small plain round pastry tip (Ateco 803)

Large flower nail

Tip coupler

Small plain round pastry tip (Ateco 802)

Petal tip (Ateco 60)

Place a cardboard round at the bottom of a 6-inch/10 cm cake ring (or a homemade cake ring made from a Crisco container). Place a layer of cake on the cardboard round inside the ring. Reserving 1 cup/235 ml of the buttercream for flower décor to finish, fit a pastry bag with a medium-small plain round tip (Ateco 803), fill with the buttercream, and pipe a layer of buttercream onto the cake so that it reaches all the way to the edge of the cake and touches the ring. Top with a second cake layer and move up the ring to contain the second layer of buttercream. Continue to fill and top until you reach the fourth and last layer of cake. Place it on top of the buttercream and smoothly pipe the top of the cake with buttercream. Transfer to the freezer to set, 20 to 30 minutes. Then, gently heat the sides of the ring and slip it up off the sides of the cake.

Note: If you have leftover buttercream from filling and topping, use it to pipe flowers. Using a medium-small plain tip (Ateco 803), pipe a small, egglike dollop onto a piece of parchment attached to a flower nail. Using a petal tip, pipe an arch starting at the bottom of the dollop and piping in an arch to cover about half the dollop. Continue piping arches, overlapping them, until you've achieved the rose size you're happy with. For simple flowers, use a petal tip and pipe flat arches onto a piece of parchment, overlapping only slightly, until you have five evenly spaced petals. Transfer the flower décor to the top of the cake.

Cake Lady

USING A BENCH OR FROSTING SCRAPER

The secret to a perfectly smooth finish on a cake is having a tool that has a perfectly straight metal edge. You can find that in a standard piece of kitchen equipment: a bench scraper. Or you can go to the hardware store and get a tile scraper. That works as well. Or you can splash out and get a custom-made frosting scraper. I have one that's my favorite. It's supertall, tall enough to scrape the sides of the tallest cake. It's made by Fat Girl Cakes and it's 12 inches/30.5 cm long. I love that thing so much.

When you use it, you have to make sure that it's perfectly level. The best kind of scraper has a perfect 90° angle that rests neatly on your turntable. All you have to do is aim the scraper at your cake so that it can just smooth the outer layer of icing. Check to be sure that the scraper is clean. One little crumb hanging onto the scraper can etch a trough onto the side of your cake. And one last thing: it helps if the scraper is not only clean but hot. Running the metal edge under scalding water and then drying it does the trick. If the idea of running back and forth to the sink doesn't appeal, you can take a page from professional pastry shops. We use heat guns to heat the blade, but a blow dryer works just as well. The hot blade gives a perfectly smooth finish to the outside of the cake that you can't get from a cold blade.

ZEBRA CAKE

I love this jaunty zebra stripe. It's quite original and criminally easy. You only have to know how to tear apart paper, or in this case, parchment. It's a very satisfying endeavor. One half sheet of parchment is more than enough to get the perfect set of zebra stripes out of Puppet Dust made from leftover cake (page 206). One way to make a very big impact with very little effort is to bake a cake in a half sheet pan, cut the cake into strips, frost it and stack it, and then turn the cake over onto its "side" so that the layers are now vertical instead of horizontal. Easy-peasy!

YOU'LL NEED

1 recipe White Party Cake (page 52),
    baked in a half sheet pan and cut into
    four 3½ x 12-inch/9 x 30.5 cm strips
1 recipe Swiss Buttercream (page 175), made
    with 1 teaspoon lemon extract
1 cup/140 g Puppet Dust (page 206)

EQUIPMENT

Pastry bag
Large plain round pastry tip (Ateco 806)

Place a cake strip on a piece of parchment. Fit a pastry bag with a large plain round tip (Ateco 806) and pipe the buttercream in long strips on the cake layer, piping them right next to each other. Use a small offset spatula to gently smooth the ridges of the buttercream. Top with a second cake layer and press gently to adhere the cake to the buttercream layer. Pipe buttercream in strips as you did with the first layer, smooth, and top with a third cake layer. Pipe and smooth one last time, topping with the fourth cake layer, and gently press to adhere the last cake layer.

Refrigerate for 10 to 15 minutes to set the buttercream and then transfer the cake to a cake platter, tipping the cake onto its side so that the cake layers are running vertically. Trim the front and back of the cake and smooth the remaining buttercream over the outside of the cake. Refrigerate the cake for 10 to 15 minutes to set the buttercream.

Tear strips of parchment into rough, long triangles and drape over the cake, alternating on either side, gently pressing to adhere them to the cake, being careful to space the parchment pieces so that there is a gap of about ½ inch/1.3 cm between the strips.

Gently press Puppet Dust onto the cake, pressing gently but firmly so the "dust" adheres to the exposed buttercream portions of the cake. Gently brush away any extra Puppet Dust that hasn't adhered to the cake off the cake platter with a pastry brush. Refrigerate the cake for 10 to 15 minutes to make sure the buttercream is set and then gently pull away the strips of parchment to reveal zebra stripes.

OMBRÉ CAKE

I love smoothing the sides of a cake. It appeals to the anal-retentive baker in me. Everything nice and neat and smooth. Just perfect. But there's a way of making all that smoothing even more satisfying, by creating an ombré effect on the side of the cake. You pipe different shades of frosting up the side of the cake as sloppily as you please and then you smooth it all out with a frosting scraper and the world becomes an elegant icing sunset.

YOU'LL NEED

2 recipes Swiss Buttercream (page 175),
    made with 2 teaspoons lemon extract
Pink gel dye
1 recipe White Cake Homemade Box
    Mix (page 38),
    baked in two 8-inch/20.5 round pans and
    torted in half, making 4 layers

EQUIPMENT

Pastry bag
Medium plain round pastry tip (Ateco 804)
St. Honoré tip (Ateco 883)

Place one recipe of the buttercream into a pastry bag fitted with a medium plain round tip (Ateco 804).

Divide the second batch of buttercream evenly among three bowls. Leave one bowl undyed. Stir in 1 drop of pink gel dye into the second bowl, and 3 to 4 drops into the third bowl. Make sure the two pinks are clearly different in shade. Set aside.

Place a cake layer on a cardboard round and transfer to a cake turntable. Pipe the plain buttercream in the pastry bag onto the first layer of cake, top with a second layer, and gently press to adhere. Pipe another layer of buttercream onto the second layer, add the third layer of cake (pressing gently to adhere), and then pipe buttercream onto the third layer, pressing the fourth cake layer onto the buttercream. Refrigerate the cake for 10 to 15 minutes to set the buttercream.

Spread the remaining plain buttercream from the pastry bag onto the cake and use a small offset spatula and a bench scraper to smooth the buttercream in a crumb coat over the top and sides of the cake

(see sidebar). Refrigerate the cake for 20 minutes to set the buttercream.

Place the plain buttercream from the reserved bowls into the same pastry bag as used before. Pipe the plain buttercream onto the top third of the side of the cake. Transfer the lighter pink buttercream to the pastry bag and pipe onto the middle third of the side of the cake. Transfer the darker pink buttercream into the pastry bag and pipe onto the bottom third of the side of the cake. Using the bench scraper, smooth the sides of the cake, scraping the excess frosting into a bowl and reserve.

Transfer the excess frosting, mixing the colors together, into a pastry bag fitted with the St. Honoré tip and pipe a wave pattern along the top edge of the cake.

DON'T LEAVE IT CRUMMY

Crumb coats on a cake are a critical component of the "Smooth" portion of the B.A.D.A.S.S. method. In fact, the smooth coat is a two-step procedure, consisting of a crumb coat and a finish coat. To crumb coat, you're coating the sides of the cake with a very thin layer of frosting, so thin that you can see through to the cake layers, trapping in any crumbs that would otherwise detach themselves and mar your finished smooth coat. The crumb coat can also be a final coat if you're going seminude. When a recipe calls for a portion of the icing or frosting to be added to the sides and top of the cake, use about a quarter of it for the purpose. Take a small or large offset spatula and spread that reserved quarter of the icing/frosting over the sides of the cake and then, using a heated bench or frosting scraper, smooth the sides of the cake (see sidebar, page 215). Refrigerate the cake for 10 to 15 minutes to set the crumb coat and then you're ready to pipe on the remaining icing/frosting for the perfect finish.

BANANA CARAMEL CAKE

This cake looks all sorts of zany, with the big yellow banana on the side, but the flavors are 100 percent elegant. The cake is moist with deeply tropical banana. The filling is an outright doozy of caramel creaminess. It's one of the most delicious and luscious fillings I've ever created. The buttercream just hints at that lovely caramel flavor, while the chocolate Puppet Dust adds a tantalizing bit of cocoa.

YOU'LL NEED

1 recipe Banana Cake (page 78), baked in a half sheet pan and cut into 3½ x 12-inch/9 x 30.5 cm strips
1 recipe Caramel Cremeux (page 144)
½ recipe Caramel Buttercream (page 178)
1 cup/140 g chocolate cake Puppet Dust (page 206)
Yellow gel dye

EQUIPMENT

Pastry bag
Medium plain round pastry tip (Ateco 805)

Place a strip of cake onto a half sheet of parchment.

Transfer the cremeux to a pastry bag fitted with a medium plain round tip (Ateco 805). Pipe strips of the cremeux on the cake layer, piping them right next to each other. Use a small offset spatula to gently smooth the filling and then top with a second layer of cake, gently pressing to adhere. Pipe a layer of cremeux on the second cake layer and smooth with the offset spatula, and then top with a third layer. Pipe the remaining cremeux on the third cake layer, smooth, and top with the last layer of cake. Wrap the parchment around the cake to cover and place in the freezer to set for 20 to 30 minutes.

Transfer the cake to a cake platter and tip the cake up on its side. Optional: Using a serrated knife, carve a gentle curve into the top of the cake, about ½ inch/1.3 cm lower in the middle of the cake than the top sides of the cake.

Add 2 drops of yellow gel dye to the buttercream and stir to combine. Spread an even layer over the cake and refrigerate for 10 to 15 minutes to set the cake. Cut a piece of parchment in the shape of a banana, using a real-life medium banana as a guide.

Gently press the banana-shaped piece of parchment onto one longer side of the cake and then gently press the Puppet Dust onto the cake, making sure the dust adheres to all those areas not covered in parchment. Brush away any extra Puppet Dust on the platter, using a pastry brush, and refrigerate the cake for 10 to 15 minutes to allow the buttercream to set. Gently peel away the parchment to reveal the banana.

PIPING!

You may think I'm being a little fussy when I say to pipe the filling rather than just taking a big ol' spoon and dumping a random amount of frosting on your cake and spreading it around willy-nilly. There is a method to my madness, however. First, if

you follow my method of piping, you'll have an even layer of frosting on each layer. When you slice into the cake, there's a beauty to the symmetry of a perfectly balanced slice. But there's more to it than just aesthetics.

Each bite gets the perfect ratio of cake to filling. You'll also make sure that you don't go nuts and put an overabundance of filling inside the cake, perhaps leaving you without enough frosting to cover the cake, if you're using the same recipe for both the filling and the finishing coat. If you don't have the assorted number of piping tips that I have, you can snip off the corner of a resealable plastic bag, fill it up, and pipe away.

CHERRY BLOSSOM CAKE

Living just outside Washington, DC, was a special way to grow up. We had such history and all the monuments to that history at our fingertips. And in the springtime, we had the blooming of the cherry blossoms. The local news gave updates as to when the blooms were peaking. If a storm was brewing, the weather person was sure to remind us that all those blossoms could vamoose with one big wind gust, so it was wise to get our tushes to the city to admire them before they vanished. My mother adored that time of year and would drag me to admire them with the sunrise. While I didn't appreciate their full beauty as a sleep-deprived kid, as an adult missing my mom every day, I certainly appreciate the fleeting grace of those flowers. In honor of them, of the country that gifted those magical trees to us (Japan), and my mother, I give you the Cherry Blossom Cake. At once elegant, a little earthy, and full of hearty citrus zing: kind of like my mother.

YOU'LL NEED

1 Matcha-Honey Sponge (page 98), baked in an angel food pan

1 recipe Tart Cherry Swiss Meringue Buttercream (page 176)

1 recipe Microwave Citrus Curd (page 124), made with yuzu

A few small French Meringues (page 202)

1 macaron, if you have a spare one handy (page 111)

1 quarter-size piece Gum Paste (page 201) to make flowers (see sidebar, page 227)

Color dust for gum paste flowers (see sidebar, page 227)

Royal Icing (page 207) for gum paste flowers (see sidebar, page 227)

EQUIPMENT

Pastry bag

Medium-small plain round pastry tip (Ateco 803)

Small plain round pastry tip (Ateco 802)

A small flower cookie cutter for gum paste flowers

Freeze the sponge cake for 20 to 30 minutes (if you have baked it ahead, then take the cake from the freezer 30 to 40 minutes before torting) and torte the cake into three even layers. Place the bottom layer of cake on a cake platter. Dam the outer and inner perimeter of the cake with a band of cherry buttercream, using a medium-small plain round tip (Ateco 803). Pipe a thin layer of buttercream within the band borders. The buttercream should not reach higher than the middle of the outer and inner buttercream bands. Spread the yuzu curd on top of the buttercream and then top with the middle layer of cake. Dam the outer and inner perimeter of the cake with a band of cherry buttercream, again using a medium-small plain round tip (Ateco 803). Pipe a thin layer of buttercream within the band borders. The buttercream should not reach higher than the middle of the outer and inner buttercream bands. Spread the yuzu curd on top of the buttercream and then top with the third layer of cake.

Refrigerate for 10 to 15 minutes to set the buttercream and then crumb coat the cake (see sidebar, page 221) with a thin layer of cherry buttercream. Refrigerate for 10 to 15 minutes to set the buttercream. Using a small offset spatula and a bench or frosting scraper, apply a smooth coat of buttercream on the sides and top of the cake. Transfer any remaining buttercream to a pastry bag fitted with a small plain round tip (Ateco 802) and pipe small dots along the bottom perimeter of the cake.

Before serving, add the meringues, macaron, and gum paste flower(s).

DIPPING YOUR TOES INTO
GUM PASTE FLOWERS AND LEAVES

You, too, can make realistic edible flowers and leaves. It just takes a few tools and some time. I suggest you start with simple blossoms where you can stamp out the whole flower and then gently work your way up to the more intricate blooms. And the lovely thing about these flowers? You can make them *way* ahead of time, essentially storing them indefinitely, if you keep them in a cool, dry place. Keep a few on hand to adorn a cake when it's feeling a little lonely.

FOR BLOSSOMS:

Lightly dust your work surface with cornstarch. Roll the gum paste to ⅛ inch/3 mm thick. Stamp out flower shapes one at a time, covering the rolled-out gum paste you aren't working on with plastic wrap to make sure it doesn't dry out. Place the flower on a soft foam surface and gently thin the petals with a gum paste ball tool. You can even use the back of a spoon for this; just be gentle. You want to make the petals thin enough that you can see light through them. Run a pin through the center of the flower and widen it enough that a toothpick can fit through. Place the finished blossoms in the cavities of a clean egg carton so they keep their shape until they dry completely. Gently apply color dust to the flower petals with a small brush. At this point, it's most common to thread a ready-made stamen through the hole you've made in the center of the flower, and to create an arrangement, attach a floral wire with floral tape to the stamen. However, in the beginning, I suggest you just use the flowers individually, and place them on your cakes when you're about to serve them and then pipe a little royal icing in the center of the flower for a sweet decoration.

FOR LEAVES:

Making leaves is similar: roll them out to the same depth as the flowers and gently smooth and thin the sides. However, there are special pads that have a channel in them. You roll the gum paste over the channel and then center a leaf cutter so that the channel reaches halfway up the leaf. You then thread a very thin floral wire into the channel and allow the leaf to dry. Dust the petals with green edible dust.

DAN'S 50TH BIRTHDAY CAKE

Our friend Dan turned 50 and invited us to celebrate with his family at their ancestral lakeside home in Maine. It has been a childhood dream of mine to have a slightly old-fashioned lakeside home, one surrounded by forest and filled with squabbling family. I was so thrilled that he'd invited us to their aquatic sanctum sanctorum that I pleaded with his wife to let me bake his birthday cake as a thank-you. She agreed. I asked her what his flavors of choice were. She responded that he loved chocolate and coffee. As it turns out *I* love chocolate and coffee, so it was a dream of a cake to make. The weekend ended up being just as dreamy as I imagined, too. And now, Dan's cake will always have a special place in my heart.

YOU'LL NEED

1 recipe I Love This Chocolate Fudge Cake (page 58), baked in two 8-inch/20.5 cm square pans, for 2 layers (do not torte)

1 recipe I Love This Chocolate Fudge Cake (page 58), baked in three 6-inch/ 15 cm square pans, for 3 layers (do not torte)

1 recipe Chocolate Cremeux (page 142)

3 recipes Espresso Buttercream (page 177)

3 cups/420 g chocolate Puppet Dust (page 206)

EQUIPMENT

Pastry bag

Medium-small plain round pastry tip (Ateco 803)

Bubble tea straws

Place an 8-inch/20.5 cm layer of cake on a cake stand. Fit a pastry bag with a medium-small plain round tip (Ateco 803) and fill with buttercream. Pipe bands of buttercream onto the cake, placing the bands right next to each other so that the top of the cake is entire covered with stripes of buttercream (you can, of course, just take a big spoon and plop a mound of buttercream on top of the layer, smoothing it out with a small offset spatula, but this way I get a perfect depth of buttercream on the cake and it looks supercool when you slice the cake).

Pipe a band of buttercream with the same tip along the edge of the cake to create a dam on top of the bottom buttercream layer and then spread a layer of chocolate cremeux on top of the buttercream layer. Top with the second 8-inch/20.5 cm square layer. Refrigerate while you work on the second tier.

Place one 6-inch/15 cm square layer of

cake on a cake board (trim a round cake board into a square if you don't have a square cake board). Pipe the buttercream and spread the cremeux as above for the 8-inch/20.5 cm square layers, but repeat the piping and layering one more time, for three layers total. Refrigerate the cake while you work on the bottom tier.

Remove the bottom tier from the refrigerator and coat with a crumb coat of Espresso Buttercream (see sidebar, page 221). Return to the refrigerator and crumb coat the 6-inch/15 cm tier.

Cut parchment into ¼-inch/6 mm-wide strips. Smooth a finishing coat of the buttercream over the 8-inch/20.5 cm and 6-inch/15 cm cakes with a bench or frosting scraper. Gently press 2 strips of parchment in an "arrow" formation on one side of the 8-inch tier and then press 2 strips, parallel to the original strips, spacing about 1½ inches/4 cm apart, on either side of the first arrow strips. Gently press chocolate Puppet Dust

over the 8-inch tier and gently brush away any excess crumbs, using a pastry brush. Return the cake to the refrigerator.

Place two parchment strips on one side of the 6-inch/15 cm cake in a V formation and then place two strips parallel to either strip, spacing them about 1½ inches/4 cm apart on either side. Gently press chocolate Puppet Dust over the 8-inch/20.5 cm tier and gently brush away any excess crumbs, using a pastry brush. Return the cake to the refrigerator.

Take the 8-inch/20.5 cm cake from the refrigerator and gently peel off the parchment strips. Insert three bubble tea straws in a rough circle in the middle of the cake, trimming them so they sit flush to the top of the cake. Take the 6-inch/15 cm cake from the fridge and gently peel away the parchment strips from the cake. Center the cake over the 8-inch cake and gently place on top, with the (hidden) straws centered right underneath the 6-inch cake.

Dan's 50th Birthday Cake, Heaven and Hell Cake, Agnes's Birthday Cake

HEAVEN AND HELL CAKE

The Heaven and Hell Cake is a real thing. I didn't make it up. It's a cake made up of white cake, chocolate cake, peanut butter filling, and a light-colored frosting on the outside. I took it one step further and made it terribly tall, to mimic the distance between the two places (or so I imagined). Luckily, there's no hell when it comes to eating this cake. Just heaven.

YOU'LL NEED

1 palm-size piece gum paste (page 227)
1 recipe Swiss Buttercream (page 175), made with vanilla extract
¼ teaspoon Dutched cocoa powder
1 recipe Devil's Food Cake (page 74), baked in 6-inch/15 cm round cake pans, for 2 layers
½ recipe Peanut Butter Mousse (page 150)
1 recipe White Cake Homemade Box Mix (page 38) baked in three 6-inch/15 cm round cake pans, making 3 layers (you'll use 2 here: reserve the third for Puppet Dust; see page 206)

EQUIPMENT

Pastry bag
Medium plain round pastry tip (Ateco 805)
Long wooden kebab skewer

Roll out the plain piece of gum paste to a ¼-inch/6 mm-thick rough oval. Using a sharp paring knife, cut out a cloud shape. Set aside to air dry.

Place ¼ cup/60 ml of the buttercream in a small bowl and stir in the cocoa powder.

Set aside.

Place a chocolate cake layer on a cardboard cake round and transfer to a cake turntable. Dam the perimeter of the cake with a band of buttercream frosting, using a pastry bag fitted with a medium plain round tip (Ateco 805). Using a small offset spatula, smooth the peanut butter mousse over the cake layer and top with a white cake layer, pressing gently to adhere the layer. Dam the white cake layer with buttercream around the perimeter, fill with mousse to the edge of the buttercream dam, and top with a chocolate layer. Refrigerate the cake for 10 to 15 minutes to set the buttercream before continuing.

Dam the chocolate layer, fill with peanut butter mousse, and top with the second white cake layer, gently pressing on the cake to adhere to the buttercream. Dam the white cake layer and fill with the remaining mousse and then top with the third and last layer of chocolate cake. If the cake feels wobbly (it's awfully tall), wrap it in plastic wrap and refrigerate the cake for 10 to 15 minutes to set the buttercream. You can also wrap the cake and place it in the freezer to set more firmly or if you want to make this portion of the cake ahead of time (you can freeze this for up to week).

Take the cake from the refrigerator and gently drive a long wooden kebab skewer through the middle of the cake. It should stick up above the top layer just a bit. The skewer helps secure the cake, since it's so tall, and it serves as an anchor for the finishing touch of the cake.

Using an offset spatula and a bench or frosting scraper (this kind of supertall cake is where my Fat Girl Cakes 12-inch/30.5 cm frosting scraper really pays for itself), coat the top and sides of the cake with a crumb coat of buttercream (see sidebar, page 221). Refrigerate or freeze the cake for 10 to 15 minutes to set the buttercream.

Coat the top and sides of the cake with a finishing coat of plain buttercream and, using the reserved cocoa buttercream, use a small offset spatula to swipe "flames" along the bottom of the cake.

Gently place the cloud on the top of the cake, centering the cloud over the skewer and gently pressing so that skewer literally skewers the cloud like a Popsicle stick, keeping the cloud in place.

AGNES'S BIRTHDAY CAKE

If given the task to make a birthday cake for someone I didn't know, I'd make this cake. It is the quintessential birthday treat, with hearty, tender yellow cake layers and smooth and pleasantly sweet chocolate filling and frosting. It's exactly the picture of the cake they should have under the entry "birthday cake."

YOU'LL NEED

1 recipe Yellow Cake (page 55), baked in two 8-inch/20.5 cm round pans to make 2 layers and each layer torted in half, for 4 layers total

1 recipe Fudgy Chocolate Frosting (page 186)

EQUIPMENT

Pastry bag

Medium-small plain round pastry tip (Ateco 80)

"Triple Petal" Russian piping tip

Place a layer of yellow cake on a cardboard round and transfer to a cake turntable. Fit a pastry bag with a medium-small plain round tip (Ateco 803), fill with the chocolate frosting, and pipe an even layer of frosting over the cake. Top with a second cake layer and gently press to adhere. Pipe another frosting layer on the second cake layer and top with the third cake layer. Pipe another even layer of frosting and then place the fourth and last cake layer on top, pressing gently to adhere. Refrigerate the cake for 10 to 15 minutes to set the frosting.

Using a small offset spatula and a bench or frosting scraper, apply a crumb coat to the top and sides of the cake (see sidebar, page 221). Refrigerate for 10 to 15 minutes to set the frosting.

Transfer about 1 cup/235 ml of the frosting to a pastry bag fitted with a "Triple Petal" Russian tip and set aside.

Using an offset spatula and a bench or frosting scraper, use the remaining frosting to smooth a finished layer of frosting on the top and outside of the cake. Pipe a decorative band of frosting along the perimeter at the top of the cake, using the Russian tip and reserved frosting.

ACRYLICS—THEY AREN'T JUST FOR NAILS ANYMORE!

When smoothing the sides of a cake, there are times when you need all the help you can get to make everything perfect and level. Most the time, a well-balanced bench or frosting scraper will do the trick of making everything straight and narrow. However, when your cake gets to a substantial height, a few cake aids can really do a lot to guide you to perfection. Personally, I use acrylic rounds (and squares). I buy them from www.cakesafe.com. What makes these rounds especially helpful is that if you're making an 8-inch/20.5 cm cake, you can get two 8¼- or 8½-inch/21 or 21.5 cm rounds, depending what you like the depth of your frosting to be on the sides of your cake. I lean towards a bit less, so I have 8¼-inch/21 cm rounds. Once you've crumb coated your cake, you place one round at the base of the cake, using the helpful guides on the acrylic to center the cake. I then make sure the top of the cake has a relatively finished coating and then place a parchment round on top. Smear a dab of buttercream onto the parchment to act

as a patch of glue when you place the second acrylic atop it. Use those handy guides to center the round. Using a large offset spatula, coat the sides of the cake with your frosting of choice (be generous and make sure the top acrylic doesn't shift) and then, keeping firm pressure on the top acrylic while turning the cake, scrape the sides of the cake with a tall icing scraper for a near perfect (and quick) finished coat. Make it even more perfect by heating and drying your icing scraper. If you make more than a few cakes a month, this is an investment worth making and a guarantee that your tallest cake won't become the Leaning Tower of Pisa.

BEEHIVE CAKE

The first layer cake that I made on my very own was a recipe from *The Winnie-the-Pooh Cookbook*: I was nine. It was called the hipy papy bthuthdth bthuthdth thuthda bthuthdy cake. That's not a typo. It's the actual name of the cake. I made if for my mother's birthday and if I hadn't already been hooked on baking, this cake certainly solidified my love.

YOU'LL NEED

2 tablespoons/28 g Marzipan (page 192)

1 ounce/28 g bittersweet chocolate, melted

1 recipe Almond Cake (page 63), baked in a half sheet pan and then the following sized rounds stamped out from the cake: 7-inch, 6-inch, 5-inch, 4-inch, and 3-inch (18, 15, 12.5, 10, and 7.5 cm)

1 recipe Honey-Pear-Lavender Cremeux (page 141)

1 recipe Honey Buttercream (page 178)

A quarter-size round brown fondant (see page 200 for homemade)

EQUIPMENT

Pastry bag

Small plain round piping tip (Ateco 2)

Medium-small plain round pastry tip (Ateco 803)

Divide the marzipan into 15 dime-size pieces and roll five of them into small ovals (I like to think of the shape as a supersize Tic Tacs). These will be the bee bodies. Roll the rest into balls and then flatten them to make wings.

Transfer the little bee bodies to a piece of parchment. Transfer the melted chocolate to a pastry bag fitted with a small plain round tip (Ateco 2) and pipe stripes along the "body" of each bee. Set aside to let the chocolate set.

Place the 7-inch/18 cm cake layer on a cake board and transfer to a cake turntable. Pipe a buttercream dam around the perimeter of the cake with a pastry bag fitted with a medium-small plain round tip (Ateco 803). Spread a little more than one quarter of the cremeux over the layer and top with the 6-inch/15 cm layer. Pipe a buttercream dam around the perimeter of the cake. Spread a little more than one third of the remaining cremeux over the layer and top with the 5-inch/12.5 cm layer. Pipe a buttercream dam around the perimeter of the cake and spread a little more than half of the remaining cremeux over the layer. Top with the 4-inch/10 cm layer and pipe a buttercream dam around the perimeter of the cake. Spread the remaining cremeux over the layer and top with the 3-inch/7.5 cm layer. Refrigerate the cake for 15 to 20 minutes to allow the buttercream to set.

Mound about ½ cup/118 ml of the honey buttercream on top of the cake and then, using a large offset spatula, apply a crumb coat to the top and sides of the cake (see sidebar, page 221). Refrigerate for 10 to 15 minutes to set the frosting.

Return the cake to the turntable. Spread the remaining frosting over the cake, using a large offset spatula, smoothing the top of the cake into a dome. Using a small offset spatula, gently place the spatula at a slight angle at the very top of the cake, applying slight pressure, and slowly turn the turntable and "wind" the spatula down the cake, still applying slight pressure, to create a spiral pattern down the cake.

Roll out the brown fondant into a 4 x 2-inch/10 x 5 cm rectangle and round the top to make the little door. Position the door at the bottom of the cake, pressing gently to adhere. This will be the "front" of the cake, so pick the prettiest side upon which to install your door.

Place the bee bodies at random intervals on the front of the cake, using the buttercream as glue. Gently insert the wings on either side of the body.

PBJ CAKE

Sometimes it takes a while for a cake idea to come together. The elements might be there but the presentation might elude me. Or I can see exactly what the cake will look like but the innards will be a mystery. This cake, the PBJ Cake, came to me fully formed. I'm sure you look at it and say, "No, duh!" just as you'd say in elementary school, eating a PBJ. It had to look like a peanut butter and jelly sandwich and it had to have all the yummy components, just in cake form. You can even mix it up and forgo the jam and add Nutella Mousse on top of the peanut butter for something utterly delightful.

YOU'LL NEED

1 recipe Peanut Butter Cake (page 80), baked in two 10-inch/25.5 cm square pans for 2 layers

½ recipe Peanut Butter Mousse (page 150)

1 cup Quick Raspberry Jam (page 128) or ½ recipe Nutella Mousse (page 149)

1 (2 ounce/55 g) piece plain Fondant (page 200)

EQUIPMENT

Pastry bag

Place a cake layer on a cake stand. Using a pastry bag without a tip, pipe the peanut butter mousse in an even layer over the top. Place in the freezer for 15 to 20 minutes to firmly set the mousse.

Spread the jam in an even layer over the mousse and top with the second layer of cake. Roll out the fondant into a square just a few centimeters smaller than the top cake layer and transfer to the top layer of the cake. Using a plastic fork or a chopstick (nothing with too sharp a point), gently make indentations into the fondant to mimic the crumb structure of a piece of toast.

COCONUT SNOWBALL CAKE

For all its tropical cred, coconut flakes scream "Winter Wonderland!" They are snow white, fluffy, and when sprinkled willy-nilly, look like delicious snowdrifts. What better way to use them than in a big ol' coconut cake snowball? This particular snowball is hiding something caramelly and delicious inside, though. So, don't be fooled into thinking that it's all cool simplicity inside because the center is layered with caramel goodness that will warm your belly and soul during the coldest months.

YOU'LL NEED

2 recipes Coconut Cake (page 85) or Coconut Cake Homemade Box Mix (page 44), divided into thirds to bake two 8-inch/20.5 cm half spheres and one 8-inch/20.5 cm round layer

1 recipe Italian Buttercream (page 177), made with coconut extract

1 recipe Coconut Caramel Filling (page 171)

1 (14-ounce/400 g) bag sweetened flake coconut

EQUIPMENT

Pastry bag

Medium-small plain round pastry tip (Ateco 803)

Place a half sphere of cake, round-side down, on a cake pedestal. Fit a pastry bag with a medium-small plain round tip (Ateco 803) and fill with about a third of the buttercream. Pipe a buttercream dam around the perimeter of the cake and fill with half of the coconut caramel filling. Top with the single 8-inch/20.5 cm round layer. Pipe a buttercream dam around the layer and fill with the remaining coconut caramel filling. Top with the remaining half sphere and press very gently to adhere. Refrigerate the cake for 10 to 15 minutes to set the buttercream.

Using a small offset spatula, spread the remaining buttercream over the outside of the cake, then smooth, using a flexible frosting scraper (I use Innovative Sugarworks' Sugar Smoother). Gently press the coconut flakes over the whole cake.

CARAMEL CAKE

I have loads of favorite sweet things. I never refuse a meringue the size of my head and as fluffy as a cloud. I can spend quality time eating a sheet tray of palmiers. I have been known to snap at anyone who gets too close to me when I've got a bowl of ganache in my hands. But it's caramel in all its iterations that steals my heart every time. Whether it's a crackling coating on a cream puff or a soft-flowing sauce drizzled (okay, I dump it), or, better yet, a chewy morsel slipped out of a square of waxed paper, that simple act of heating sugar to the point that it changes from brilliant white to slightly golden to coppery brown is my weakness. So, I made a cake to celebrate my utter devotion to all things caramel.

YOU'LL NEED

1 recipe Gesine's Tried-and-True Yellow Cake in its Butterscotch variation (page 70), baked in two 8-inch/20.5 cm round pans, torted in half to make 4 layers
1 recipe Caramel Buttercream (page 178), divided
1 recipe Firm Caramel Coating (page 203)
2 recipes Feuilletine (page 167)

EQUIPMENT

Pastry bag
Medium-small plain round pastry tip (Ateco 803)
Large star pastry tip (Ateco 828)

Place a layer of cake on a cardboard round and transfer to a cake turntable. Set aside 1 to 2 cups/235 to 475 ml of caramel buttercream for décor. Fit a pastry bag with a medium-small plain round tip (Ateco 803), fill with the remaining caramel buttercream, and pipe an even layer of buttercream over the layer. Top with a second cake layer,

pressing gently to adhere. Pipe another even coating of buttercream over the second cake layer. Top with the third layer of cake and pipe an even layer of buttercream over it. Top with the fourth and last cake layer. Refrigerate the cake for 10 to 15 minutes to firm the buttercream.

Smooth the remaining buttercream over the top and sides of the cake, using a small offset spatula and a bench or frosting scraper. Refrigerate for 10 to 15 minutes.

Cover the cake with the firm caramel topping, gently centering the caramel along the top of the cake and gently smoothing the caramel layer down the sides of the cake, pulling gently so that the caramel coating covers the sides of the cake. Trim away any excess caramel along the bottom of the cake. Fit a pastry bag with a star tip (I use Ateco 828), fill with the reserved buttercream, and pipe décor along the perimeter at the top of the cake. Fill in the space at the top of the cake with some of the feuilletine. Decorate the bottom of the cake with the remaining feuilletine by gently pressing it with your palm along the perimeter.

DOUBLE-BARREL WEDDING CAKE

I wanted to make my own wedding cake but sanity prevailed. I still made the cookie treats that guests took away, though. Instead, my mom and I wrote out the recipe we were happy with, handing it off to the caterer and giving them the German baker's stare as warning that if they didn't get it right, we'd be unhappy. As it turns out, the cake was lovely. The outside was chocolaty and the inside was a velvety almond flavor studded with almond toffee. Now that Ray and I are close to our 20th anniversary and talking about renewing our vows, I'm thinking of our cake. This time, I'll make it. And this is the very one I'd make. All white, this time, and decorated with the things that make me happy. An owl for my mother (her nickname was Eule as a kid, "owl" in German). The inside is layered with marzipan and studded with fresh strawberries, two of my mom's favorites. Wheat sheathes for my love of baking, acorns for the trees that stud our property, symbols of new life, and rice flowers for the beauty of a life well lived with the partner I love. A pretty tall order, so it's a pretty tall cake.

YOU'LL NEED

1 recipe Marzipan (page 192)

2 recipes Famous WASC Homemade Box Mix (page 40), baked in four 8-inch/20.5 round pans, torting in half, making 8 layers

3 recipes Macerated Strawberry (page 122)

3 recipes Italian Buttercream (page 177), made with lemon extract

8 ounces/225 g plain Fondant (page 200)

1 recipe Stabilized Sweet Whipped Cream (page 131)

EQUIPMENT

Pastry bag

Medium plain round pastry tip (Ateco 804)

Long wooden kebab skewer

Impression molds of choice

2 sheets edible rice paper to make paper flowers (see sidebar, page 247)

Divide the marzipan into 7 equal-size pieces. Roll each into a ball and roll into a round, just about 8 inches/20.5 cm in diameter and trimmed to 7¾ inches/19.5 cm round.

Place a layer of cake on a cardboard round. Brush the cake lightly with the juices from the macerated strawberries and top with a round of marzipan.

Divide the strawberries into 7 equal portions.

Fit a pastry bag with a medium round tip (Ateco 804), fill with the Italian buttercream, and pipe a dam around the perimeter of the cake. Top with ⅟ of the strawberries and then spread ½ cup/118 ml of the whipped cream to coat the strawberries. Top with the second layer and continue lightly brushing with

juices, topping with marzipan, damming, filling with strawberries, coating with whipped cream and topping with a cake layer, until you reach the fourth layer of cake. Press on the cake layer gently and freeze the cake for 20 to 30 minutes to set.

Check your freezer and refrigerator to make sure you have enough height to store your cake when it has double the layers. Make room now, rather than later. You'll thank yourself when the time comes.

Continue lightly brushing with juices, topping with marzipan, damming, filling with strawberries, and coating with whipped cream until you reach the eighth and final layer. Gently drive a long wooden kebab skewer down the middle of the cake for stability and freeze the cake for 20 to 30 minutes to set the buttercream and cream.

Using a large offset spatula and a tall icing scraper, coat the top and outside of the cake with a crumb coat of buttercream (see sidebar, page 221). Refrigerate for 10 to 15 minutes to set.

If using, now is the time to attach acrylic rounds (see sidebar, page 235). Using a large offset spatula and a tall icing scraper, smooth a finishing coat over the sides of the cake. Refrigerate the cake for 10 to 15 minutes to set the frosting and before removing the acrylics.

Roll out the fondant to just over ¼-inch/6 mm depth and gently press into your desired impression molds. Trim the sides and gently press to the buttercream to adhere.

Before serving, attach the paper flowers.

Cake Lady

MAKING SIMPLE EDIBLE PAPER FLOWERS

I adore painstakingly crafted, unbelievably realistic gum paste flowers. I revel in the time it takes to make the most intricate of them, scheduling a good few hours to spend meditating over the smoothing, veining, and subtle brushing on of powdered, lustrous colors. But there's something to be said for the utter whimsy and modernity of edible paper flowers. They are ethereal and bewitchingly iridescent. And they are ridiculously easy to make.

You'll need

- Edible rice paper
- Edible glue
- Fondant (page 200)
- Edible writing markers (optional)

Cut petal shapes from the paper. Cut a notch in each petal. Dab on a tiny bit of edible glue and secure the petals in a curve, and then use a touch of edible glue to attach the flowers to each other, overlapping slightly. Allow to dry and then place a small round of fondant in the middle of the flower. If attaching the flowers to buttercream, first "glue" the flower to a small knob of fondant, otherwise the moisture of the buttercream will make the flowers soggy.

You can use edible markers to color the paper petals in jaunty hues as well!

SKULL CAKE

A friend of mine throws a party on the Day of the Dead. Everyone who comes has to bring a dish that represents the memory of someone they have lost. One by one, they stand up on the table, dish in hand, and speak of their loved one's memory and how the dish honors them. Isn't that wonderful? I've laced this cake with the things I love about Mexico, the epicenter of the Dìa de los Muertos celebrations. The cake is full of great chocolate with a kick of flavor and spice. And then there's the skull: an homage to the colorful and whimsical skulls that signify the celebration.

YOU'LL NEED

½ recipe Gum Paste (page 201), divided into seven equal pieces. Leave one of the pieces white. Dye each remaining piece one the following colors, using 1 drop of dye for each: orange, yellow, red, purple, green, and blue

1 recipe Chocolate Cake Homemade Box Mix (page 48), made with 1 teaspoon ground cinnamon in the dry ingredients and baked in two 8-inch/20.5 cm round pans and torted in half to make 4 layers

1 recipe Chocolate Truffle Filling (page 183), made with cinnamon oil and cayenne pepper

1 recipe Zippy Dark Chocolate Ganache (page 180), made with lime oil

¼ cup/21 g Dutched cocoa powder

Royal Icing (page 207) or edible glue

EQUIPMENT

Pastry bag

Medium-small plain round pastry tip (Ateco 803)

Roll out the gum paste to slightly thinner than ⅛ inch/3 mm thick and about 8 inches/20.5 cm across (you'll be trimming the pieces to fit the guide), working with one piece at a time, making sure the other pieces are well covered in plastic wrap. Cut into ¼-inch/6 mm-wide pieces and shape according to the skull template (page 312). Allow to air-dry overnight to completely harden.

Place a cake layer on a cardboard round and transfer to a cake turntable. Fit a pastry bag with a medium-small round tip (Ateco 803) and fill it with chocolate truffle filling. Pipe an even layer of chocolate truffle filling over the cake, top with a second layer of cake and press gently to adhere. Pipe another layer of chocolate truffle filling and then top with the third layer of cake, pressing gently to adhere. Pipe a layer of chocolate truffle filling over the cake and top with the fourth and last layer of cake, pressing gently to adhere. Refrigerate for 10 to 15 minutes to allow the filling to set.

Using a small offset spatula and a hot bench or frosting scraper, smooth a crumb coat of ganache over the top and sides of the cake (see sidebar, page 221). Return the cake to the refrigerator for 5 to 10 minutes to set.

Spread a smooth finish coat of ganache over the cake, using an offset spatula and a hot scraper. Trace the skull template (page 312) onto a piece of parchment, cut it out, and place on the side of the cake, gently rubbing it to adhere. Refrigerate the cake for 5 minutes to just set the ganache.

Place the cocoa powder in a small bowl and dip a dry pastry brush into the cocoa, gently knocking off any excess. Gently pat and brush the cake with cocoa so it adheres and creates a suedelike effect. Gently peel off the skull parchment.

Using a small dab of royal icing or edible glue, coat the back of the gum paste pieces and put in place within the "skull" outline left behind by the parchment. Press gently to adhere the pieces, but not so hard that they crack. They are delicate once dry.

Hummingbird Cake and Seminaked Cake (Sticky Toffee Pudding) with Caramel Topping

SEMINAKED CAKE (STICKY TOFFEE PUDDING) WITH CARAMEL TOPPING

A simple, square cake, ever so lightly frosted so that the caramel-rich layers underneath peek through, topped with caramel drifting in waves down the sides, and bordered with golden orbs of fondant, dancing along the bottom layers, making for such an elegant look. The cake and frosting themselves won't disappoint in the taste department, either, the cake studded with sweet and tender dates and laced with coffee and rum, and the buttercream enlivened with molasses-infused brown sugar. This gem of a cake is sure to brighten any event.

YOU'LL NEED

1 recipe Sticky Toffee Pudding Cake (page 83), baked in two 8-inch/20.5 cm round pans and torted, to make 4 layers

½ recipe Swiss Buttercream (page 175), made with light brown sugar instead of granulated sugar

4 ounces/115 g white Fondant (page 200)

Wilton Gold Color Mist

¼ recipe Firm Caramel Coating (page 203)

EQUIPMENT

Pastry bag

Medium-small plain round pastry tip (Ateco 803)

Place a layer of cake on a cardboard square. Transfer to a cake turntable. Using a pastry bag fitted with a medium-small round tip (Ateco 803), pipe an even layer of buttercream over the cake, top with a second layer of cake, and press gently to adhere. Pipe another layer of buttercream and then top with the third layer of cake, pressing gently to adhere. Pipe a layer of buttercream over the cake and top with the fourth and last layer of cake, pressing gently to adhere the layers to the buttercream. Refrigerate for 10 to 15 minutes to set the buttercream.

Using a small offset spatula and a bench scraper, coat the cake in a smooth coat of frosting and then, using a hot scraper, gently smooth out the sides with enough pressure that the scraper reveals patches of cake beneath the frosting while still leaving a few small patches of buttercream on the sides of the cake.

Roll out the fondant to ⅛ inch/3 mm thick and stamp out thirty 1-inch/2.5 cm rounds (I use the opening top of a large pastry tip to stamp out the rounds) from the fondant. Cut 10 of the rounds in half, place them on a half sheet of parchment, and spray with a light dusting of gold luster spray. Allow the gold luster to dry and then place them side by side along the base of the cake. Place the remaining 20 rounds on the parchment and then use the round cutter to stamp out a curved V shape from the bottom of each round so that they fit snugly between the first row of half rounds. Spray them with the luster spray, allow to dry, and then position in a second row.

Place the caramel between two sheets of parchment and roll into a rough 8-inch/20.5 cm square. Center the caramel on top of the cake and gently pull down on the caramel to create a "dripping" effect.

HUMMINGBIRD CAKE

This cake is the perfect balance of sweetness and texture. Pineapple and banana bring a fruitiness to the cake layers, and pecans baked in the layers and coating the outside of the cake give a lovely crunch. The soft cream cheese frosting offers a tanginess to balance all that beautiful fruity sweetness. And let's not forget the beautiful hummingbird that my Ray drew with edible markers on a piece of fondant. Replicating the beauty may be a challenge, but it's worth a try! If you don't have the artistic skills, you can place a small hummingbird image over the fondant and use a sharp skewer to gently trace the drawing (without ripping through the paper) to create an indentation on the fondant that you can trace with the edible markers.

YOU'LL NEED

1 recipe Hummingbird Cake, baked in two 8-inch/20.5 cm round pans and torted, to make 4 layers

1 recipe Cream Cheese Frosting (page 190)

2 ounces/55 g plain Fondant (page 200)

2 cups/200 g pecans, lightly toasted, cooled, and finely chopped

Edible writing markers

EQUIPMENT

Pastry bag

Medium-small round pastry tip (Ateco 803)

Place a cake layer on a cardboard round. Transfer to a cake turntable. Using a pastry bag fitted with a medium-small round tip (Ateco 803), pipe an even layer of frosting over the cake, top with a second layer of cake, and press gently to adhere. Pipe another layer of frosting and then top with the third layer of cake, pressing gently to adhere. Pipe a layer of frosting over the cake and top with the fourth and last layer of cake, pressing gently to adhere. Freeze the cake for 20 to 25 minutes to set the icing.

Spread the remaining icing over the cake, using a small offset spatula, and use a bench or icing scraper to smooth the top and sides of the cake. Refrigerate for 15 to 20 minutes to set the icing.

Roll out the fondant into a rough 5 x 4-inch/12.5 x 10 cm rectangle, between ⅛ and ¼ inch/3 and 6 mm thick. Cut a 4 x 3-inch/10 x 7.5 cm oval from a piece of parchment and use the parchment as a guide to cut an oval from the fondant with a sharp paring knife. Transfer the piece of parchment to the side of the cake, pressing lightly to adhere. Gently press the pecan pieces onto the top and sides of the cake and refrigerate for 15 to 20 minutes to set.

Place an image approximately the size of the fondant (I prefer a hummingbird for obvious reasons) centered over the fondant. Use a sharp skewer to gently trace the image (hard enough to make an indentation in the fondant but not so hard that it rips through the paper). Remove the parchment and use the edible markers to trace the image and color it in.

When you're just about ready to serve the cake, gently peel the parchment from the cake and replace with your fondant image, pressing gently to adhere.

MAPLE BARK CAKE

Each spring, when the trees are budding across most of the country, we in Vermont are putting on our rubber boots and trampling through snow-patched expanses of mud, our trees still very bare. But while we don't enjoy the spring being experienced by the rest of the continental 48, we get something far better: sap. Ray and I bore holes and gently hammer taps into our sugar maples until the sap starts to trickle out. Every day, we collect what is liquid gold in these parts. We boil down the sap until it thickens and takes on that unmistakable hue and scent of maple syrup. And each time, we squeal in delight and we thank goodness for Vermont's very peculiar brand of springtime. This cake is a love letter to our adopted home state and the most delicious natural treasure.

YOU'LL NEED

1 recipe Maple Cake (page 56), baked in three 6-inch/15 cm round pans to make 3 layers

1 recipe Maple Espresso Cream Cheese Frosting (page 190)

¼ cup/21 g Dutched cocoa powder

2 ounces/57 g Fondant (page 200)

Wilton Gold Color Mist

EQUIPMENT

Pastry bag

Medium-small plain round pastry tip (Ateco 803)

1 (2-inch/5 cm) maple leaf cookie cutter (I use a plunger-style cutter that also stamps in a bit of veining on the leaf: the 2-inch/5 cm Ateco 1983 cutter)

Place a cake layer on a cardboard round and transfer to a cake turntable. Fit a pastry bag with a medium-small plain round tip (Ateco 803), fill with the cream cheese frosting, and pipe an even layer of frosting over the cake layer. Top with the second and fill it with frosting. Top with the third and final layer of cake. Gently press on the top of the cake to adhere the layers to the frosting and transfer the cake to the freezer for 15 to 20 minutes to set the frosting.

With an offset spatula, smooth an even layer of frosting on the top of the cake. Then, dip a small offset spatula into the remaining buttercream frosting and coat the sides of the cake, using short sideways strokes, making each a little shorter or longer, to mimic bark.

Dust the cake with cocoa powder. Roll out the fondant to between ⅛ and ¼ inch/3 and 6 mm thick and, using the maple leaf cutter, stamp out 6 to 8 maple leaves. Place the leaves on a sheet of parchment and spray with a light coating of gold luster spray. Allow the spray to dry, 10 to 15 minutes, and then gently apply the leaves in a random scatter onto the cake.

GINGERBREAD CAKE

I look at this cake and it makes me ridiculously happy. It's the perfect cake for a big holiday party. It's the perfect cake for a winter birthday. It's the perfect cake for a holiday wedding. It's just the perfect cake. Period.

YOU'LL NEED

1 recipe Gingerbread Cookies (page 208), baked in 2-inch/5 cm and 3-inch/7.5 cm heart shapes, tree shapes, gingerbread person shapes, and 1 house shape

1 recipe plain Royal Icing (page 207), made to a piping consistency (see sidebar, page 259)

2 recipes Gingerbread Spice Cake (page 84), one of the recipes baked in two 8-inch/20.5 cm round pans and torted to make 4 layers, and the other baked in three 6-inch/15 cm round pans and torted to make 6 layers

3 recipes Swiss Buttercream (page 175), made with 1 tablespoon orange extract

EQUIPMENT

Pastry bag

Small plain round piping tip (Ateco 2)

Medium-small plain round pastry tip (Ateco 803)

4 bubble tea straws

2 long wooden kebab skewers

At least one night before, or up to a week prior to assembling the cake, place the baked cookies on a sheet pan and pipe the royal icing onto the cookies. Allow to set, uncovered, at room temperature. Once the icing is set, you can store the cookies at room temperature in a resealable plastic bag before placing on the cake.

Place an 8-inch/20.5 cm round of cake onto a cardboard round and transfer to a cake turntable. Fit a pastry bag with a medium-small plain round tip (Ateco 803), fill with buttercream, and pipe an even layer of frosting over the layer. Top with the second 8-inch cake layer and press gently to adhere. Pipe a second layer of frosting over the cake layer and place the third 8-inch cake layer atop the frosting, pressing gently to adhere. Pipe one last layer of frosting and place the fourth and last 8-inch layer on the cake, pressing gently to adhere. Transfer the cake to the refrigerator for 10 to 15 minutes to set the buttercream.

Using a small offset spatula and a bench or frosting scraper, smooth a crumb coat of buttercream over the top and sides of the cake (see sidebar, page 221). Return the cake to the refrigerator for 10 to 15 minutes to set the buttercream. Using a bench or frosting scraper, smooth a finishing coat over the top and sides of the cake. Return the cake to the refrigerator while you work on the second cake.

Place a 6-inch/15 cm round of cake on a cardboard round and transfer to a cake turntable. Fill, stack, skim coat, and finish coat the 6-inch cake layers just as you did the 8-inch layers, and refrigerate for 10 to 15 minutes to set.

Insert four bubble tea straws in a circle about 5 inches/12.5 cm in diameter into the 8-inch/20.cm cake. Use scissors to trim the straws so they are flush with the top of the cake. These will act to keep the 6-inch/15 cm cake from sinking into the 8-inch cake beneath them. Place the 8-inch cake onto a cake stand. Center the 6-inch cake in the middle of the 8-inch cake, over the straws, gently lowering. Use any extra buttercream to smooth over any nicks that may have occurred during the assembly.

Place 2 long wooden kebab skewers into the middle of the top cake, a few inches from each other, making sure they stick out an inch/2.5 cm from the top of the cake. Place the gingerbread people on the cake, directly in front of the skewers so they act to prop up the cookies, gently pressing down on the cookies to plant their feet into the buttercream.

Place the remaining gingerbread shapes around the cakes, piping a small dollop of buttercream onto the back of the cookies to act as glue to attach them to the cake.

PIPING WITH ROYAL ICING

Royal icing is a magic tool in decorating. When piped onto cookies, it sets hard and firm, allowing you to transport the cookies without smearing the decoration. You can get pretty intricate with the stuff, but even just a simple outline of a cookie does wonders for its looks. There are a few tricks to doing it right, but they don't take long at all to master.

Using a stand mixer to mix the icing makes it much smoother, but you can mix it all by hand in a large bowl and get loads of steps on your Fitbit.

Start with the least amount of water suggested for a piping consistency icing. Add more water a drop at a time until you get to the right consistency.

For piping consistency, you shouldn't have to struggle getting the icing out of the piping tip: the icing should flow slowly and, once piped, should keep its shape without any change in shape at all.

For a medium consistency, the icing, once piped, should relax a bit and should be relatively easy to nudge to meet up and "melt" into the icing next to it, but shouldn't drip or flow.

For flooding consistency, the icing should flow easily but not be completely liquid. It should be the consistency thicker than maple syrup but thinner than honey. When piped, it should immediately flatten.

RUDY'S ROOTIN' TOOTIN' FIRST BIRTHDAY CAKE

Our little friend Rudy was turning one and having a Wild West–themed birthday party. I had to go all out on his cake because he's the cutest little cowpoke in Vermont. It would also be his first real taste of cake, so I made sure to give him options so he could have all the options!

YOU'LL NEED

1 recipe Gingerbread Cookies (page 208) made in house shapes measuring 4 inches/ 10 cm wide x 6 to 8 inches/15 to 20.5 cm tall (cut freehand or you can use the house cutters in R&M International's Gingerbread House Bake Set), for 12 large cookies

1 recipe Royal Icing (page 207)

1 recipe Gum Paste (page 201)

Edible writing markers

4 recipes French Strawberry–Lemon Yogurt Cake (page 64), baked in 12-inch/30.5 cm square pans for 4 layers

2 recipes Italian Buttercream (page 177), made with 2 teaspoons lemon extract

2 recipes Fruit Cremeux (page 146), for filling the French Strawberry– Lemon Yogurt Cake

Sky Blue gel dye

2 recipes Everyone's Favorite Carrot Cake (page 60), the two batters divided equally among three 10-inch/25.5 cm round pans to make 3 layers

1 recipe Italian Buttercream (page 177)

1 recipe Cream Cheese Frosting (page 190)

1 recipe Chocolate Cake Homemade Box Mix (page 48), baked in two 8-inch/20.5 cm round pans, torted in half to make 4 layers

1 recipe Helga's Chocolate Buttercream (page 179)

1 recipe Italian Buttercream (page 177), made with 1 teaspoon orange extract

1 sleeve graham crackers, ground into a powder in a food processor to make 1¼ cups/135 g

EQUIPMENT

Pastry bag

Medium plain round pastry tip (Ateco 804)

18 large bubble tea straws

3 extra-long wooden/bamboo skewers (should measure 15½ inches/39 cm long)

At least one night before, or up to a week prior to assembling the cake, place the baked cookies on a sheet pan and pipe the royal icing onto the cookies to outline and decorate. Allow to set, uncovered, at room temperature. Once the icing is set, you can store the cookies at room temperature in a resealable plastic bag before placing on the cake.

Roll out the gum paste to ¼ inch/6 mm thick. Cut out a cactus shape that's about 5 inches/12.5 cm tall, a small boy or girl figure, and a 6-inch/15 cm circle. Use the edible markers to color in the cactus, add detail to

the figure, and draw a wagon wheel on the circle. Allow to dry, uncovered, to harden overnight. Keep any reserve gum paste well covered to finish the cake.

Place a 12-inch/30.5 cm layer of the French Strawberry–Lemon Yogurt cake on a cardboard square and transfer to a cake turntable. Fit a pastry bag with a medium plain round tip (Ateco 804), fill with lemon buttercream, and pipe a dam around the perimeter of the cake. Spread one third of the fruit cremeux over the layer and top with a second layer. Pipe a dam of buttercream around the perimeter of the cake and spread another third of the fruit cremeux over the cake and top with a third layer. Pipe a dam of buttercream around the perimeter of the cake and spread the last third of fruit cremeux on the cake and top with the fourth and last layer. Transfer to the freezer for 30 to 35 minutes to set.

Transfer about ¼ cup/60 ml of the lemon buttercream to a small bowl and add a very small dollop of Sky Blue dye and stir until incorporated. Set aside.

Using an offset spatula and a bench or icing scraper, spread a skim or crumb coat of lemon buttercream over the top and sides of the cake (see sidebar, page 221). Refrigerate for 10 to 15 minutes to set.

Using an offset spatula and then a bench scraper, spread a finish layer of buttercream over the top and sides of the cake and then, using a small offset spatula, smear small, random dollops of the blue-dyed buttercream on

the sides of the cake and *then*, using a bench or icing scraper, smooth the sides and top of the cake, thereby smoothing and smearing the blue dollops of icing so that they look like lazy clouds. Transfer the cake to the fridge while you build the remaining cakes.

Place a 10-inch/25.5 cm layer of carrot cake on a cardboard round. Fit a pastry bag with a medium plain round tip (Ateco 804), fill with the plain buttercream, and pipe a dam around the perimeter of the cake. Spread half of the cream cheese frosting over the layer and top with a second carrot cake layer. Pipe a buttercream dam around the perimeter of the cake and spread the rest of the cream cheese frosting over the layer and top with the third and final layer. Transfer the cake to the freezer for 20 to 25 minutes to set.

Using an offset spatula and a bench or icing scraper, spread a skim or crumb coat of plain buttercream over the top and sides of the cake. Transfer the cake to the refrigerator to allow the buttercream to set, 15 to 20 minutes.

Transfer about 2 tablespoons of the plain buttercream to a small bowl, dab with a small amount of Sky Blue gel dye, and stir to combine.

Using an offset spatula and a bench or icing scraper, spread a finish layer of the remaining undyed buttercream over the top and sides of the cake and then, using a small offset spatula, smear small, random dollops of the blue-dyed buttercream on the sides of the cake. Using a bench or icing scraper, smooth the sides and top of the cake, thereby smoothing and smearing the blue dollops of icing so that they look like lazy clouds. Transfer the cake to the fridge while you build the remaining cake.

Place an 8-inch/20.5 cm round of chocolate cake on a cardboard round. Fit a pastry bag with a medium plain round tip (Ateco 804) and pipe one third of the chocolate buttercream over the cake in an even layer. Place a second chocolate cake layer on top of the chocolate buttercream and pipe another third of the chocolate buttercream over the cake layer. Place a third cake layer on top of the chocolate buttercream and pipe the remaining chocolate buttercream on the cake layer. Top with the fourth and last layer. Transfer the cake to the refrigerator for 10 to 15 minutes to allow the ganache to set.

Using an offset spatula and a bench or icing scraper, spread a skim or crumb coat of the orange buttercream over the top and sides of the cake (see sidebar, page 221). Transfer the cake to the refrigerator to allow the buttercream to set, 15 to 20 minutes.

Transfer about 2 tablespoons of the orange buttercream to a small bowl, dab with a small amount of Sky Blue gel dye, and stir to combine.

Using an offset spatula and a bench or icing scraper, spread a finish layer of the undyed buttercream over the top and sides of the cake and then, using a small offset spatula, smear small, random dollops of the

blue dye on the sides of the cake. Using a bench or icing scraper, smooth the sides and top of the cake, thereby smoothing and smearing the blue dollops of icing so that they look like lazy clouds. Grab a handful of graham cracker powder and gently press against the lower bottom of the cake, pressing some of the powder lower and, as you turn the cake, some higher, to create a mountain effect on the side of the cake. Transfer the cake to the fridge to set the buttercream, 10 to 15 minutes.

Take the 12-inch/30.5 cm cake tier from the refrigerator and place on a cake platter. Center a 10-inch/25.5 cm cardboard round on the top of the 12-inch cake and press gently into the top of the cake to leave an impression. This is your guide for arranging the straws. Insert 10 bubble tea straws within the confines of the 10-inch circle, spaced evenly: 7 on the outer perimeter and 3 closer to the center of the circle. Clip each straw so that each sits flush to the top of the cake's frosting.

Carefully center the 10-inch/25.5 cm cake atop the 12-inch/30.5 cm cake.

Center an 8-inch/20.5 cm cardboard round on top of the 10-inch/25.5 cm cake and press gently to provide a guide for the straws. Insert the straws evenly within the confines of the 8-inch/20.5 cm guide, 5 on the outside and 3 on the inside. Clip each straw so that each sits flush to the top of the cake's frosting.

Carefully center the 8-inch/20.5 cm cake over the 10-inch/25.5 cm cake. Drive a long wooden skewer, sharp end down, through the middle of the top cake down through to the very bottom, using a rubber mallet or a hammer to gently tap the skewer through the cardboard rounds. Use the second skewer to continue poking the first skewer down to the bottom. Then insert the second and third skewer on either side of the first skewer, spaced about ½ inch/1.3 cm from the middle skewer, and gently tap the skewers into the cake just as you did the first but allow about 4 inches/10 cm of each skewer to remain above the top of the cake. Place the wagon wheel right in front of the two skewer "stands," allowing the wheel to lean against them.

Place the cookies around the bottom tier, 3 on each side. Press each cookie gently against the cake to adhere. If they aren't stable, dab any extra frosting or royal icing on the back of the cookies to act as glue.

Place the cowboy or girl on the top of the 12-inch/30.5 cm tier, leaning it against the 10-inch/25.5 cm tier, and then place the cactus next to it. Roll out a reserved piece of gum paste into a ⅛-inch/3 cm thick, 8-inch/20.5 cm-long "rope." Use a brown edible marker to tint the rope. Gently loop one end into a 1 inch/2.5 cm-diameter circle and pinch the "end" to the rope to seal. Place the loop around the top of the cactus and gently insert the other end of the rope into the cake, next to the cowboy or cowgirl's hand.

CARROT CAKE

One morning, after making a live television appearance demonstrating a few chocolate recipes for early risers, I was getting ready to leave when I someone called to me from down a long corridor, "You! Your carrot cake! It was the best thing at my wedding." I get this a lot. My carrot cake recipe has a way of making people yell at me from across large expanses. Ever since I published the first version of the recipe, almost ten years ago, I've had the pleasure of hearing of happy memories of weddings and birthdays and anniversary parties where my carrot cake made an appearance. It's an incredibly simple recipe, both the cake and the frosting, that's easy enough for anyone to make for a special occasion, which is perhaps what makes it so wonderful. And, let's not forget, it's a pleasure to eat. It's so good, in fact, that it will have people yelling at you about it from across the room to compliment your baking.

YOU'LL NEED

1 recipe Cream Cheese Frosting
  (page 190)
Leaf Green gel dye
Orange gel dye
1 recipe Everyone's Favorite Carrot
  Cake (page 60), baked in two 8-inch/
  20.5 cm round pans and torted in half
  to make 4 layers
Marzipan rabbit (see sidebar, page 267)

EQUIPMENT

Pastry bag
Medium-small plain round tip
  (Ateco 803)
Grass piping tip (Ateco 234)
Small plain round piping tip
  (Ateco 2)

Set aside 1 cup/235 ml of the cream cheese frosting in a small bowl and stir in 1 to 2 drops of green dye.

Set aside ½ cup/118 ml of frosting in another small bowl and stir in 1 drop of orange dye.

Place a cake layer on a cardboard round and transfer to a cake turntable. Fit a pastry bag with a medium-small round tip (Ateco 803) and fill with the remaining undyed frosting. Pipe an even layer of cream cheese frosting onto the layer, top with the second cake layer, pressing gently to adhere the cake to the frosting, and pipe another even layer of cream cheese frosting. Top again with the third layer of cake, pressing gently to adhere, and pipe a final layer of cream cheese frosting on the cake layer. Gently press the fourth and final layer on top of the frosting. Place the cake in the freezer for 15 to 20 minutes to set.

Using a small offset spatula, smooth a crumb coat over the top and sides of the cake (see sidebar, page 221) and return the cake to the freezer to set the frosting, 10 to 15 minutes.

Spread the remaining frosting over the top and sides of the cake, using an offset spatula and a bench or frosting scraper, smoothing the top and sides of the cake. Return to the freezer to set the icing, 10 to 15 minutes.

Fit a pastry bag with the grass tip and fill with the green frosting. Pipe shallow rounds of grass up the sides of the cake, stopping halfway up.

Pipe a longer patch of grass in the top center of the cake, around 4 inches/10 cm in diameter.

Fit a pastry bag with the medium-small piping tip (Ateco 803) and fill the bag with the orange frosting. Pipe carrots around the top perimeter of the cake and pipe a band of dots above the grass band along the sides of the cake.

Fit a pastry bag with the small round piping tip (Ateco 2) and fill with the remaining green frosting. Pipe carrot greens at the ends of each carrot.

Place the sweet little marzipan rabbit in the middle of your grass patch.

THE MAKING OF A MARZIPAN RABBIT

Once in a while, a sweet little marzipan rabbit makes everything better, and since they are notoriously fond of carrots, there's no better place to set one than atop a carrot cake. You can make one out of fondant just as easily, but it won't be as yummy.

You'll need

8 ounces/225 g Marzipan (page 192)
Edible writing markers
Edible confectioners' glue

Equipment

Toothpicks

Break off a 1-ounce/28 g and a $^1/_2$-ounce/14 g piece of marzipan and form each into an egg shape.

Take the smaller egg-shaped piece and gently etch a smile and a little notch for the nose on the narrower end of the egg shape. Using a pink marker, color the tip of the nose. Using a black marker, make two dots toward the fatter end of the egg, for eyes.

Take the larger egg-shaped piece and place it, wider side down, on your work surface. Drive a toothpick (you may have to trim it a bit so it doesn't stick up past the bunny head once you attach it) down the middle of the egg (sorry, bunny), making sure there's a bit sticking up out of the egg. Center the head over the exposed toothpick and gently press the head down onto the body, using the toothpick as the anchor for the head.

Shape 2 more $^1/_2$-ounce/14 g pieces of marzipan into 1-inch/1.5 cm narrow ovals (the ears) and gently make an indentation in the middle of both, using the dull edge of a knife. Use a pink edible marker to slightly tint the inside of each ear.

Snap a toothpick in half and drive each piece about $^1/_4$ inch/6 mm up the ear, leaving about $^1/_4$ inch sticking out of the ear. Attach the ears to either side of the head, using the exposed portions of the toothpick.

Take 2 dime-size pieces of marzipan and shape into teardrops. Gently flatten the narrower ends, place a drop of edible glue on the flattened end, and press onto the side of the bunny body.

Take 2 nickel-size pieces of marzipan and shape into teardrops. Flatten the entire teardrop slightly and place a small dollop of edible glue onto the narrower end. Place the narrower ends underneath the bunny and gently bend the portions that are sticking up toward the body slightly, for bunny feet. Gently make indentations with the dull edge of a knife at the tip of the foot, for toes. You can use marzipan for the carrot or pipe a little carrot with cream cheese icing left over from the carrot cake onto the bunny's chest to make it look like she's nibbling on a treat.

SUPER RAY'S BIRTHDAY CAKE

Ray loves superheroes. I love Ray. Ray loves lemon. I love Ray. Ray loves cake. I love Ray . . . and making cake. That's all to say that when Ray's birthday approaches, I have the best time making him a cake, putting into it all the things that make him happy, like this superhero-themed extravaganza built for my very own superhero husband.

YOU'LL NEED

Cornstarch for dusting

1 recipe Gum Paste (page 201), dyed yellow

1 recipe Lemon–Poppy Seed Cake (page 76), baked in two 9-inch/23 cm round pans and torted in half, for 4 layers

2 recipes Swiss Buttercream (page 175), made with lemon extract, divided

1 recipe Lemon Cream (page 125)

2 recipes Gesine's Tried-and-True Yellow Cake (page 70), baked in four 8-inch/20.5 cm round pans to make 4 layers

½ recipe Stovetop Mango Curd (page 123)

2 pints/680 g fresh blueberries

1 recipe Stabilized Sweet Whipped Cream (page 131)

1 pound/453 g black fondant (for something so inky dark, I buy fondant instead of making it. My favorite brand is Fondarific.)

1 recipe Royal Icing (page 207)

EQUIPMENT

3-inch/7.5 cm cookie-cutter letters

Toothpicks

Pastry bag

Medium-small plain round tip (Ateco 803)

4 bubble tea straws

Dust a clean work surface with cornstarch. Roll out the yellow gum paste to a little over ¼ inch/6 mm thick. Firmly stamp out the applicable letters for the birthday girl or boy. In my case, I used *R*, *A*, and *Y*. Insert toothpicks into the letters so that half of the toothpick is embedded in the letter and half is sticking out below it. Place the letters on a flat surface in a cool, dry place to dry out completely, preferably overnight.

Place a 9-inch/23 cm layer of lemon–poppy seed cake on a cardboard round and transfer to a cake turntable. Fit a pastry bag with a medium-small plain round tip (Ateco 803) with 1 recipe of lemon-flavored Swiss buttercream (reserve the remaining recipe for the yellow cake). Pipe a dam around the perimeter of the cake layer and smooth a third of the lemon cream over the cake layer. Top with a second layer, pipe a dam and fill with lemon cream, and repeat with the third layer. Place the fourth and last cake layer on top and transfer the cake to the freezer for 10 to 15 minutes to set the filling and buttercream.

Using a small offset spatula and a bench

or frosting scraper, smooth a crumb coat of buttercream over the top and sides of the cake (see sidebar, page 221). Return the cake to the refrigerator for 10 to 15 minutes to set the buttercream. Using a bench or frosting scraper, smooth a finishing coat over the top and sides of the cake. Return the cake to the refrigerator while you work on the second cake.

Place an 8-inch/20.5 cm round of yellow cake on a cardboard round. Pipe a dam around the perimeter of the cake with the reserved second recipe of lemon buttercream. Pour a third of the mango curd over the layer, spreading with a small offset spatula, then place one third of the blueberries over the layer. Smooth one third of the whipped cream over the blueberry-covered layer. Continue to dam, fill, and stack the second and third yellow cake layers, placing the fourth and final cake layer on top. Place the cake in the refrigerator for 10 to 15 minutes to set the frosting. Follow the same process to skim coat the yellow cake with the lemon buttercream, return it to the refrigerator for 10 to 15 minutes to set, and then add the finish coat to the yellow cake, as you did the lemon–poppy seed cake, and refrigerate to set.

Insert four bubble tea straws in a circle about 5 inches/12.5 cm in diameter into the 8-inch/20.5 cm yellow cake. Use a scissor to trim the straws so they lay flush with the top of the cake. These will act to keep the yellow cake from sinking into the lemon–poppy seed cake beneath it. Place the 9-inch/23 cm lemon–poppy seed cake on a cake stand. Center the 8-inch cake on the middle of the 9-inch cake, over the straws, gently lowering. Use any extra lemon buttercream to smooth over any nicks that may have occurred during the assembly. Refrigerate the stacked cake while you work on creating a fondant cityscape and mask.

Dust an even coating of cornstarch over a flat and very clean work surface and roll out the fondant to about ¼ inch/6 mm thick, being careful not to get a lot of cornstarch on the surface of the fondant because it's hard to get that white dust off! Using a sharp paring knife or an X-ACTO blade, cut out "building" shapes and windows and then gently press them onto the sides of the bottom tier of the cake.

Cut out the mask and pipe royal icing details for eyebrows and other details, if you'd like to, and attach to the upper tier of the cake.

Carefully insert the letters into the first tier.

STICKY BUN LAYER CAKE

If you can have coffee cake for breakfast, why can't you have a sticky bun layer cake for breakfast? I can't think of one reason why not. And to make this cake extra sticky, you can fill the center with a scrumptious, caramely German chocolate cake filling and drizzle the outside with even more caramel. This, in my considered opinion, is truly a breakfast of champions.

YOU'LL NEED

1 recipe Maple Sticky Bun Cake (page 72) baked in two 8-inch/20.5 cm round pans to make two layers

1 recipe German Chocolate Cake Filling (page 170)

1 recipe Caramel Buttercream (page 120)

1 cup/99 g toasted pecans

¼ cup/56 g melted caramel, from store bought caramels

Place a cake layer on a cardboard round and spread the filling evenly over the layer and top with the second layer. Press gently to adhere the layers to the filling and refrigerate for 10 minutes.

Using a large offset spatula and an icing scraper, coat the top and outside of the cake with a crumb coat of buttercream (see sidebar, page 221). Refrigerate for 10 to 15 minutes to set.

Using a large offset spatula, spread the remaining buttercream over the top and outside of the cake and then create a swirl pattern on the top and sides of the cake with the spatula. Drizzle the cake with the caramel and pecans.

GIANT PUMPKIN CAKE

Are you a cake or a pie person? If your answer is yes, then boy, is this the cake for you because it's got both. It's composed of two layers of a tender pumpkin Bundt cake, one on top and one on the bottom. Inside, there are two layers of flaky pie dough. And smack dab in the middle, pie filling. You get to decide which filling; you can go with pecan or pumpkin. Both are excellent choices. And to make sure everything stays happily together, the inside layers are held together with white chocolate–pumpkin ganache. And let's not forget the finishing touch: a pumpkin ermine frosting finishes the outside, along with a jaunty fondant stem and a few tendrils, straight from the pumpkin patch.

YOU'LL NEED

1 recipe Pumpkin Cake (page 81), batter divided in half, each portion baked in a 9-inch/23 cm Bundt to make 2 shallow Bundt layers

1 recipe White Chocolate Pumpkin Ganache (page 181)

1 recipe You Flake (page 108), baked to make two 8-inch/20.5 cm round layers

1 recipe Pumpkin Pie Filling (page 160) or Pecan Pie Filling (page 162)

1 recipe Ermine Frosting made with pumpkin purée (page 185)

8 ounces/225 g brown fondant (when fondant is dyed very dark, I prefer to buy it rather than make it. Fondarific is my preferred brand.)

Two or three gum paste leaves (see page 227)

EQUIPMENT
Wooden skewer

Place one Bundt layer, rounded-side down, on a cardboard round and transfer to a cake turntable. Spread one quarter of the pumpkin ganache over the top of the Bundt cake in an even layer. Place a flake layer over the ganache and then spread another quarter of the ganache over the flake layer (do this gently, as it *is* flaky and delicate). Top with the chilled and firmed pumpkin or pecan filling. Spread another quarter of the ganache over the pumpkin or pecan filling and then top with the second flake layer. Spread the remaining ganache and top with the second Bundt cake layer, rounded-side up. Using an offset spatula, spread a thin layer of pumpkin ermine frosting over the cake, making sure to fill any deeper gaps around the middle of the cake. Use a flexible frosting scraper (I use Innovative Sugarworks' Sugar Smoother) to really smooth and round out the pumpkin shape. Transfer the cake to the refrigerator for 15 to 20 minutes to set the frosting.

Using an offset spatula, spread dollops of frosting in a sweeping motion, starting at the base of the pumpkin and bringing it to the top, to create a ribbed effect. Spread any remaining frosting in the middle cavity to fill the gap.

Pinch off a 1½-inch/4 cm dollop from the brown fondant, cover with plastic wrap, and set aside. Roll the larger portion of the brown fondant into a 4-inch/10 cm-long and 1½-inch/4 cm-wide cylinder. Flatten the top end and roll the piece between your hands to make it a bit narrower through the middle.

Place the "stem" onto a piece of parchment, flattened (top)-side up. Gently press along the edge of the fondant to flatten and to make a skirt around the entire perimeter of the stem. Place the stem in the middle of the cake.

Roll the remaining fondant into a thin rope and cut into 5- to 6-inch/12.5 to 15 cm-long pieces. Wrap the pieces around a wooden skewer to create tendrils and then slip off and place around the stem, trailing down the sides of the cake. Insert leaves near the tendrils.

WORLD CAKE

Sometimes you want a cake that makes a big impression. What could be bigger than the whole wide world? What's great about this cake is that you need only to get your hands on half sphere baking molds. Usually, they're used to make various ball cakes of the sport variety: tennis ball, golf ball, basketball, baseball. You get the gist. But if you take a little more time with a pastry bag and a few continents, you can make the world in cake. It's on this rare occasion that I use American Crusting Buttercream (page 189) because it works beautifully in transferring buttercream patterns (in this case continents) seamlessly onto a buttercream-coated cake. For this cake not to be *too* much about that yummy but super-sweet frosting, the majority of the cake is actually cake layers. Specifically Carving Cake—very much like a hearty pound cake—which is pretty darn tasty all on its own and sturdy enough to carry the world on its shoulders.

YOU'LL NEED

2 recipes American Crusting Buttercream (page 189), one recipe dyed with green gel dye and the other recipe dyed with blue gel dye

2 recipes Vanilla (page 88) or Chocolate (page 89) Carving Cake, two thirds of the batter divided between two 8-inch/20.5 cm half sphere cake pans and the remainder baked in one 8-inch/20.5 cm round pan, for a total of three layers

EQUIPMENT

Continents in Mirror Image template (page 314)
Pastry bag
Small plain piping tip (Ateco 2)

Place the Continents template underneath a piece of parchment so that you can see the image through the parchment. Tape the graphic in place.

Fill a pastry bag fitted with a small plain tip (Ateco 2) with green buttercream. Trace the outline of each continent and then fill them in. You don't have to be perfect. You don't even need to have that steady a hand while you do this. The continents will look more authentic for it. Transfer the parchment to a sheet pan and freeze for 10 to 15 minutes, or until the images are very firm but not frozen solid.

Place 1 half sphere cake layer on a cake platter, rounded-side down. Spread 1 cup/235 ml of the green buttercream over the layer and then top with the 8-inch/20.5 round layer. Spread 1 cup/235 ml of green

buttercream over the 8-inch layer and top with the second half sphere, round-side up, to form a sphere. Transfer the cake to the refrigerator for 10 to 15 minutes to allow the buttercream to set.

Using a small offset spatula and a flexible frosting scraper (I use Innovative Sugarworks Buttercream Shaper), and coat the cake with a crumb coat of blue frosting (see sidebar, page 221). Refrigerate the cake for 10 minutes. Spread a smooth finishing layer of frosting over the sphere, using a small offset spatula and the flexible frosting scraper. Return the cake to the refrigerator for 15 to 20 minutes, or until very cool and the frosting feels set.

Take the piped continents from the freezer. To make the transfer easier, use a scissor to separate some of the continents so that you can concentrate on one area at a time. While you transfer one section, keep the rest in the freezer.

Flip the parchment over so the icing portion faces the world and, holding the parchment slightly above the cake, position the continents in the right hemisphere. Once you're in the right latitude and longitude, place the parchment on the cake, icing touching icing, and gently rub the continent to transfer the mirror image to the cake. Gently peel back the parchment. The continent should have cleanly transferred to the cake. If it seems warm and is still sticking to the parchment, stop peeling and transfer the cake and parchment to the fridge to set a bit more. When things are feeling nice and cool, continue rubbing and peeling until the continents have all transferred and you have the world before you in cake.

FRAISIER CAKE

In the early summer, when strawberries are in season, this is the cake that I dream of. It uses strawberry in the mousse, around the mousse, and on top of the mousse. It uses strawberry for decoration and for taste. It is, quite frankly, a celebration of strawberries. In fact, the word *strawberry* is baked right into the French name for the cake: *fraise* means "strawberry." Now isn't that just perfect?

YOU'LL NEED

2 pints/700 g fresh strawberries

1 recipe Fraisier Sponge (page 97), baked in one 9-inch/23 cm round pan and torted for 2 layers

1 recipe Fresh and Easy Strawberry Mousse (page 148)

1 recipe Fruit Glaze Topping (page 197)

¼ cup/60 ml Royal Icing (page 207), at piping consistency (see sidebar, page 259)

A few small gum paste flowers (optional; see sidebar, page 227)

Fresh rosemary sprigs (optional)

EQUIPMENT

Pastry bag

Small plain round piping tip (Ateco 2)

Line the sides of a 9-inch/23 cm springform pan with a 5-inch/12.5 cm tall x 30-inch/76 cm-long strip of parchment so that the ends overlap and the parchment acts as a tall ring within the pan.

Select 10 unblemished and similarly sized strawberries, hull them, and cut them in half lengthwise.

Place a cake layer in the bottom of the pan. Place the halved strawberries inside the pan, lining the perimeter, pointy side up and flat side touching the parchment. Pack the strawberries as close together as you can so that there are no gaps.

Set aside about ½ cup/118 ml of mousse in a small bowl and refrigerate. Carefully pour the remaining mousse into the pan, aiming for the middle of the cake layer, and, using a small offset spatula, gently push the mousse to the sides of the cake and smooth out the top.

Place the second cake layer on top and press gently to adhere. Spread the reserve mousse in a smooth layer over the cake. Transfer the cake to the freezer to set, 30 to 40 minutes, or until the mousse on the top

layer is very firm, almost hard.

Make the top glaze and allow to cool until slightly thickened but still spreadable. A consistency similar, if slightly thinner, to honey is perfect. If it's too thin, it will merely soak into the cake instead of sitting on top and setting into a glaze. Take the cake from the freezer and pour the glaze over the top of the finished cake, starting in the middle of the cake layer and gently pushing the glaze to the edge, making sure not to push the glaze over the edge of the cake layer. It shouldn't drizzle down the sides of the cake. You can leave about a ½-inch/1.3 cm perimeter of the cake bare of glaze just to be certain you don't go over the sides (you'll be lining the edge with strawberry slices to make up for that naked gap).

Return the cake to the freezer to completely set but not freeze, 15 to 20 minutes. Release the sides of the springform, leaving the parchment surrounding the cake.

While the glaze is setting, slice the remaining strawberries into ¼-inch/6 mm-thick rounds. You'll need about two dozen 1-inch/2.5 cm rounds and a few tips from the sliced strawberries.

Place the strawberry rounds around the perimeter of the cake, on top of the glaze, overlapping slightly.

Fill a pastry bag fitted with a small plain round piping tip (Ateco 2) with the royal icing. Pipe overlapping circles onto the glaze, just inside the strawberry circles.

Place a few strawberry tips, gum paste flowers (if using), and rosemary sprigs (if using) on top of the cake. Peel off the parchment.

APPLE CIDER CAKE

Germans have a knack for filling all manner of dessert with whipped cream and surprises. This dessert is an homage to my favorite German cake with an autumnal twist. The main element, at least the one you see, is a whipped cream–based pumpkin cider mousse that's sandwiched between two moist layers of applesauce cake. Buried inside the mousse, like little secret jewels, are cream puffs filled with chocolate *or* pumpkin pastry cream (it's your cake; you choose which flavor you want to use—or go with both). When you slice into the cake, the secret yumminess is revealed.

YOU'LL NEED

1 recipe Applesauce Cake (page 77), baked in one 9-inch/23 cm round pan and torted for 2 layers

4 large red apples, sliced into paper-thin slices (you can use a mandoline), placed in a large bowl of ice water with ¼ cup/60 ml lemon juice to keep them from browning

1 recipe Apple Cider–Pumpkin Mousse (page 152)

1 recipe Pâte à Choux (page 172)

1 recipe Firm Caramel Coating (page 203), rewarmed for dipping

1 recipe Chocolate Pastry Cream (page 140), Salted Pastry Cream (page 136) or Pumpkin Pastry Cream (page 138)

1 recipe Stabilized Sweet Whipped Cream (page 131)

EQUIPMENT

Skewer or chopstick
Pastry bag
Small round pastry tip (Ateco 802)
St. Honoré tip (Ateco 883)

Line the sides of a 9-inch/23 cm cake pan with a 5-inch/12.5 cm x 30-inch/76 cm-long strip of parchment so that the ends overlap and the parchment acts as a tall ring within the pan.

Place a cake layer into the bottom of the pan. Place the best apple slices inside the pan, lining the perimeter, touching the parchment. Pack the apple slices as close together as you can so that there are no gaps.

Pour the mousse into the cake ring and, using a small offset spatula, spread the mousse to the sides and smooth the top. Transfer the cake to the refrigerator while you coat and fill the pâte à choux puffs.

Carefully dip the tops of about 8 cream puffs into the caramel, taking care to coat only the top, and transfer to a piece of parchment to set, naked-side down.

Poke a pilot hole into the sides of 8 or 9 of the remaining uncoated cream puffs (however many will fit in your cake: you can

freeze any unused choux puffs in a resealable plastic bag) with a skewer or a chopstick. Fit a pastry bag with a small round tip (Ateco 802) and fill with your pastry cream of choice. Insert the tip into the pilot hole and apply gentle pressure to fill the cream puff. It should start to feel heavier. Once the coated cream puffs are set, poke a pilot hole in the bottom of each of them and fill with the remaining pastry cream.

Take the cake from the fridge and carefully insert the uncoated and filled cream puffs into the mousse deep enough that they are covered in mousse. Place the second cake layer on top of the mousse and press gently. Transfer the cake to the freezer and allow to set, 40 to 45 minutes.

Gently turn the cake out of the cake pan, leaving the parchment band in place.

Spread 1 cup/235 ml of the whipped cream in an even layer over the top of the cake. Fit a pastry bag with a St. Honoré tip and fill with the remaining whipped cream. Pipe a decorative border around the perimeter of the cake. Place cream puffs on top of the cake inside the St. Honoré band. Peel off the parchment.

BLACK FOREST CAKE

Chocolate, cherries, whipped cream, and a bit of booze. That's what pastry dreams are made of and it's what makes this most traditional of German cakes something straight out of a fairy tale. I up the magical quotient by topping the cake with marzipan toadstools and a bit of cake moss.

YOU'LL NEED

½ recipe Mürberteig (page 116), baked in an 8-inch/23 cm round pan for 1 layer

¼ cup/80 g apricot jam

1 recipe Light Chocolate Sponge Cake (page 101), baked in two 8-inch/23 cm round pans and torted for 4 layers

1 recipe Stabilized Sweet Whipped Cream (page 131) and made with Kirschwasser

1 recipe Schwarzwald Cherry Filling (page 126)

2 cups/280 g chocolate Puppet Dust (page 206)

3 to 4 marzipan toadstools (see sidebar, page 288)

Cake moss (see sidebar, page 288)

EQUIPMENT

Pastry bag
Medium plain round pastry tip (Ateco 804)

Place the Mürberteig round onto a cake stand and spread with an even layer of apricot jam. Place a chocolate sponge layer onto the apricot jam, pressing gently to adhere.

Fit a pastry bag with a medium plain tip (Ateco 804) and fill with the whipped cream. Pipe a dam around the perimeter of the cake and spread a third of the Schwarzwald cherry filling on the cake. Pipe a shallow layer of whipped cream on top of the cherry filling and top with the second layer of cake. Continue adding layers of sponge cake, damming and topping with cherry filling and whipped cream, until you reach the fourth and last layer of cake. Place that on top of the whipped cream and press lightly to adhere. Transfer the cake to the freezer for 30 to 35 minutes to set.

Using an offset spatula and a bench or icing scraper, smooth the remaining whipped cream over the top and sides of the cake. Freeze for 30 to 35 minutes to set.

Gently press the chocolate puppet dust onto the sides of the cake. Place the marzipan toadstools and cake moss on top of the cake.

TOADSTOOLS AND MOSS, OH MY!

You'll need

Marzipan (page 192)

Red gel food coloring

Vodka

Swedish sugar

Cuttings from green
or vanilla cake

Equipment

Small paintbrush

Toadstools are such magical fungi and easy to make. To make the cap, take a ½-inch/1.3 cm round piece of marzipan and gently flatten on your palm to double the diameter. In a small bowl, combine 2 drops red gel food coloring and a few drops of vodka to thin the dye. Using a small paintbrush, paint the top of the toadstool red. Sprinkle the still damp toadstool with Swedish sugar and set aside to dry, about 1 hour. For the "stem," take a ¼-inch/6 mm round piece of marzipan and form into a ½-inch/1.3 cm-long cylinder. Brush one end of the cylinder with water to just dampen and then place the cap on top, pressing gently to adhere.

For moss, I simply save trimmings from any green (Matcha cake is perfect) or vanilla cake, as when you trim any doming from the cake and freeze. Place the pieces in small patches on your cake. If using a lighter, vanilla cake, I brush the cake with a dusting of green powder food coloring to get the full moss effect.

LINZER MACARON CAKE

At my baking school, Sugar Glider Kitchen, my most popular class is Macaron Madness! We start off making petite macarons, the kind that most people know and love. But once the students have finished piping and our shells are waiting the requisite time outside the oven to form tough little skins, I show my eager pupils the delights of the macaron cake. Using the same batter we used to pipe our slightly larger than 1-inch/2.5 cm dollops, I spin the batter (the *macaronage*) into a giant round layer. And then I pipe another. I usually have enough batter left over to pipe some smaller shells and some hearts. And when I'm finished, a student will invariably break the silence and say, with complete incredulity, "Wait. That could be a cake!" "Yes, indeed!" I reply, to everyone's delight.

YOU'LL NEED

1 recipe Nut Dacquoise (page 111), made with 1 teaspoon Speculoos Spice Mix, piped into two 10-inch/25.5 cm rounds and a few smaller macarons for décor

1 recipe Red Currant German Buttercream (page 178)

1 pint/255 g red raspberries

EQUIPMENT

Pastry bag

Medium plain round pastry tip (Ateco 804)

Place one dacquoise round on a cake platter, spiral-side down. Fit a pastry bag with a medium plain round tip (Ateco 804) and fill with buttercream. Pipe an even layer of buttercream over the dacquoise on the cake stand, leaving about ½ inch/1.3 cm of the outer rim naked. Place raspberries along the perimeter, pointy side up, along the naked edge. Use a small offset spatula to gently smooth the buttercream and spread it up to the raspberries. Gently press the raspberries into the buttercream to "glue" them in place. Top with the second dacquoise layer, spiral-side up.

Use the remaining buttercream to sandwich small macaron shells. Arrange them on the top of the cake, using any remaining raspberries to prop them up.

Merveilleux, Pavlova Cake, and Linzer Macaron Cake

PAVLOVA CAKE

Pavlova Cake: layers of meringue, slathered with a tart lemon cream, and then covered with a Swiss Meringue overcoat. It's as elegant as a tulle tutu but far more delicious. And like the Linzer Macaron Cake, it just happens to be gluten-free! That's a sweet win-win.

YOU'LL NEED

1 recipe Swiss Meringue Topping
(page 176)

1 recipe Pavlova-style Meringue
(page 115), baked as four 8-inch/
20.5 cm layers

1 recipe Microwave Citrus Curd
(page 124), made with lemon

EQUIPMENT

Pastry bag

Medium plain round pastry tip
(Ateco 804)

Fit a pastry bag with a medium plain round tip (Ateco 804) and fill with Swiss meringue. Place a dime-size dollop of Swiss meringue on a cake stand and place a Pavlova layer on the cake stand. Pipe a dam around the perimeter of the Pavlova layer and spread a third of the curd over the Pavlova layer. Pipe a thin layer of Swiss meringue over the curd and place a second Pavlova layer on the Swiss meringue. Press very gently to adhere the Pavlova layer to the Swiss meringue. Continue damming, filling with curd, and topping with Swiss meringue until you reach the fourth and final layer. Top with the final layer and transfer the cake to the freezer for 20 to 25 minutes to set the curd and Swiss meringue.

Using a small offset spatula, spread an even layer of Swiss meringue over the top of the cake so that it just starts to peek over the edge and then, using long upward strokes, start at the bottom of the cake and swipe a dollop of meringue up the side of the cake to meet the overhanging meringue. Continue all around the sides of the cake. Serve immediately.

MERVEILLEUX

If you wish to know what the latest dessert trend will be, look to Paris. The French invented the macaron craze. They brought éclairs back to the front of the pastry case. And now, there's the *merveillleux*. There are shops that only sell this delightful treat of tiny meringue layers layered with a very stiffly whipped heavy cream. It's devilishly simple, but cute as a button and insanely tasty.

YOU'LL NEED

1 recipe Pavlova-style Meringue (page 115), baked into eighteen 3-inch/7.5 cm rounds

1 recipe Cocoa Cream (page 131) or 1 recipe Caramel Cream (page 134)

1 large bittersweet chocolate bar (I use Lindt's 70% bar)

EQUIPMENT

Pastry bag
Small plain round pastry tip (Ateco 802)

Line up 9 meringue rounds on a parchment-lined sheet pan.

Fit a pastry bag with a small plain tip (Ateco 802) and fill with cocoa cream. Pipe an even layer over a meringue round and top with a second meringue. Pipe a small mound of cocoa cream on top of the second layer. Continue filling and building the remaining meringues until you have 9 meringue stacks. Place the sheet pan with the assembled meringues into the freezer to set, 20 to 25 minutes.

Pipe whipped cream around the sides of the meringue stacks and, using a small offset spatula, smooth the cocoa cream around the sides and over the top to create a dome. Transfer the meringue stacks back to the freezer for 20 minutes to set.

Gently warm but do not melt the edge of the chocolate bar, using a blow dryer, then scrape chocolate shavings from the warmed chocolate with a vegetable peeler onto a parchment-lined sheet pan. Continue warming and shaving until the chocolate is all shaved. Transfer the shaved chocolate to the freezer to set, about 5 minutes, and then gently press the chocolate shavings onto the top and sides of the cream-coated meringue stacks.

TIRAMISU CAKE

By piping ladyfinger batter into rounds to mimic cake layers, you'll have a tiramisu that's fit for a celebration. All the delicious flavors and textures remain; it's just the presentation that gets a well-deserved face-lift.

YOU'LL NEED

½ cup/99 g granulated sugar
½ cup/118 ml brewed hot coffee
1 recipe Tiramisu Cream (page 132)
1 recipe Ladyfinger Sponge (page 100), piped into four 8-inch/20.5 cm round layers
½ cup/42 g Dutched cocoa powder

EQUIPMENT

Pastry bag
Medium plain round pastry tip (Ateco 804)

Stir the granulated sugar and coffee together in a small saucepan, then bring to a simmer until the sugar has melted into the coffee and the coffee simple syrup is thickened.

Place a dime-size dollop of tiramisu cream on the middle of a cake platter and place a ladyfinger sponge round on the platter. Using a pastry brush, brush a generous layer of coffee simple syrup onto the sponge layer.

Fit a pastry bag with a medium plain round tip (Ateco 804), fill with tiramisu cream, then pipe an even layer over the sponge and sift an even dusting of cocoa onto the cream. Place a second sponge round on the cream layer and brush with a generous layer of coffee simple syrup. Pipe an even layer of tiramisu cream over the sponge and sift an even dusting of cocoa onto the cream, then place a third layer of ladyfinger sponge on top. At this point, if the cake doesn't feel completely stable, carefully transfer the cake to the freezer to set, about 30 minutes. Refrigerate the remaining tiramisu cream.

Brush the sponge layer with the coffee simple syrup and pipe an even layer of the tiramisu cream over the layer, coating with a sifted layer of cocoa and then topping with the fourth and last sponge layer. Transfer back to the freezer for 20 minutes, refrigerating the remaining tiramisu cream.

Using a small offset spatula and a bench or icing scraper, smooth an even layer of tiramisu cream over the top and sides of the cake. Transfer the cake back to the freezer for 10 to 15 minutes. Transfer the remaining tiramisu cream to the pastry bag with the medium round tip and pipe cream kisses in an arch onto half of the top of the cake. Sift cocoa over the little mounds. Refrigerate until ready to serve, within a few hours of assembly; don't try to hold this cake for much longer.

SWISS ROLL CAKE

For a cake that would be perfectly happy as an art exhibition, look no further than the Swiss Roll Cake. There's no better time to let your imagination go wild, so feel free to ignore my love of all things fruity and pipe any design you like on the outside. In fact, go doubly wild because this recipe makes *two* cakes.

YOU'LL NEED

1 recipe Swiss Roll Sponge (page 106), baked in a half sheet pan, edges trimmed and cut in half to make two cakes, each measuring about 8 x 12 inches/20.5 x 30.5 cm

1 recipe Stabilized Sweet Whipped Cream (page 131)

2 cups/275 g fruit of choice, diced into ½-inch/1.3 cm or smaller pieces, if needed

Place the cake pattern-side down and spread half the whipped cream onto the surface of the cake without the pattern. Stud the cream with half of the fruit pieces. Roll up the cake, starting at the shorter end, as tightly as you can without smushing all the cream out the sides. Wrap the cake in plastic wrap and freeze for 20 to 25 minutes to set. Fill and roll the second cake, wrap in plastic wrap, and freeze 20 to 25 minutes to set.

PRINCESS CAKES

We know the green cake—that's the Princess cake that survives in bakeries everywhere—but legend has it that when the baker who invented this confection in the 1940s first presented it, it had two companions. So, there were three cakes in all to honor the three princesses of Sweden. I've taken it upon myself to invent two more to make the set complete again.

FOR EACH CAKE, YOU'LL NEED

1 recipe Vanilla Bean Pastry Cream (page 135) for either the green or the pink Princess Cake, or 1 recipe Chocolate Pastry Cream (page 140) for the cocoa Princess Cake

½ recipe Stabilized Sweet Whipped Cream (page 131)

1 recipe Genoise (page 92), plain for the green Princess Cake, honey-lavender for the pink Princess Cake, or the chocolate genoise for the cocoa Princess Cake, baked in two 8-inch/20.5 cm round pans and torted in half for 4 layers

1 cup/320 g Quick Raspberry Jam (page 128) for the green Princess Cake, 1 cup/320 g store-bought blueberry jam for the pink Princess Cake, or 1 cup/300 g store-bought orange marmalade for the cocoa Princess Cake

1 recipe Marzipan (page 192), dyed green, pink, or brown with added cocoa powder, as appropriate to desired color cake. For the traditional green Princess Cake, before dyeing the marzipan green, pinch off a quarter-size piece of marzipan and, using Americolor Soft Pink gel dye, dip a tooth-pick into the dye and add a small smear onto the piece and knead to distribute the color (reserve the pink marzipan separately to make a rose)

1 pink marzipan rose for the green Princess Cake, a small meringue kiss (page 202) for the pink Princess Cake, and chocolate shavings for the cocoa Princess Cake

Transfer 1 cup/235 ml of the pastry cream to a small bowl, cover with plastic wrap, and refrigerate until needed. Stir the remaining pastry cream to loosen and fold in ½ cup/118 ml of the whipped cream to lighten it. Cover and refrigerate until needed.

Line an 8-inch/20.5 cm half sphere cake pan with plastic wrap, making sure that the plastic wrap overhangs the sides of the pan all around.

Place a cake layer of Genoise inside the pan and gently pat the cake in place to make sure that it's sitting flush with the sides of the pan. Spoon about 1½ cups/355 ml of the whipped cream on top of the cake layer and spread in an even layer.

Slightly trim the sides of a second layer of cake so that it fits snugly on top of the cream. Spoon the lightened pastry cream over the cake and smooth with a small offset spatula. Place a third genoise layer on top of the light-ened cream and spread the reserved cup/235 ml of pastry cream over the third layer.

Spread the jam over the fourth and last layer of genoise and place it, jam-side down, on top of the pastry cream layer. Cover any exposed cake with plastic wrap and freeze for 45 minutes to an hour to set.

Roll out the marzipan between two sheets of parchment into an 18-inch/45.5 cm-diameter circle.

Place a cardboard round onto the bottom sponge layer and flip the cake over and onto a cake stand. Carefully remove the half sphere pan and peel off the plastic wrap.

Peel off the top layer of parchment from the marzipan. Carry the marzipan to the cake, using the bottom sheet of parchment. Use the parchment to center the marzipan over the cake and then carefully peel off the parchment. Gently smooth the marzipan over the cake.

For the traditional green Princess Cake, make a pink rose with the reserved pink marzipan (see sidebar, page 193). I put a little meringue kiss on top of the pink Princess Cake, and some chocolate shavings on the cocoa Princess Cake.

CHOCOLATE MIRROR CAKE

Layers of supple chocolate cake, chocolate mousse, and some crispy feuilletine would be enough to knock anyone's socks off, but cover it all in a sexy, shiny chocolate glaze and then sprinkle it with some Schoko Crossies, and you've get a blue ribbon cake on your hands.

YOU'LL NEED

1 recipe Deep Dark Chocolate Mousse (page 158), Fruit Mousse (page 154), or Coconut Mousee (page 156)

1 recipe Chocolate Genoise (page 94), baked in two 8-inch/20.5 cm round pans and torted in half for 4 layers

1 recipe Simple Chocolate Coating (page 191)

2 recipes Crispy Caramelized Rice Puffs (page 166)

1 recipe Chocolate "Black Out" Mirror Glaze (page 198)

1 recipe Schoko Crossies (page 168)

Place 2 cups/475 ml of the chocolate mousse into a small bowl, cover with plastic wrap, and refrigerate until needed.

Line an 8-inch/20.5 cm bowl with plastic wrap, making sure the wrap extends over the rim of the bowl. Line the bottom of the bowl with one layer of cake, gently pressing it down into the bowl. Brush the layer with a thin layer of chocolate coating and, before it sets, sprinkle with an even layer of the caramelized rice puffs, about ½ cup/75 g. Gently drizzle the rice puffs with more chocolate coating. Transfer the cake to the freezer for

5 minutes to set the chocolate coating.

Spoon half of the mousse into the bowl, on top of the rice puffs. Spread with an offset spatula to create an even layer. The mousse should reach the top of the cake layer. Top with a second cake layer and brush the cake with the chocolate coating. Sprinkle with ½ cup/75 g of caramelized rice puffs in an even layer and then gently drizzle with more chocolate coating. Transfer the cake to the freezer for 5 minutes to set the chocolate coating.

Spoon the remaining chocolate mousse over the rice puffs and smooth with an offset spatula. Top with a third cake layer. Cover the cake with plastic wrap and freeze to set, 1 to 2 hours.

Place a cardboard round over the bottom cake layer and turn the cake over. Gently remove the bowl and peel off the plastic wrap. Using a small bench scraper and a flexible icing scraper, coat the outside of the cake with a smooth layer of the reserved mousse. Return the cake to the freezer, 1 to 2 hours, to allow the mousse to set. It must be completely set and ice cold before you can glaze it.

Prepare the glaze. When it has come to temperature (105° to 100°F/40.5° to 43°C), place a cooling rack over a parchment-lined sheet pan. Hold the cake over the cooling rack and pour the glaze over the cake, tilting it from side to side to make sure that all sides of the cake are coated. Immediately transfer the cake to a cake stand and refrigerate the cake for ½ hour to set the glaze. You can scrape up any glaze runoff and use again (you'll have to reheat to 105° to 110°F/40.5° to 43°C).

Once set, gently press the remaining caramelized rice puffs along the lower third of the cake and then sprinkle the top of the cake with Schoko Crossies.

ROYAL PURPLE VELVET MIRROR GLAZE CAKE

I'm of the opinion that Red Velvet could really up its game in the fashion department. For such an eye-catching cake layer, it's an awful shame that it's always dressed in humdrum (yet delicious) cream cheese frosting. And it's always wearing the same color! Why not pink? Or blue? Wait a second, I know: how about purple? For something with as regal a moniker as "velvet" in the title, I think purple is the right way to go. So, I'm going give our most American cake a little royal makeover in purple and I'll go back in time and layer it with vintage ermine and then drape it in a glamorous cape of violet mirror glaze. And then, let's just go ahead and make it look like a crown worthy of a coronation and make this the queen of cakes.

YOU'LL NEED

1 recipe Royal Purple Velvet Cake
 (page 87), baked in two 8-inch/20.5 cm
 round pans and torted in half for 4 layers
1 recipe Ermine Frosting (page 185)
1 recipe Mirror Glaze (page 194), made
 with purple gel dye
1 recipe Swiss Buttercream (page 175)
 for décor and flowers

EQUIPMENT

Pastry bag
Medium-small plain round pastry tip
 (Ateco 803)
Russian rose tip

Place a layer of cake on a cardboard round and transfer to a cake turntable. Fit a pastry bag with a medium-small plain tip (Ateco 803) and fill with ermine frosting. Pipe an even layer of frosting over the cake and top with the second cake layer. Continue to pipe and stack layers until you reach the fourth

and last layer. Place the last layer on the cake and gently press to adhere the cake layers to the frosting. Transfer the cake to the freezer for 20 minutes to set the frosting.

Using an offset spatula and a bench or icing scraper, coat the cake with a skim or crumb coat (see sidebar, page 221) and return the cake to the freezer for 10 minutes to set.

Using an offset spatula and a flexible icing scraper, coat the cake with a smooth finish coat, rounding the edges of the cake with the flexible scraper. Return the cake to the freezer for at least an hour before glazing. The icing must be ice cold and hard.

Place a cooling rack over a parchment-lined sheet pan. Hold the cake in one hand over the cooling rack and pour the glaze in an even stream over the cake, tilting the cake to make sure the top and sides are completely coated. You can reheat and reuse the glaze that has gathered on the parchment.

Place the cake on the cake stand and refrigerate for 1 hour before decorating with piped buttercream roses (see sidebar, page 310) and serving.

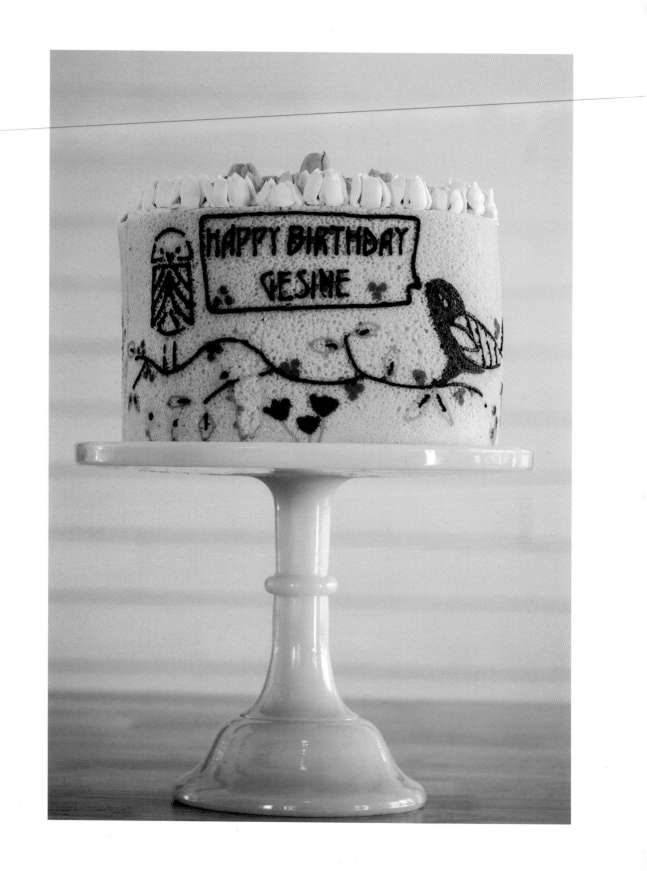

"IT'S MY BIRTHDAY AND I'LL BAKE IF I WANT TO" CAKE

There's a very good reason I don't want anyone else making my birthday cake: I don't want anyone else having all the fun! That's why I like to call it "It's My Birthday and I'll Bake If I Want To" Cake. I also take the opportunity to try new things. To experiment and go a little zany while sticking with flavors and textures I think are delightful. And I swear, I share.

YOU'LL NEED

1 recipe Chiffon Cake (page 102), made with Key lime juice, baked in two 8-inch/20.5 cm round pans and torted in half for 4 layers

1 recipe Coconut Dacquoise (page 114), piped into four 8-inch/20.5 cm rounds

1 recipe Quick Raspberry Jam (page 128), made instead with strawberries

1 recipe Key Lime Cheesecake (page 163)

1 recipe Passion Fruit French Buttercream (page 188)

1 recipe patterned joconde décor sides (page 104)

Buttercream Russian flowers (see sidebar, page 310)

EQUIPMENT

Pastry bag
Large plain round pastry tip (Ateco 808)

Place a chiffon cake layer on a cardboard round and transfer to a cake turntable. Spread a third of the jam over the layer and top with a dacquoise layer.

Fit a pastry bag with a large plain tip (Ateco 808) and fill with the cheesecake filling. Pipe a third of the cheesecake filling over the layer. Top with a second chiffon round, and continue to spread with jam and dacquoise and fill with cheesecake filling until you reach the fourth and last layer. Place the fourth cake layer on top and press down gently to adhere. Transfer the cake to the freezer to set, 40 to 45 minutes.

Spread an even layer of passion fruit French buttercream over the top and sides of the cake. Return the cake to the freezer to set, 10 to 15 minutes.

Trim and apply your joconde sides, pressing gently to make sure they adhere to the buttercream. Top with buttercream Russian flowers (page 310).

Cake Lady

MAKING BUTTERCREAM RUSSIAN FLOWERS

You will need	*Equipment*
Swiss Buttercream (page 175)	Pastry bags
Gel dye	Russian flower tips

For buttercream Russian flowers, divide Swiss buttercream among as many bowls as colors you are using. Thoroughly stir the gel dye into the buttercream. For the perfect Russian tip piping consistency, your buttercream should be between 65° and 68°F/18° and 20°C.

If you'd like to make a multicolored Russian tip flower, fit a pastry bag with a Russian tip. Dip a small offset spatula into the color you'd like to just coat the outside of the flower and scrape the color onto the sides of the bag, starting at the tip and spreading the buttercream up. You want a thin layer. For the main color, use a small offset spatula to spread the buttercream inside the bag. For a middle color, fill a second pastry bag with the interior color, and snip off just a small corner of the bag. Plunge the bag into the middle of the color-streaked pastry bag, as low as you can go, and then apply gentle and constant pressure to fill it with buttercream as you lift the bag out.

To pipe the flowers, hold the tip just about at the top of the cake but not touching the cake. Apply gentle pressure, keeping the bag steady, and pipe an anchor of frosting onto the cake without moving your pastry bag. Once you have some buttercream adhering, continue to gently press and lift the bag up. Once you're about ½ inch/1.3 cm above the cake, stop applying pressure. For some Russian tips, the tulip tips specifically, the petals look better longer, so keep pressure on the bag longer as you lift.

Note: I suggest you practice piping with plain buttercream on a piece of parchment that you've securely taped down on your work surface. This way, you can start understanding the amount of pressure you need for each type of tip.

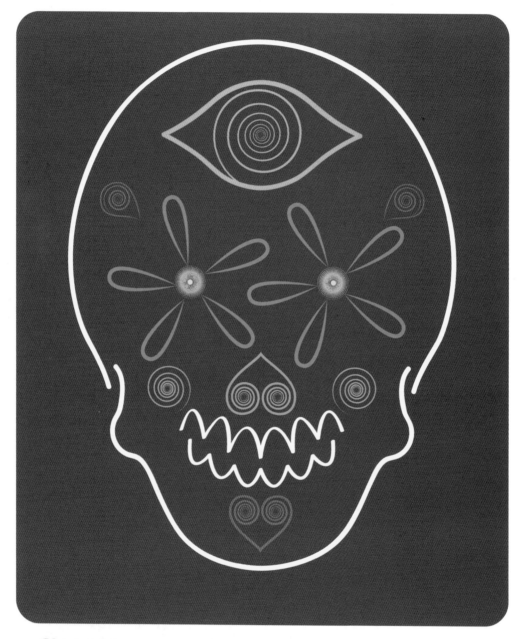

Acknowledgments

The biggest thank you to Laura Nolan, literary agent extraordinaire and true friend, who never once lost faith in me. You are as good a person as you are an agent.

Raymo, I've never had as much fun as when we're doing a project together. You're the best partner a wife and baker could have.

And thank you to all my baking students who inspire me to create and share new things every day.

Index

Note: Page references in *italics* indicate photographs.

Notes

Notes

Notes